Armistice 1918

ARMISTICE 1918

1918

By Bullitt Lowry

THE KENT STATE UNIVERSITY PRESS
Kent, Ohio, and London, England

© 1996 by The Kent State University Press, Kent, Ohio 44242
All rights reserved
Library of Congress Catalog Card Number 96-7600
ISBN 0-87338-553-5
ISBN 0-87338-651-5 (pbk.)
Manufactured in the United States of America
04 03 02 01 00 99   5 4 3 2

Library of Congress Cataloging-in-Publication Data

Lowry, Bullitt, 1936–
    Armistice 1918 by Bullitt Lowry.
        p.   cm.
    Includes bibliographical references and index.
    ISBN 0-87338-553-5
    1. World War, 1914–1918—Armistices.   I. Title.
    D641.L68   1996   96-7600
    940.4'39—dc20   CIP

British Library Cataloging-in-Publication data are available.

Contents

Maps

Preface

In October 1918, the Germans asked the Allied and Associated Powers for an armistice. Victory was coming to the Allies and the United States because of the Germans' failure in their 1918 offensive and the effect of that failure on the other Central Powers—Bulgaria, the Ottoman Empire, and Austria-Hungary.

The Bulgarians, with German aid ended and their front collapsing, had already asked for an armistice, which the Allies granted at the end of September, and Bulgaria left the war. The leaders of the Ottoman Empire also wanted out of the war as quickly as possible. They saw the morale of their soldiers fading, British armies advancing from three directions, and further German help blocked because of Bulgaria's surrender. Finally, Germany's oldest and most important ally, Austria-Hungary, was spinning apart, with national group after national group claiming the right to decide its own destiny. That situation, explosive for years, was now getting worse daily.

In all cases, the decisive point, geographically and chronologically, was Germany and its failed 1918 offensive. Begun in March, the offensive was General Erich Ludendorff's fierce attempt to end the war before fresh American troops could tilt the balance. By midsummer, the offensive's second phase had lost momentum, and Allied counterattacks started the great German retreat.

The constantly worsening military situation led Ludendorff, late in September, to demand that the German government get an immediate armistice from the Allied and Associated Powers. What Ludendorff wanted was a respite to set up a strong defensive line, so that the Germans could negotiate peace from strength. That overture toward a negotiated peace, however, tumbled headlong into surrender, the armistice of November 11, 1918.

This book examines the making of that armistice. It looks in detail only at France, Great Britain, and the United States, because it was the leaders of those three nations who wrote the armistice, not the Germans. Once the Germans decided to ask for an armistice, they were acted upon, not actors. This book discusses the armistices made with the other Central Powers, too, but it was the German armistice, far more than those others, that shaped European and world events during the months and years that followed November 11.

Before the autumn of 1918 and the German overture, the Allies and the United States had done practically nothing to prepare armistice terms. Individually, Great Britain, France, and the United States had undertaken extensive investigations of matters that a potential peace treaty would cover. They had not looked at armistice terms or at how those terms should relate to peace.[1]

Furthermore, historical precedents gave the leaders little guidance. In the half-century before World War I, armistices (ones that ended wars, not just temporary pauses in hostilities) sometimes came about after the clear defeat of one nation. With defeat obvious and complete, the victor might grant moderate armistice conditions because there was no danger that the beaten country could reassert itself during the period between the armistice and the peace treaty. Bismarck's new German Empire gave France such an armistice in 1871.[2] A more common experience in the years before World War I was that, while fighting continued, diplomats came to agreement on preliminary peace terms. The soldiers then stopped fighting, and the diplomats wrote a definitive treaty based on the agreement just reached. That was the case at the end of the Austro-Prussian War.[3] The Spanish-American War contained both elements, defeat and agreement to a preliminary peace.[4] In the Mad Hatter's tea party of the Balkan Wars, both defeat and prior diplomatic agreement created armistices at one stage or another.[5] These conflicting models from the preceding half-century offered no clear signposts for armistice makers in the fall of 1918. The leaders of the Allied nations and the United States had to break new ground.

Nor had those leaders agreed among themselves on what gains they wanted the end of the war to bring them. Revolutionary Russia's separate peace with the Central Powers had left the Allied wartime secret treaties in diplomatic disarray. Moreover, to avoid quarrels that might undermine wartime cooperation, Allied and American leaders had deliberately postponed joint discussion of their individual war aims.

Certainly, the leaders of the Allies and the United States—the American president insisted his nation was not an Ally but "associated" with the Allied effort—had hopes for what their individual nations would get, but they had no common program. The French had fervent ambitions directed toward reducing Germany's strength and territory and augmenting France's. President of the United States Woodrow Wilson had a peace program, his Fourteen Points, but he had never officially submitted that plan to the Allies. Three days before Wilson presented his Fourteen Points to Congress, the British prime minister gave a speech in which he took much the same line the American president would. Nevertheless, whatever similarities might exist between the British and American programs, the leaders of those two nations had not agreed on war aims, and grave differences over matters such as neutral rights and reparations might well make accord impossible.

Early in October 1918, facing the German request for an armistice to arrange a peace based on Wilson's Fourteen Points, the Allied leaders drifted. As October passed, their feelings solidified, at first more implicitly than explicitly. After four terrible years of war, the Allies wanted complete victory and the satisfaction of all those hopes for which they had suffered fearful losses of men and treasure.[6]

Therefore, when the Allied leaders began to put armistice terms together, their drafts of military and naval clauses began to merge with their visions of peace terms. As deliberations continued over what answer to give Germany, the armistice terms grew imperceptibly to become a preliminary peace. That is the most important conclusion reached in this book: the armistice with Germany became a preliminary peace, one that fulfilled many Allied dreams.

The Germans wanted Wilson's Fourteen Points to shape the coming peace treaty. During the armistice discussions, the Allies, too, formally agreed to the Fourteen Points, albeit with several amendments and reservations. Critics of every stripe since 1918 have debated how free that agreement left the peacemakers. The conclusion reached in this book is that the Fourteen Points, both as Wilson wrote them and as Wilson and his representatives explained them to the Allies, were murky and ambiguous. Because they did not constitute a precise guide for peacemaking, common agreement to them meant little.

This book also will evaluate several arguments made over the years about the German armistice. First are the related questions of whether it came too soon or too late. The argument that the Allies and the United States granted an armistice too soon has its origin in postwar German claims that their army was never really defeated. To prove those claims false, critics said, the Allies should have waited to sign an armistice until the German people saw some tangible sign of defeat. In the end, critics argued, this delay might have given the world a more lasting peace.

The converse of this argument, the claim that the armistice came too late, stems from charges made that the Allies unnecessarily delayed presenting the armistice to Germany. During that delay, men died to no purpose. Speed here could have been the first step to a peace of reconciliation, a peace that might have lasted longer than the Treaty of Versailles did.

A variant of those two positions is the retrospective wish that the armistice had been either harsher or milder. That is, either it should have been unconditional, like the German surrender in World War II, or it should have left the Germans with enough strength to resist the outrageous demands of the Versailles Treaty the following year. Those arguments, too, are assessed.

As it was, the harsh armistice of November 11, although it was not an unconditional surrender, did incapacitate Germany. Once the German leaders signed it and carried out its terms, they could not take up the fight again. They would no longer have any means of resistance, and even if the German people had seen no tangible symbol of military defeat, they would eventually have to submit to whatever final peace terms the Allies and the United States chose to dictate.

Another element to note during the armistice negotiations is civil-military relations. It is a subject that has puzzled many analysts, especially in the Cold War years, and civil-military relations have caused problems in every modern nation. The issue is how a government should use the services of technical experts, and it perplexed the leaders of 1918 no less than modern leaders.

To examine all these matters, a historian can now look at the entire period from the German request for an armistice on October 3, 1918, to the signature on November 11 through the eyes of those involved—politicians, military leaders, and diplomats. Historical data are malleable, and memory concerning the armistice is fallible. Perhaps because the First German Note of October 3 did lead, finally, to an armistice, later recollections of participants drift into assumptions of inevitability, contrary to what really happened. On top of that, persons who wrote in the 1930s or later lived in a world in which the peace after World War I had failed, and many of them unconsciously recast their memories in the light of that realization. Therefore, I have tried to limit my sources as much as possible to data and opinions and remarks set down almost simultaneously with the events described. I have used later accounts and analyses only with great caution.

The personal papers of all the major British and American participants are now available to scholars. The French left fewer materials, and many of the French collections that do exist—for example, the papers of President of the Republic Raymond Poincaré and Minister of Foreign Affairs Stephen Pichon—are sparse.

French governmental records show the same pattern. The French ravaged their own records during World War II, deliberately destroying documents in the Ministry of Foreign Affairs as the Germans entered Paris. Later, during the occupation, the Germans collected French documents on the armistice and peace conference, and many of them were burned or lost during the chaos at the end of the war. Nevertheless, the French materials that still exist are accessible, and the richer archives of Great Britain and the United States are entirely open.

Previous studies have looked at the armistice with Germany, but all of them suffer from lack of the data that archival and manuscript research offer. Other than participants, authors who have looked at the armistice in detail include Sir Frederick Maurice in 1943; Harry Rudin in 1944; Brigadier C. N. Barclay in 1968; the dean of French diplomatic scholars, Pierre Renouvin, also in 1968; Gordon Brook-Shepherd in 1981; and Stanley Weintraub in 1985.[7] General Maurice wrote without archival support, although he knew many of the people involved. Harry Rudin, like Maurice, wrote under the shadow of World War II. Although some manuscript materials were open when he wrote, the major governmental collections were still closed, and the difficulties of travel during the war years kept him from using private papers. Therefore, he wrote entirely from published documents. Brigadier Barclay's study is interesting because it, like Maurice's a generation before, is the product of a military pen, but Barclay examined no archival sources, and his work contains serious errors of fact and interpretation. Pierre Renouvin used some French archival material, but he crossed neither the English Channel nor the Atlantic Ocean to put that material into context. Gordon Brook-Shepherd, a distinguished diplomatic correspondent and an editor of the *Sunday Telegraph,* used manuscript materials only for color in his work. Finally, Stanley Weintraub's excellent study is an evocation, a superb, dramatic recreation of the last moments of the war and what it meant to the peoples of the world. His book is not, nor did he intend it to be, a close study of the diplomatic maneuvers of October and November 1918.

Just such a close study is now possible, and with it, an examination of the motives and calculations of the people who drafted the armistice. The chapters of this book cover events chronologically. The earliest event discussed in detail is the Bulgarian surrender, which set in motion the German request to President Wilson that he arrange an armistice between Germany and its enemies. The first stage of Wilson's correspondence with the Germans was contemporary with a conference of Allied prime ministers meeting, by chance, when the Germans made their request. After the prime ministers dispersed and while Wilson continued his exchanges with the Germans, the British and French tried to define their own policies in case an armistice with Germany should become reality. In both countries, that process was complicated and painful.

At the end of October the Allied prime ministers met once again, this time in company with a representative from the United States. What had been internal quarrels and discussions now moved into the diplomatic arena. In meetings from October 29 to November 4, the Allied leaders and the United States' representative agreed on terms to offer Germany.

From November 8 to November 11, Allied and German representatives met in the Forest of Compiègne, near Rethondes, north of Paris. The Germans protested the harshness of the terms. In response, Allied representatives amended a few items and then told the Germans that they must accept the terms or the war would continue. On November 11, 1918, the Germans and the Allied and Associated Powers signed the armistice, which went into effect that morning at 11:00 a.m.

I need to note several idiosyncrasies of style. In the footnotes, I have usually changed titles to proper names. Thus, a document sent as "Secretary of State to the Special Representative" becomes "Lansing to House." When archival material has been published, such as in the *Foreign Rela-*

tions of the United States volumes, I have generally quoted from, and cited, the published text, unless there are substantial differences between the published and unpublished versions. Finally, I have treated quotations from procès-verbaux as if they were direct quotations, not indirect ones.

The number of persons who have helped this study come to fruition is great. I should like to note particularly Professors Harold Parker and Joel Colton, each of whom taught me a little of what they know about history and how to write it. The Faculty Research Committee of the University of North Texas gave me assistance that let me consult European archives. My greatest debt, of course, is to my wife, Sharon, who had faith.

Introduction

The Situation, September 1918

Near La Capelle in northern France on the evening of November 7, 1918, a bugler sounded the truce while three automobiles carried a few quiet Germans slowly across no-man's-land.[1] The guns of the 166th French Infantry Division were silent as the little group wound through the shell craters and tangled barbed wire. When the Germans entered the Allied lines, two French officers met them, and they changed to waiting Allied automobiles. After midnight, having driven southwestward through desolate, moonlit country, the Germans and their French escort boarded closed railroad cars. In the morning they arrived at the Forest of Compiègne, and there Allied representatives gave armistice terms to the Germans. On November 10, the German government instructed its delegates to accept them.[2] Soldiers in the trenches and workers in the factories, who in 1914 had held the extravagant hope that the carnage would end by the war's first Christmas, had begun to fear the war might never stop. Now, just before dawn on November 11, the Germans signed an armistice, and that day, at 11:00 A.M., the guns of the Western Front fell silent for the first time in more than four years.

Military events of the previous four months had forced the Germans to accept the armistice terms of the Allied and Associated Powers. On the crucial Western Front, the German spring offensive of 1918, and the attacks that followed it, gradually slowed, and the two sides reached equilibrium in July. From that time, Allied and American soldiers drove the

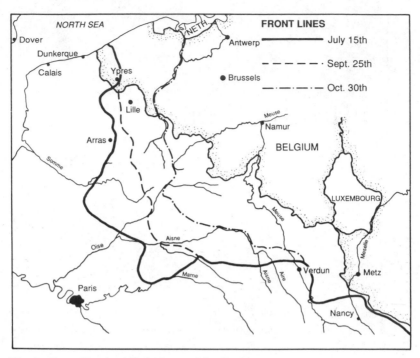

Western Front, Showing Allied Advance, July–October 1918

German army steadily backward in France and Belgium. In all these battles, Germany lost enormous numbers of soldiers. The manpower reserves of Great Britain and France, the senior European Allied nations, were no greater than those of the Germans, but the soldiers of that behemoth of the New World, the United States, were pouring across the Atlantic. If the war lasted into 1919, those additional men meant that Germany must face almost two million fresh enemy soldiers.

The "Black Day" of the German army—so named by the German commander—was August 8. After the defeat Germany suffered that day, German resistance eroded. In the four weeks after August 8, soldiers of the Allies and the United States recaptured all the territory they had lost to the German offensive the previous spring, and their advance was continuing without pause.

The German withdrawal remained orderly. Their defeats might still become a rout, but in September had not done so. Still, a great Allied offensive that began on September 26 made strong progress against the Germans along the entire Western Front. Most important of all, Germany's declining military fortunes meant that it could no longer provide criti-cally necessary military assistance to its allies, the Ottoman Empire, Austria-Hungary, and Bulgaria.

On the seas, too, the Allies were supreme. The German fleet had not ventured from harbor since the battle of Jutland in 1916. German subma-rines were still attacking Allied and American shipping, but the convoy system and other antisubmarine measures had reduced the submarine threat from a fearful peril to a military nuisance. The Austro-Hungarian fleet, wracked like the Dual Monarchy itself with nationalist rebellions, rotted in harbor.

In the Near East, the Ottoman Empire was collapsing. Internal revolt and Allied forces operating from Egypt and India were pushing the Turk-ish leaders to seek peace. Beginning on September 19, 1918, a great British offensive through Palestine destroyed the three German-Turkish armies guarding the southern flank of the Turkish heartland. The British took Damascus on October 1, and even the Anglo-Indian army in Mesopotamia, after long, terrible years, began to roll up the Turks facing them.

On the European continent, internal collapse was driving Austria-Hungary from the war. Austro-Hungarian leaders told their allies with increasing urgency that by December 1 they must withdraw from the war.[3] On September 14, the Austro-Hungarian Foreign Office sent a circular letter to all warring governments suggesting negotiations preliminary to a peace.[4] The Allied nations and the United States rejected this initiative almost immediately in the hope that a victory at arms might spare them the pitfalls of negotiation. Still, the only Allied force operating in strength against the Austro-Hungarian homeland was the Italian army, and after its ghastly defeat at Caporetto in 1917, it was only marginally effective. The Italians were unable to exploit the situation fully.

Nevertheless, the Italian leaders wanted more territory on the east coast of the Adriatic than Italy's allies had granted them in wartime treaties. Before they entered the war on the Allied side, they had received prom-ises from Great Britain, France, and Russia in the Treaty of London (1915) that when the war ended, Italy would receive large parcels of territory in the Alps and along the Adriatic coast. Now, the Italians saw the Treaty of London as only a first step to more extensive annexations in the Balkans.

French leaders opposed any increase in Italian territory beyond what they had agreed to give in the Treaty of London, but generally they sup-ported the Treaty of London line. The British, too, accepted the Italian boundary set in that treaty, although with no great enthusiasm. The United

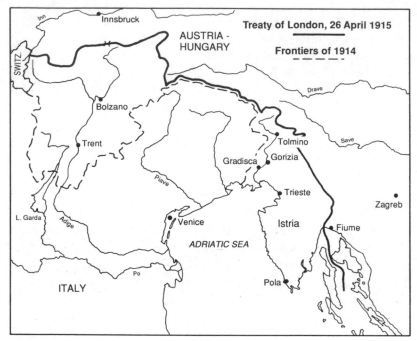

Italian Frontier, 1914, and Treaty of London Line (1915)

States' leaders had never signed the Treaty of London, and insofar as these matters involved them, they proposed a policy of ethnic self-determination.[5] Self-determination would deny the Italians most of the Adriatic territory promised in the Treaty of London and give that land, instead, to either Yugoslavia or Serbia.

The Kingdom of Serbia was, like Italy, an Allied nation. Unhappily for Allied unity, it claimed much of the same territory that Italy wanted. In 1915, the Central Powers had defeated the Serbians and occupied that nation, but the Royal Serbian Army had refused to surrender. It fought its way over the mountains and eventually joined with Allied forces in the southern Balkans, being, thereafter, an army without a country. During the war, some ethnic Serbs and other Slavs established the Yugoslav ("South Slav") Committee. The Yugoslav Committee wanted to include the Kingdom of Serbia in a Greater Yugoslavia, whereas exiled leaders of the occupied Kingdom of Serbia wanted to bring all territories where Slavs lived into an enlarged Kingdom of Serbia. Cooperating uneasily under the 1917 Declaration of Corfu, the Yugoslav Committee and the

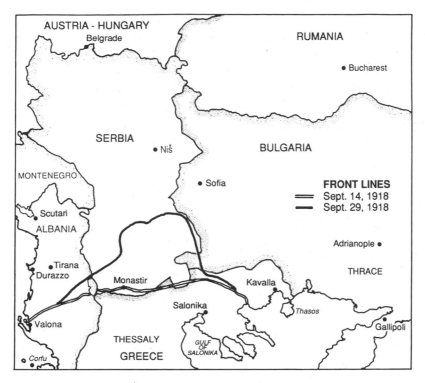

The Balkans and the Army of the East

Kingdom of Serbia fully agreed on only one policy: to oppose any Italian inroads into Slavic territory.

Not only was there a potential Serbian-Yugoslavian-Italian conflict, but other Balkan nations provided further complications. The leaders of Rumania, an Ally defeated in 1917 and driven from the war in May 1918, still nursed ambitions of growing at the expense of friends and foes alike. The Greeks, too, reluctant additions to the Allied side in 1916–17, had visions of territorial gains in Macedonia, as well as a keen interest in parts of Turkey.

The major Allied force in the southern Balkans, born in the withdrawal of soldiers from the military disaster of Gallipoli, was the Army of the East, based at Salonika.[6] In the early fall of 1918, that force was under the overall command of a French general and was a thoroughly multinational army. A predominantly British force under a British commander made up its right flank, the area closest to Constantinople. In the center and on the left flank was a mixed group of French, Italian, Greek, and Serbian soldiers.

That Army of the East faced Bulgaria, the weakest of the Central Powers, and on September 15, 1918, began a new offensive. By September 22, it had cut the enemy forces in two, and the Bulgarian army was in full retreat. A week later, Bulgaria surrendered, beginning the cascade of events that led directly to the end of World War I.

1

The Conference of Prime Ministers and the First German Note

On September 25, the Bulgarians decided to ask for an armistice. They lacked German aid, their front was crumbling, and they faced the Army of the East's renewed offensive as well as mutiny in their own forces. With no hope of victory left, Bulgarian representatives met with the commander of the Allied army facing them.[1] The French general who commanded that army, Louis Franchet d'Esperey, drew up the armistice conditions he wanted to impose on Bulgaria and sent them to the French prime minister, Georges Clemenceau, for approval.[2] Clemenceau endorsed them and cabled a copy to London, which the British approved, too.[3]

The Bulgarians accepted those terms, the Salonika Armistice, without objections on September 29.[4] The Salonika Armistice required the Bulgarians to evacuate the Greek and Serbian territory they still held. The Army of the East would stay on in the Bulgarian territory it already occupied, and Allied soldiers would have the right of transit through the rest of Bulgaria. The Bulgarians had to demobilize all but three divisions and surrender the equipment of the demobilized divisions to Allied supervision. Finally, the Salonika Armistice gave Bulgaria's allies, Germany and Austria-Hungary, only four weeks to withdraw their military units from Bulgaria.

Not only did the Bulgarians accept those terms readily, but they had something more in mind. A Bulgarian delegate told Franchet d'Esperey that Bulgaria might reenter the war, this time on the Allied side. That is, if the Allies gave Bulgaria peace terms, not just armistice terms, Bulgaria would become an Allied nation. The abdication of the wartime tsar of Bulgaria on October 3 made that change more feasible.[5]

In the meantime, American actions were disturbing the Balkan situation. The United States, a nation "associated" with the Allies in the war against Germany and Austria-Hungary, had never declared war on the other two Central Powers, Bulgaria and the Ottoman Empire. The Bulgarians, at the same time that they sent representatives to the Army of the East, had also asked President Woodrow Wilson to "use his influence" with the Allies to end the bloodshed.[6]

Wilson eagerly agreed to help the Bulgarians get an armistice "if the Bulgarian Government will authorize him to say that the conditions of the armistice are left to him for decision."[7] To cap it off, the American State Department on October 2 sent a circular letter to all Allied capitals stating that any peace with Bulgaria must form part of a general settlement of the war.[8] That is, the United States was insisting on taking a hand in Balkan affairs although it had not joined the Allies in making war there.

French reaction against American interference was sharp. Even before the United States' circular letter arrived, the French prime minister ordered the commander-in-chief of the Army of the East to have nothing to do with any Americans. Clemenceau told the British ambassador in Paris, "We must make it clear that the Allies have a free hand in a war which is ours and not America's."[9] He stayed angry. Days later, Clemenceau said he could reduce the official response he planned to give the United States to "This has nothing to do with you. Go to the devil."[10]

Yet, perhaps because of Wilson's pressure, Clemenceau backed away from drafting immediate peace terms for Bulgaria. To the British prime minister, he claimed that the difficulty in reaching a Bulgarian settlement came from greed in the Balkan nations.[11] The defeat of Bulgaria had "overexcited hungers that it will not be easy to satisfy." He added that ultimately there should be "one single and large peace." The British agreed with him that Bulgaria could not become an Anglo-French ally immediately.[12]

Behind all this talk was the fact that adding Bulgaria to Allied ranks would require a peace treaty. The British and French could not possibly exclude the Americans from participating in formal discussions over that settlement, and neither Clemenceau nor the British were ready yet to accept American involvement in Balkan affairs. The result was that Bulgaria would get no quick peace treaty. Whatever promises Allied representatives had held out to the Bulgarians—and there seem to have been some—evaporated in the months that followed. In the end, the Bulgarians could expect treatment no more generous than the other Central Powers got.[13]

Bulgaria's surrender changed the strategic situation dramatically. First, it isolated Turkey geographically and freed the Army of the East to attack Turkey-in-Europe. Second, with the Salonika Armistice, the British and French gained access to their former ally, Rumania. Out of the war since the Peace of Bucharest the previous spring, the Rumanians now could reenter the conflict and possibly attack the Hungarian provinces of Austria-Hungary in concert with Franchet d'Esperey's Army of the East. Third, the Army of the East might join the Italian army in an assault on southern Austria.

The Allied leaders thus had to decide among three courses of action: to attack Turkey-in-Europe, to attack Hungary, or to attack southern Austria. The British were the first to suggest that the leaders meet, to which Clemenceau answered that he wanted no formal conference on Balkan matters.[14] He never gave any explicit explanation for opposing a formal meeting, but it was probably because a formal meeting had to have representatives from the United States. He did tell the British ambassador in Paris that he was ready to meet informally with only the Italian and British prime ministers.

British Prime Minister David Lloyd George concluded that a meeting was essential, informal or not, and he went to Paris late on October 4.[15] The next morning, he began his day with a pile of French memoranda about the Balkans.[16] About noon, he went to the Ministry of War, where he met with Clemenceau and the Italian prime minister, who had just arrived from Rome.[17]

No official record of that first conversation exists, but discussions over the next three days reflect its substance. In this first meeting, the Allied prime ministers argued over command in the Balkans. Lloyd George wanted to pull the British general commanding the east wing of the Army of the East, General Sir George Milne, from under the command of General Franchet d'Esperey and have him attack Constantinople independently. Although the British had pride of place in the Army of the East, because that force was the lineal descendant of the soldiers who had stormed ashore at Gallipoli in 1915, the French recently had shouldered the heavier Allied burden in the region, eight French divisions against four British ones. For that reason, it was difficult for the British to sustain their wish that they alone should carry out the attack on Constantinople, the part of a Balkan campaign likeliest to yield lasting, concrete gains. Reaching no decisions at their first meeting, the Allied leaders met again late that afternoon and began to discuss the Army of the East, this time with a secretary present.[18]

They were not meeting as the Supreme War Council, the directing body set up late the previous year, but informally as a "Conference of Prime Ministers," with some other cabinet members present. The United States' diplomatic liaison officer to the Supreme War Council had already gone to the French Foreign Office to ask what was happening. In the past, he had attended meetings of the Supreme War Council and reported the discussions to Washington. Now, "he was all agog to know what we were discussing at the Conferences and why we did not have a Supreme War Council," the secretary of the British cabinet noted in his diary.[19] "We could hardly tell him that we were holding Conferences, instead of the S[upreme] W[ar] C[ouncil], because President Wilson would not declare war on Turkey and Bulgaria."

At their noon meeting, the Allied leaders had agreed they wanted to hear Marshal Ferdinand Foch, commander-in-chief of the Allied armies on the Western Front, assess the changed Balkan situation.[20] When Foch came to the afternoon meeting, Lloyd George summed up British aims for his benefit. The main British intention at that moment, the prime minister stressed, was to get the Ottoman Empire out of the war as soon as possible. He wanted to attack Turkey immediately and not wait for the outcome of any drawn-out Danubian campaign. If the Allies could force the Ottoman Empire out of the war, he said, the British could redeploy their soldiers from the Near East to the Western Front—a plan that is, incidentally, a clear sign that Lloyd George did not expect a speedy end to the war.

To Clemenceau's intense irritation, Foch supported a tentative British proposal to take sixty thousand men from Egypt and land them in Thrace, where they would constitute an independent British command.[21] At this meeting, however, the Allied leaders reached no conclusions concerning the Ottoman Empire, deferring discussion of military operations against Turkey to some later session.

As the Allied leaders began their late afternoon talks, they suddenly learned about a potentially far more important matter. Clemenceau announced interception of a message from the German government to Woodrow Wilson. In it, the Germans asked President Wilson to arrange an armistice that would allow preparation of a peace treaty based on his peace program, the Fourteen Points.[22]

Between September 26 and September 28, the German military leaders had concluded it was no longer possible to win the war, a judgment precipitated by the Bulgarian request for an armistice.[23] Here, late in September, the Germans were prepared to admit lack of success in the war, but not defeat. What they hoped for in a peace settlement was a Wilsonian arrangement on their west, with Alsace remaining German, in exchange for a free hand to the east.

The emperor reorganized the German cabinet, and on October 3, the Germans sent their request for an armistice to President Wilson.[24] In an independent move, the Austro-Hungarians, too, sent Wilson a note asking him to arrange an armistice.[25] Thus, the two principal enemy nations were each appealing for an armistice through the offices of the American president. From the Allied point of view, the problem was that these notes had gone directly to Wilson, not to the Allies. If the Allied leaders sent the president any comments or suggestions, he might resent their interference.

It was the afternoon of October 6 before the prime ministers officially discussed the subject they had certainly been mulling over for the past twenty-four hours: this German request for an armistice.[26] To put the subject into perspective, it is necessary to remember that the First German Note, as it came to be known, was not the first peace initiative of the war. The First German Note did finally lead to an armistice, so it has gained a historical status that makes it seem a critically important document. On October 6, 1918, there was no more reason for the Allied leaders to assume that this overture would lead directly to peace than, for example, the Prince Sixtus letter or the other peace proposals of 1917 had.[27] To assess the work of the Allied leaders early in October, it is necessary to recognize that they saw the First German Note as a good sign, indeed an excellent one, but in their eyes, it by no means assured an early German surrender.[28]

The First German Note was brief.[29] In its entirety, it read:

The German Government requests the President of the United States of America to take steps for the restoration of peace, to notify all belligerents of this request, and to invite them to delegate plenipotentiaries for the purpose of taking up negotiations. The German Government accepts, as a basis for the peace negotiations, the program laid down by the President of the United States in his message to Congress of January 8, 1918, and in his subsequent pronouncements, particularly in his address of September 27, 1918. In order to avoid further bloodshed the German Government requests to bring about the immediate conclusion of a general armistice on land, on water, and in the air.

At first, none of the Allied prime ministers seems to have put much concentrated thought on armistice terms for Germany. As the secretary of the conference phrased it laconically in his later recollections, "It was decided that work should be started on the German armistice terms in case anything came of it."[30] Underlining the surprise the German note created is the dearth of civilian or military staff studies on the problems of an armistice.[31]

Now, Lloyd George suggested that the prime ministers draw up general principles for an armistice and then refer the matter to their military leaders. For the first condition, he proposed requiring the German army to retreat behind the Rhine, leaving Alsace and Lorraine as a neutral barrier. The Italians added that, like the line of the Rhine, the Allies should require the German and Austro-Hungarian forces facing Italy to fall back beyond Istria. Lloyd George said he doubted the Austrians would accept such a provision, but he was quite willing to insert it in the draft armistice. His easy acceptance of the Italian proposal, despite his belief that the Austrians would reject it, is a sign that he did not take the First German Note as a promise that the war was coming to an immediate end.

Other proposals for items to include in an armistice with Germany followed, and the prime ministers eventually created a brief guide of eight points. The Central Powers must evacuate their soldiers from France, Belgium, Italy, and Luxembourg.[32] The Germans must retire behind the line of the Rhine and evacuate their troops from Alsace and Lorraine, although the Allies would not occupy those provinces. The "same condition" would apply on the Italian Front, and the Central Powers must withdraw their soldiers from Serbia and Montenegro. The Central Powers must take immediate steps to evacuate their forces from Russian and Rumanian territory, and all enemy soldiers had to leave the Caucasus. Finally, submarine warfare would cease.

This eight-point guide was a military document, not a political one. The prime ministers had overlooked some important items, but they could add them to the document without changing its essentially military character. For example, the eight-point guide established no time limits within which the Central Powers had to carry out the actions required. Without

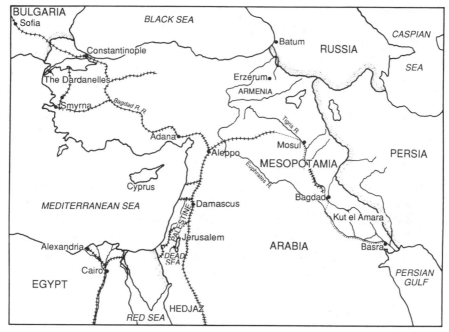

Near East

time limits, the Germans could withdraw their army in a leisurely fashion and entrench it behind the Rhine, but adding time limits would not change the basic military nature of the document.[33]

The eight-point guide did little more than restore the prewar balance of power. The Central Powers could simply withdraw to their 1914 frontiers in the west and south. True, the Rhineland, Alsace-Lorraine, and the Trentino would be stripped of enemy soldiers, but in the eight-point guide, the Allied prime ministers did not propose occupying those areas. The prime ministers required submarine warfare to cease, but they did not demand the surrender or internment of German submarines; nor did they mention the German and Austrian surface battle fleets.

An armistice based upon the eight-point guide would give the Allies an end to hostilities, but it would give them none of their war aims. What happened between this time and early November was a gradual transformation of Allied armistice proposals until they came to embody a great number of war aims. When that transformation was complete, the Allies would receive the fruits of victory not in a later peace treaty but in the armistice itself. The armistice would become a preliminary peace, and a harsh one.

After drawing up their eight-point guide for a German armistice, the prime ministers turned once more to the subject of the Ottoman Empire. This time, they discussed the armistice terms they might impose on Turkey.[34] In earlier, secret meetings with Allied representatives, the Turkish sultan had insisted on only two points in an armistice: first, he must remain on the throne, and second, the core of Turkey must remain an independent nation. Neither of the sultan's demands seemed excessive to the prime ministers.

With that much agreed to, Lloyd George presented a set of armistice terms for Turkey that the British cabinet had drafted, and he added that the Turks might want more than only armistice terms. They were likely to ask for a peace treaty. Therefore, he said, the Allied prime ministers had to decide immediately how much territory Turkey would keep. Lloyd George noted that it would be easier for the Allies to settle the matter quickly among themselves than to postpone decisions to a peace conference, for, like the situation with Bulgaria, the United States was not at war with the Ottoman Empire.

It might have been easier for the Allies to deal with Turkey than with Bulgaria. Territorial problems vexed any attempt to draw up a peace with either enemy, but for the Ottoman Empire, the Allies had already made arrangements among themselves—the so-called secret treaties. For a Turkish settlement, the most important of these treaties was the Anglo-French Agreement of 1916, better known as the Sykes-Picot Agreement. The British had also made pledges to the Arabs to encourage their revolt against the Ottoman Empire. Because of the Russian Revolution, an extension of the Sykes-Picot Agreement, the St. Jean de Maurienne Agreement of 1917, was never ratified, and an August 1917 Anglo-Italian Agreement met a similar fate. All these pacts, even if they had never been properly ratified, had created a framework for agreement on Turkey.

Nevertheless, to Lloyd George's proposal that the Allies settle peace terms for Turkey among themselves, the French foreign minister, Stephen Pichon, responded primly that it would be improper to discuss a Turkish peace treaty without President Wilson.[35] Because Pichon, known popularly as "Clemenceau's little bow-wow," was incapable of independent thought, this sentiment was no doubt Clemenceau's. Despite Pichon's opposition, Lloyd George persisted, but he received no support, and his proposal died.

The Allied leaders, however, went on to discuss the British draft armistice conditions for Turkey. After adding several items at French and Italian suggestion, they formally adopted the British cabinet's draft. According to this draft armistice, the Ottoman Empire must demobilize all its armed forces, open the Straits, allow Allied use of Constantinople as a base, and grant the Allies access to the Black Sea. The Turks must surrender their entire fleet, which the Allies would intern. Allied forces could occupy important strategic points, and the empire must withdraw its soldiers to its 1914 frontier.

When, how, and by whom the Allies would give these terms to the Turks was not yet clear; nor was there any certainty that the Turks would accept them. The draft Turkish armistice was noticeably harsher than the Bulgarian one—the demobilization of all forces and surrender of the fleet—but the document did not foreshadow the division of the Ottoman Empire among the Allies. Yet the secret treaties provided for precisely such a division of the Ottoman Empire, except for its Turkish core, and that is what Lloyd George had wanted to settle without Woodrow Wilson's interference.

The following morning, the British leaders met with Marshal Foch to discuss manpower needs for the coming year.[36] In the face of Foch's insistence that the Allies prepare for a supreme effort in the spring of 1919 and his truculent demand for more men, the British claimed they had no reserves in Britain or the Empire. They told Foch they could not even maintain all their present divisions in 1919 at their current strength. Foch was pressing the British very hard to provide manpower, which seems extravagant in view of the great increase in the United States' forces already taking place. If Foch had any confidence that the Germans would surrender in the next few months, any thought that the First German Note would lead to an armistice, then he had every reason to avoid a confrontation with the British over manpower, a subject fraught with diplomatic peril. At this meeting, the British prime minister put Foch off with occasional bitter exchanges, and they settled nothing.

That afternoon, the Conference of Prime Ministers reassembled to a seething crisis.[37] General Franchet d'Esperey had just issued orders to the Army of the East that created a new army on his eastern flank in Thrace, where Britain's Sir George Milne had been the commander.[38] A French general would command that new army, which would include five divisions: three Greek, one British, and one French. Franchet d'Esperey ordered this new army to march on Constantinople, while he sent General Milne and other forces under Milne's command north toward Rumania.[39] Franchet d'Esperey issued those orders simultaneously with, but in ignorance of, Lloyd George's plan to carry out the landing of sixty thousand men from Egypt on the eastern flank of the Army of the East and then to have those men march under independent British command against Constantinople. That is, the British and the French were each trying to do the other out of the prize of Constantinople. Franchet d'Esperey's troop dispositions, Lloyd George said, were "unfair" to the British, who had carried out most of the fighting against Turkey.[40] Bitterly, Lloyd George added that Franchet d'Esperey was not behaving like an Allied commander: "His plan was mainly political, not military." Therefore, said Lloyd George, the British government would remove General Milne from French command.

Suddenly, Allied unity was in peril. But Clemenceau disavowed Franchet d'Esperey's plan and Lloyd George graciously proposed a compromise. By its terms, Milne would remain in command of the east wing and march on Constantinople, he would stay under Franchet d'Esperey's orders, and Lloyd George would withdraw his proposal that the new forces landing in Thrace be under an independent British command. Clemenceau accepted this formula.[41] Through this agreement, those new forces in Thrace would fall under Franchet d'Esperey's orders, in name, at least. But petty bickering was souring the alliance at the moment of victory. Great Powers' competition for the spoils of war was becoming as much a factor in events as military operations.[42]

With the unpleasantness concerning orders for the Army of the East settled for the moment, but with its echoes still hanging in the air, the prime ministers turned again to the subject of an armistice with Germany. Clemenceau said he had asked Foch about occupying strategic points—for example, places in Alsace and Lorraine. Clemenceau was beginning the process of turning the eight-point guide into a political document. To the French, the return of Alsace and Lorraine, the Lost Provinces of 1871, symbolized victory. The eight-point guide only neutralized them. Clemenceau's suggestion about occupying strategic points might be a first step toward occupying the provinces as a whole.

Clemenceau reported Foch as saying that the Allies should require "all that is necessary from Germany, but not more," an elastic measurement because Foch also warned the Allies to guard against German treachery. Nevertheless, Foch insisted that "the Allies must not open themselves to the reproach of exposing thousands of men to be killed simply because they would not accede to reasonable conditions." Concluding his report of Foch's views, Clemenceau made the point that if the Allies granted

Germany an armistice, it must be for only a short duration, so that the pause would not sap the Allied soldiers' "keenness for victory."

Clemenceau saw an armistice as only a brief and temporary suspension of hostilities. He proposed making it for only three days. In that short time, the Allies would ask definite questions of the Central Powers, such as whether they would cede Alsace-Lorraine, the Trentino, and the German colonies in the peace terms to come. If the Allies received acceptable answers, the armistice would continue; if they did not, the armistice would end. That is, Clemenceau would allow a brief pause to agree on preliminary peace terms.

Lloyd George claimed he feared an armistice. Once fighting had stopped, it would be "difficult, if not impossible," to take up arms again. Before the Allies granted any armistice at all, he wanted to know what terms Germany would accept. That is, in contrast to Clemenceau, Lloyd George wanted to arrive at an agreement on preliminary peace terms before granting a cease-fire.

This concern about whether Allied forces could resume hostilities after a pause, actually an assessment of the soldiers' morale, was one of the forces that drove the Allied leaders during the next four weeks to include more and more political elements in the armistice. The truth about the soldiers' morale is difficult to discern. In 1917, large portions of the French army had mutinied, and the army chiefs had restored order only with great difficulty.[43] The British had kept order among their own forces, but their men were weary, and the Italian soldiers had never recovered from their 1917 defeat at Caporetto.

Allied victories since June 1918 and the increasing number of the United States' soldiers on the Western Front were combining to raise Allied morale. The leaders, however, were not sure how deep that feeling ran. They could not tell if improved morale was only a temporary enthusiasm or a permanent sentiment.[44] Foch, who said later that "victory gave wings" to the soldiers, was more optimistic than the political leaders and probably more optimistic than the facts justified.

With no final decision made on terms for Germany, the prime ministers referred their eight-point guide and the question of armistice terms to the Military Representatives to the Supreme War Council, a technical committee that met at Versailles. The Supreme War Council itself, composed of the "Prime Minister and a Member of the Government of each of the Great Powers," included no military members.[45] The Supreme War Council received military advice from the Military Representatives, to which each nation appointed a general, and it was natural for the prime ministers to ask them for advice now. The prime ministers sent their eight-point guide to the Military Representatives on the evening of October 7, requiring recommendations by the next afternoon—obviously too quickly for detailed study.

The Military Representatives met the next morning. The prime ministers had told them to meet as a "military and naval committee," and not formally, perhaps because naval representatives were to meet with them. Unlike the prime ministers' wish to avoid American involvement in their discussions, which had prompted them to come together as a conference rather than as the Supreme War Council, the prime ministers expected American participation in this committee meeting. Notice of the meeting went to the United States' Military Representative, General Tasker Bliss.

Bliss knew about the First German Note only from the newspapers, and he lacked instructions.[46] He concluded that the reason for the prime ministers' requesting an opinion from the military and naval committee was to use him as a medium through which to send their views to Washington, which would happen when he reported whatever occurred at the meeting. Temporizing, Bliss did not attend, excusing himself on the grounds of illness; he did, however, send his chief of staff and a naval captain, warning them to take no action whatever.[47]

The Military Representatives and the naval leaders turned the prime ministers' eight-point guide into a more precise document and added several items.[48] The military and naval committee kept the prime ministers' clauses requiring the immediate evacuation of French, Belgian, Luxembourgeois, and Italian territory and demanding that the German army retire behind the Rhine. Much the same conditions would apply on the Italian-Austrian border. Like the prime ministers, the military and naval committee operated on the assumption that armistice terms for Germany should include armistice terms for Austria-Hungary as well, which was reasonable enough. Although it was conceivable that Germany might fight on for a time if Austria-Hungary surrendered, it was impossible for Austria-Hungary to stay in the war without Germany. Like the eight-point guide, the military and naval committee's draft required the evacuation of Serbia and Montenegro, and it added Albania to the list. The Central Powers must evacuate the Caucasus and begin to evacuate all pre-1914 Russian and Rumanian territory.

To those conditions, the military and naval committee added a requirement that the Central Powers return all Allied prisoners without reciprocity. Indeed, the Allies would use German and Austrian prisoners "for reparation of the willful damage done" in the war. The military and naval committee also added a provision stating that the Allied blockade would remain in force, which the prime ministers had assumed but not made explicit.

The committee added the time limits for German withdrawal that the prime ministers had not set in their eight-point guide, requiring the enemy withdrawal to take place within four weeks. That would force the Germans to abandon much of their heavy equipment and cause the disorganization of retreating German army units as well. The Germans themselves estimated that an orderly withdrawal would require two or three months.[49] Thus far, the committee's draft did not differ substantially from the prime ministers' eight-point guide, except possibly for the forced labor they wanted to exact from prisoners of war. Then the military and naval leaders made additions that changed the nature of the document.

"The first essential of an armistice is the disarmament of the enemy under the control of the Allies," their report read. To that end, the military and naval committee required that the Germans surrender "all arms, munitions of war and supplies" between the front lines and the "left bank of the Rhine." Because that zone held most of the German forces, this provision would require the Germans to surrender most of their arms. "I don't see what guarantee we shall get worth having unless we disarm the brutes," the British chief of the Imperial General Staff wrote in his diary.[50]

The second addition the military and naval committee made was to the naval terms. Where the prime ministers had required only that submarine warfare stop, the military and naval committee demanded the internment of sixty German submarines in Allied ports. The prime ministers' draft did not mention enemy surface fleets, other than including them in the general suspension of hostilities. The military and naval committee directed all enemy surface warships to withdraw to ports specified by the Allies.

The military and naval committee made a third major addition to the eight-point guide: "The Government of Germany," the report of the military and naval committee read, "is in a position peculiar among the Nations of Europe in that its word cannot be believed, and that it denies any obligation of honor."[51] Therefore, the Allies must require that Germany furnish "material guarantees on a scale which will serve the purpose aimed at by a signed agreement in cases amongst ordinary civilized nations." To fulfill this requirement, the military and naval committee demanded Allied occupation of parts of Alsace and Lorraine.

In Alsace and Lorraine, the Allies would occupy the "fortresses" of Metz, Thionville, Strasbourg, and Neuf-Brisach. Those cities may have been fortresses, but their importance lay more in their being railroad centers. The Allies would not occupy the whole of Alsace and Lorraine, to be sure, but the occupation of those four cities would require the maintenance of lines of communication to them. Because Strasbourg and Neuf-Brisach are on the extreme eastern boundary of the provinces and commanded railroad crossings over the great military barrier of the Rhine River, the Allies would control the eastern approaches to the provinces. The difference between the number of troops involved in occupying the provinces and the number necessary to occupy strategic points and maintain lines of communication connecting them to the Allied forces in France was small, although in international law there is an important distinction between occupying certain centers and occupying a whole province.

Finally, the military and naval committee, deferring to British sentiment, required the surrender of Heligoland to the Allies. Since the beginning of the war, the British, who had ceded the island to Germany in 1890, had reproached themselves for lack of foresight. Throughout the war, the island, which lies about forty miles off the mouth of the Elbe, had served Germany as a superb submarine base.

Including the time limits the prime ministers had omitted, requiring disarmament, and demanding the occupation of strategic points in Alsace and Lorraine were the most important changes the military and naval committee made. Putting in time limits did not change the character of the document. The other provisions did. Where the prime ministers had created a document that retained, but did not increase, the military supremacy of the Allies and the United States, these new clauses would magnify that supremacy.

While the members of the military and naval committee were working on their terms for the Conference of Prime Ministers, Marshal Foch, at Clemenceau's direction, was preparing his own draft.[52] Foch's terms for the Western Front went further than the military and naval committee's terms.[53]

First, like the eight-point guide and the committee's draft, Foch required the evacuation of countries "invaded contrary to all right." He nominated to that list not only the nations of Belgium, France, and Luxembourg, but also the provinces of Alsace and Lorraine. That is, Foch would end any ambiguity over an Allied occupation of Alsace and Lorraine. Like the invaded portions of France, Alsace and Lorraine would be restored immediately to the French nation. Foch also would require the Germans to carry out the evacuation of all this territory even more rapidly than the military and naval committee had ordered. The committee had given the Germans four weeks to evacuate Allied territory and Alsace-Lorraine; Foch insisted that they do it in two.

Another clause was ominous. Foch demanded "possession of securities [gages] for the reparations to be exacted for the destruction perpetrated in Allied countries." To gain that deposit against future claims, Foch demanded the occupation of the German territory on the left bank of the Rhine within thirty days. With this clause, Foch was suggesting that the peace treaty would contain enormous financial claims against Germany, contradicting Woodrow Wilson's hope for a peace without indemnities.[54]

The proposal to occupy the left bank had another aspect as well. Voices in France had demanded the annexation of the left bank as a suitable outcome of the war.[55] Although Foch made no claim for annexation in this draft of terms, occupation of this large and valuable part of the German Empire hinted at later acquisition.

Foch also required "a suitable military base of departure." He demanded bridgeheads across the upper Rhine at Rastadt, Strasbourg, and Neuf-Brisach. The bridgeheads would consist of thirty-kilometer semicircles on the right bank. So the military and naval committee had required the occupation of only the western end of those bridges in Alsace, but Foch was demanding territory on the eastern bank.

Occupation of bridgeheads farther north could serve a military purpose, but bridgeheads on the upper Rhine were militarily pointless. Bridgeheads downstream, at such transportation hubs as Koblenz or Mainz, could facilitate an offensive into vital areas of Germany, but bridgeheads at Rastadt, Strasbourg, and Neuf-Brisach opened only into Baden and led nowhere, although they controlled three of the four Rhine crossings between Karlsruhe and Switzerland. The only purposes for holding them would be to disrupt north-south movement of German forces or to protect Alsace from a counterattack that was unlikely to occur.[56]

To those three propositions, Foch added a requirement that the Germans surrender intact all the military equipment and supplies they could not remove within the strict time limits he demanded. Superficially, at least, that requirement was less harsh than the military and naval committee's terms, which demanded the surrender of all German arms and munitions between the Western Front and the Rhine. Foch also required the return of all French and Belgian railway equipment the Germans had seized during the war. With railroads transporting and supplying the armies of 1918, the surrender of rolling stock would limit the mobility of the German army and make its evacuation less orderly.

In summary, Foch produced a document far more political than the one the members of the military and naval committee had crafted. He demanded what was, in effect, the immediate retrocession of Alsace and Lorraine. Second, he demanded occupation of the entirety of the left bank, which presaged either enormous reparations claims or territorial demands or both. Third, he required bridgeheads across the upper Rhine that had no great military significance.

When the Conference of Prime Ministers heard both the military and naval committee's draft and Foch's terms, one of the British representatives remarked that they "amounted virtually to an unconditional capitulation."[57] Lloyd George objected to both sets of terms. "Between an absolute negative and an answer such as was proposed by the military representatives and Marshal Foch he preferred a simple 'No,'" he said. "Their document amounted to a 'No' with a swagger." Clemenceau responded that provisions that seemed severe at present "might be absolutely necessary in two or three months' time," which suggested neither moderation nor a belief in an immediate end to the war. Alone among the prime ministers at this time, Clemenceau supported the harshest military recommendations.

The position here is imbalanced. Lloyd George (with the support of the Italians) was leaning to the judgment that the Allies should limit armistice terms to only that which was necessary to keep the Germans from improving their position.[58] Even Clemenceau did not believe he could get what he wanted in an armistice. "The general view," the secretary of the meeting wrote in his diary, "was that we were not in a position to impose" terms like the military and naval committee's or Foch's.[59] Yet the prime ministers had no enthusiasm for terms as light as those that were feasible. What they could demand was not enough; what they wanted seemed impossible. It is strange that none of them realized yet that if the war was to end decisively in their favor, the Allies must have—lacking a rout of the German army—some version of a preliminary peace.

Because President Wilson had not yet responded to the First German Note, the prime ministers were under no pressure to reach conclusions, and discussion was fitful. Clemenceau said that the Allied leaders should postpone decision, and Lloyd George agreed. With the two drafts of armistice terms as well as their own eight-point guide in their pockets, the prime ministers adjourned to await developments, agreeing tacitly to stay in Paris for another day in case Wilson answered the First German Note by that time.[60]

He did, and early on the morning of October 9, the Allied leaders received the text of the First Wilson Note.[61] It was brief. In it, Wilson asked if the Germans accepted the Fourteen Points.[62] He also required the evacuation of Allied territory as a precondition to any armistice. The prime ministers met again that afternoon, and Clemenceau began the discussion with the judgment that President Wilson's note was an "excellent document."[63] Without consulting the Allies, Clemenceau said, the president had required the Germans to evacuate Allied territory. After the Germans had evacuated this territory, the Allies could consult with their military advisers to draw up further necessary conditions. To do anything else at the present time, Clemenceau said, "would play into the hands of the Germans."

Lloyd George objected sharply to Clemenceau's suggestion that the prime ministers do nothing more for the moment. It was becoming clear, he said, that Germany was a defeated nation, and the Germans would certainly accept the Fourteen Points. He, however, had serious reservations about some of them, especially the freedom of the seas, and he wanted to know more about some of the other points as well. Moreover, the mere evacuation of Allied territory was not enough. If the Allies did nothing, the Germans would agree to the Fourteen Points, evacuate Allied territory, and then say they accepted Wilson's proposal and that the armistice was now in effect.

He returned to the point he had made two days before: "Once an armistice was declared we should never be able to start the war again." If the Allies could get their hands on Alsace-Lorraine, the Trentino, Trieste, and the German colonies, they would achieve the greater part of their aims. If the Allies agreed to an armistice that gave them only the evacuation of Allied territory, and then negotiations broke down, they might have nothing to show for years of bloodshed.

Lloyd George offered the draft of a telegram he proposed sending to Wilson.[64] After praising Wilson's precondition that the Germans evacuate Allied territory, it went on to say that armistice terms "can be fixed only after consultation with the military experts and according to the military situation at the precise moment when negotiations take place." The Italians supported Lloyd George, and Clemenceau, after arguing that the telegram was unnecessary, finally agreed grumpily to sending it.[65] The Conference of Prime Ministers also cabled Wilson, asking him to send someone to meet with the Supreme War Council.[66] Past events suggested that if President Wilson did send anyone, it would be his friend, Colonel Edward M. House, who had already represented the president in Europe on several occasions.

With the sending of these two telegrams, the prime ministers adjourned. They made no public announcement about the German request for an armistice. Indeed, they had made few firm decisions regarding the Germans. The prime ministers were not convinced that harsh armistice terms, such as those the military and naval committee proposed or those Marshal Foch had drawn up, were possible. Yet their war aims included provisions that a peace negotiated with Germany as an equal could never gain. None of the prime ministers was prepared to make a compromise peace, but lenient armistice terms would leave the German army in substantially its current condition. With a powerful army still in existence, the Germans could reject a later peace treaty that gave the Allies everything they wanted.

The prime ministers worried, also, about President Wilson's Fourteen Points, which had suddenly become central to events. Unexpectedly, the Allies found that a document to which they had never assented, or been asked to assent, had become critical to negotiations. But the prime ministers had reached no accord among themselves on what they wanted to substitute for Wilson's program; nor were they unanimous in believing that Wilson's Fourteen Points were unacceptable. The prime ministers neither agreed to them nor agreed to make common cause in opposing them.

Even if they united to oppose Wilson, it would only be worthwhile to make a stand against him, at the likely cost of disrupting military unity, if it were certain that the German overtures would bear fruit. Past events allowed the prime ministers to walk cautiously. The chances were good that nothing immediate would come of the First German Note. If so, they could deal with President Wilson at leisure. Politicians develop few instincts so well as the ability to avoid a crisis if no crisis is needed.

The days of discussion in Paris had also shown sharp divisions between Great Britain and France. Problems between the two were clearest in discussions over the Balkans, but there was an undercurrent of unease over other matters as well.[67] Poor Franco-Italian relations had caused concern in the days before the Paris meetings. Although Franco-Italian relations saw no great improvement, they were a less serious difficulty than they might have been otherwise, now that the war was going well.

Much had happened in a ten-day period. Bulgaria had gone out of the war with the Salonika Armistice, Turkey was sinking, and Germany and Austria-Hungary had both sent messages to President Wilson asking him to arrange an armistice. The prime ministers, buoyed up by those events as well as by substantial victories in the Saint Quentin sector of the Western Front, had sound grounds for optimism.

During the next three weeks, it began to appear more and more likely that the overtures of the Germans and Austro-Hungarians would lead to an armistice. The leaders of the Allied nations would meet again at the end of the month, this time in company with a representative of the United States. During the intervening weeks, the Allied leaders grappled with defining exactly what they wanted from an armistice and from a peace, while President Wilson negotiated with the Germans.

2

Woodrow Wilson, the Fourteen Points, and the German Notes

The Germans would accept the Fourteen Points, and the Allied leaders would eventually assent to the Wilsonian program with only two formal reservations. Thus, according to Harry Rudin writing in 1944, the Allied and Associated Powers and the Germans agreed, with two open and explicit exceptions, to make a peace based on the Fourteen Points. "The pre-armistice agreement," Rudin wrote, "deprived the [Allied and Associated Powers] of the legal and moral right to do as they pleased with Germany, a right they could be presumed to have acquired under an unconditional surrender."[1] Other commentators, too, have declared that Allied and German agreement to the Fourteen Points created a set of obligations that restricted what the Allied and Associated Powers should demand of Germany in the peace treaty. "Many persons believe," John Maynard Keynes wrote in the fall of 1919, "that the armistice terms constituted the first contract between the Allied and Associated Powers and the German Government."[2]

What these critics fail to realize is that the Fourteen Points were too imprecise to constitute the basis for a peace treaty. Wilson had not set forth a rigorous guide for action. Few of his Fourteen Points made definite statements, and qualifying phrases sapped the precision from what was left. In addition, Wilson himself amended many of his points during the course of 1918. The resulting vagueness of the Fourteen Points ruled out their ever serving as a contract, although it was their very lack of precision that made them negotiable and a program that the Allies could accept.

To a great degree, the course of negotiations with Germany would depend on Woodrow Wilson's mind and personality. There is no doubting Wilson's idealism and his commitment to humanity; yet he was certainly too conscious of his own principles, and he subordinated people to issues. Wilson also assumed that all right-thinking people shared his ideals, which meant that his opponents were wrong, and probably evil as well. Lloyd George, who would be shut in a room for five months with the president during the peace conference, wrote later that Wilson "was the most extraordinary compound I have ever encountered of the noble visionary, the implacable and unscrupulous partisan, the exalted idealist and the man of rather petty personal rancours."[3]

It is ironic that a person who had constructed youthful fantasies about being the prime minister of Great Britain and holding Parliament in thrall with his oratory should have the speeches he delivered during 1918 become central to events at the end of the war. On January 8, 1918, to a joint session of Congress, Wilson had presented his Fourteen Points as the basis of the peace the United States sought.[4]

The first of the Fourteen Points, "open covenants openly arrived at," Wilson said later, did not prohibit confidential discussions.[5] It was his second point, the "freedom of the seas," that became the most controversial.[6] In his original statement, Wilson meant to give absolute protection to the maritime rights of neutral nations, but he consistently avoided saying so. Memories of the British blockade still rankled, but during 1918 Wilson was not overly solicitous about allowing the few remaining neutrals the maritime rights he had demanded for the United States before that nation entered the war.

Qualifications weakened both the third point, which proposed the removal "of all economic barriers," and the fourth point, disarmament. The economic clause suggested the removal of trade barriers only "so far as possible," and the fourth point, the disarmament clause, asked only that armaments be reduced "to the lowest point consistent with domestic safety." For reasons he never made clear, Wilson considered the League of Nations and the first three clauses—open covenants, freedom of the seas, and reduction of economic barriers—the "essentially American" war aims. He did not include the fourth point, which asked for a degree of disarmament, as an American war aim.[7]

When Wilson drafted his fifth point, the "absolutely impartial adjustment of all colonial claims," he intended it to nullify the treaties the Allies had made with one another before the United States entered the war.[8] But even if he gained the abrogation of those treaties, he left the future of colonial territories uncertain, because he gave the interests of colonial peoples only equal weight with the claims of governments, and equality might very well be in the eye of the beholder.

Events dealt harshly with his sixth point, the evacuation of Russia. When he issued the Fourteen Points, the Bolsheviks and the Germans were negotiating peace, and in March 1918, Lenin's Bolsheviks accepted ignominious peace terms from Germany and Austria-Hungary, the Treaty of Brest-Litovsk. After that peace treaty, the Allied nations and the United States intervened in Russia, so that by the time Germany requested an armistice in October 1918, the forces operating in Russia were Allied and American as well as German and Austrian. By October, too, both the Allies and the Germans were supporting puppet governments in the territory of the Russian Empire. Complicating the Russian question still further were Allied fears that Bolshevism might spread to infect other areas of shattered Europe.

The next seven points, the territorial points, contain more ambiguity than appears with casual reading. The seventh point, requiring the evacuation and restoration of Belgium, was the most definite of all of them, but Wilson left restoration undefined. His eighth point demanded the evacuation of France and righting "the wrong done to France by Prussia in 1871 in the matter of Alsace-Lorraine." Righting it did not necessarily mean France's annexing the Lost Provinces, but by October, Wilson saw the impossibility of any Franco-German compromise and said that the French must get the provinces back. Nevertheless, their return might very well be against the wishes of many of the provinces' inhabitants, indeed, of a majority in some districts.

The ninth point, the "readjustment" of Italian frontiers, implied territorial gains for Italy. But although Point Nine endorsed the incorporation of *Italia irridenta* into the Kingdom of Italy, the Italians wanted more. The Treaty of London (1915), which had brought Italy into the war on the Allied side, gave Italy non-Italian territory along the Austrian frontier. The Allied nation of Serbia and the Yugoslav Committee claimed some of the land that the Treaty of London gave Italy. Even worse, Italian hopes now far exceeded the Treaty of London line. Point Nine, if it were honestly applied to include only "clearly recognizable lines of nationality," would deny Italy many of the Treaty of London gains and certainly any greater claims. In his speech, Wilson drew no precise boundaries, and he ignored the Treaty of London.

The tenth point asked that the peoples of Austria-Hungary get the "freest opportunity of autonomous development," and by the fall of 1918, this point was dead. By this time, the Allies and the United States had recognized, to varying degrees, the claims of successor nations. Something of the same problem affected the eleventh point, in which Wilson discussed the Balkans; even worse, Point Eleven was naïve. Wilson asked that boundaries be set "along historically established lines of allegiance and nationality," and such lines simply did not exist between Balkan nations. Two wars in the Balkans just before the World War served as conclusive proof that boundaries were malleable and that the leaders of those nations calculated in terms other than common interest.

Wilson's twelfth point, on Turkey, demanded free passage through the Dardanelles, and like the Austro-Hungarian article, it asked that Turkey's subject nationalities have the opportunity for autonomous development. It was just barely possible to reconcile this clause with the secret treaties on the Ottoman Empire, if "absolutely unmolested opportunity of autonomous development" for the non-Turkish peoples—in Syria, Mesopotamia, Jordan, Lebanon, Palestine, and Arabia—meant their coming under the control of some European nation.

His thirteenth point asked for the restoration of an independent Poland with access to the sea. In this case, as in every case of setting boundaries in central Europe, Wilson assumed clearer geographical divisions than really existed. Moreover, Poland could gain access to the sea only by incorporating into the new nation indisputably non-Polish populations.

Events had moved past these seven territorial points. Wilson admitted he saw difficulties in enacting them, but he believed a fair settlement could be reached through self-determination, a solution far simpler to propose than to apply. Even in western Europe, clear ethnic frontiers did not exist, and in central and eastern Europe, the problems were greater. For example, Italians formed a majority or large minority in many of the cities, such as Trieste, along the Adriatic's eastern coast, but almost no Italians lived in the rural areas that surrounded and supported those cities. In the less developed areas of eastern Europe, such as Galicia and eastern Poland, the peasants had little concept of nationality to self-determine.

Wilson may have imagined long lines of peaceful citizens waiting patiently to cast a ballot determining their future nationality, but even if the Allied nations could maintain order while people voted, only special and rare territories were susceptible to judgment by plebiscite. The territory had to be contiguous with the national soil of the choices offered. The frontier could not, or should not, cut across any vital economic or military interests of either nation. The area a plebiscite judged had to be small enough to provide for the decisions of compact minorities, but large enough to avoid creating a border that was an insane checkerboard. All this is not to say that self-determination was inferior to other and more traditional ways of establishing boundaries. All methods have faults, and perhaps the faults of self-determination were less than the faults of Absolutist diplomacy. But self-determination was no panacea for the territorial ills of the world.

Wilson's fourteenth and last point called for the formation of a "general association of nations." None of the Allies had any real objection to creating what people already were calling the League of Nations. Three days before Wilson's January 8 speech, Lloyd George had proposed some sort of international organization.[9] The French might deprecate such an organization unless they could turn it into an armed alliance, but they did not oppose it. Wilson believed that it was central to the peace settlement. It would be, he said in a mixed image, "the pillars on which the house will stand."[10]

During 1918, Wilson made three additional speeches amending and adding to his program.[11] On February 11, he presented self-determination as a necessary ingredient for the territorial settlements. Then, on the Fourth of July, he stressed that nations must live under a "reign of law." To further the reign of law and because he believed democracies were less warlike than other systems, Wilson stated that "every arbitrary power anywhere that can separately, secretly, or of its single choice disturb the peace of the world" must be destroyed or rendered impotent. That thought reappeared in Wilson's later negotiations with the Germans.

On September 27, Wilson made the last of his speeches on American war aims. In that September speech, he stressed particularly his aversion to secret treaties, perhaps as an opening salvo in an attack on the interallied arrangements he knew he must face in drawing up a peace treaty.

These four speeches, the Fourteen Points and the three subsequent speeches that Wilson delivered during 1918, constituted the Wilsonian program. They can be interpreted as an earnest and methodical attempt to root out the causes of war, but for Wilson's program to work as he hoped, it needed precisely defined elements. Nations must agree to and then follow clear rules, not unilaterally developed perceptions of self-interest, and the fuzzier Wilson's clauses were, the likelier it was that some nation would act contrary to the spirit behind his program. But ambiguity made the Fourteen Points negotiable and was their only chance of winning international acceptance. In a world in which national sovereignty was king, leaders would reject the diminution of their freedom that precisely defined rules entailed.

Wilson could not have both precision and agreement. To the degree that his program was imprecise, it was acceptable to the Allied leaders. Any compromise making it less precise would make it even more acceptable. Wilson could further his ideals only through an imprecision that would prevent his achieving his goals.

Wilson never formally submitted his program to the Allies. The omission was deliberate, because trying to force the Allies to accede to an American policy might have sapped the war effort.[12] Perhaps as a consequence of his never having asked them to make formal comments, the Allies had raised only limited objections to his program. The French wondered what "restoration" of invaded territory might mean, and the British objected strongly to the freedom of the seas. All the Allies objected when Wilson's statements seemed to conflict with the gains promised them in the secret treaties for which they believed they had paid, and paid again, in blood. But the Allies had no great objection to most of Wilson's program, so long as it was loosely defined.[13]

While the Allied prime ministers sat in Paris waiting for Wilson to respond to the First German Note of October 3, Wilson, aided by his intimate friend and adviser Colonel Edward M. House, labored over an answer to the Germans. Colonel (honorary) House came from a wealthy Texas family. With a talent for making himself amiable to men of power, House had become a professional friend to a series of political leaders. He was certainly perceptive and able, but as Wilson's adviser on diplomatic affairs and, later, as Wilson's representative in the negotiations with the Allies over the armistice, House tended to be overly flexible in debate. In complex diplomatic negotiations, he sometimes surrendered too much to gain a chimerical agreement. Lloyd George, from a later vantage point, would describe House as having a well-balanced but not powerful mind: "When I recognize that he was honourable in all his dealings, it is not inconsistent with this characteristic to say that he possessed craft. It is perhaps to his credit that he was not nearly as cunning as he thought he was."[14] Clemenceau, who generally saw little good in his fellow men, genuinely liked House, and Clemenceau's chief military aide later was fulsome in House's praise.[15]

In considering his answer to the First German Note, Wilson inclined, at first, toward leniency. He told the British chargé "with a smile that the position was a difficult one, as the Central Powers were professing to be accepting his own terms."[16] Wilson's draft response gradually became less lenient.[17] Public passions in a democracy, once roused, take on a life of their own, and Wilson was under far greater popular pressure to be pitiless than to be forgiving. Because the United States' off-year congressional elections were less than a month away, Wilson had to bear in mind strident public and congressional outcries against a moderate peace, and any number of close associates were advising him to be stern in his negotiations with the Germans.[18]

In contrast, his secretary of state advised him to return a conciliatory reply.[19] Secretary of State Robert Lansing was upset at the public's cry for vengeance, complaining that the people were "almost savage in their vindictiveness." He wrote that persons who encouraged the clamor, such as Republican senator Henry Cabot Lodge and former president Theodore Roosevelt, were "either intellectually dishonest or intellectually defective."[20]

Even without judging the intellectual honesty or intellectual soundness of his opponents, the president would have made a political mistake in embracing moderation here, and the First Wilson Note, sent on October 8, took a middle course. It avoided specific commitments; Secretary Lansing called it a "query, not a reply."[21] The Germans, in their note, had accepted the Fourteen Points only as a basis for discussion, and Wilson asked whether the German government fully accepted his Fourteen Points and later statements. Wilson added that he could not propose an armistice to the Allied governments so long as the armies of the Central Powers were occupying Allied territory.

In his last paragraph, Wilson asked the ambiguous question of "whether the Imperial Chancellor is speaking merely for the constituted authorities of the Empire who have so far conducted the war." Wilson was truly disturbed at having to negotiate with the German autocracy, but what he planned in its stead is uncertain. He rejected Allied intervention to reorganize the German nation by force, and he considered radical change in the German government extremely dangerous to hopes for stability.[22] Whatever his objections to dealing with autocracy, he seemed at this moment to have no alternatives to doing so.

With the pressure of the First German Note removed, the president showed his irritation at what he thought had been Allied interference. It was messages from General Bliss reporting the eight-point guide and the military and naval committee's draft terms—Bliss's personal boycott of the military and naval committee's meeting did not bar him from information—that set the president off.[23] Wilson ordered Secretary Lansing to demand an explanation of Allied actions from Sir William Wiseman, a semiofficial British representative, who was the main contact between House and the British Foreign Office.[24]

On October 9, Wiseman went to the Department of State, and Lansing read him two of Bliss's telegrams.[25] One of those telegrams included the unfortunate phrase that the Allies had "agreed upon" various principles for the armistice. Wiseman tried to soothe Lansing, explaining that the prime ministers had simply taken the opportunity, because they were meeting already, to discuss "terms which [the] Allies would require should any acceptable request for an armistice be formulated in the future."[26]

Not satisfied with Wiseman's explanations of the day before, Wilson ordered Lansing to call in the British chargé d'affaires (the British ambassador was in England) and the French and Italian ambassadors.[27] After a flurry of telegrams, the three diplomats selected the French ambassador, the senior among them, to speak for all three to President Wilson.[28] The French ambassador talked with the president for almost an hour. Wilson declared that the "very fact of [the] Allied Prime Ministers having discussed terms of an armistice had caused him considerable astonishment. Personally, he had never contemplated [the] question of an armistice at [the] present time and in [the] present temper of [the] German people." Wilson went on that he was "surprised that this question should have been discussed at all without previous consultation with him." The president claimed that his reply to the Germans did not allow for a lengthy exchange of views. The Germans could reply only yes or no. His note to the Germans had also asked whether they understood his previous statement that he would refuse to deal with a government that had no honor. Because he had said that, he told the French ambassador, "he did not anticipate a favourable reply" to his note. If the Germans did say yes to his questions, he would "naturally refer the matter without further delay to [the] European Allies and this of course would be a question for [the] military authorities at Versailles to decide upon."

The French ambassador seems to have calmed Wilson, and by October 13 the situation apparently no longer troubled the president. Possibly, as time went by, the cascade of events made what the Allied leaders had done in Paris seem less important. When Wilson spoke with Wiseman on October 13, he was "friendly and cordial" and showed he was "very pleased" with the way things were going.[29] The "misunderstanding" about the Conference of Prime Ministers, Wiseman reported, "has been explained to his complete satisfaction."

The Allies had won a point in this exchange. They had informed Wilson of their thinking, and Wilson had promised he would seek the advice of the Allies and the "military authorities at Versailles" before committing the United States to any particular plan for Germany. Although he might carry on negotiations without asking Allied support for his decisions, he had told the Allies he would not, in the end, act unilaterally, if indeed he had ever intended doing so.

The Germans had received Wilson's First Note with mixed feelings, for it neither accepted nor rejected their request for an armistice. That the note contained no requirements crippling the German army cheered the German military leaders, but the Allied advance on the Western Front was continuing without pause. The Germans tried to make the best of the situation.[30] The Second German Note, sent on October 12, stated that the German government accepted the Fourteen Points without reservation.[31] At the instigation of the German Army Command, the Germans asked for assurances that the Allies also accepted the Fourteen Points. That move was a shrewd one, because it was likely to bring about strains in the ranks of Germany's enemies, and it was certainly an appropriate question for the Germans to raise.

Then the Germans, as Lloyd George had feared, tried to trap Wilson. To bring about an armistice, the Germans said, they would evacuate Allied territory as the president had suggested, and they proposed that Wilson arrange "the meeting of a mixed commission" of Allied and German representatives to plan that evacuation. The assumption the Germans hoped to convert into reality was that an armistice—a cease-fire—would follow immediately upon evacuation, without the imposition of any other terms.

Finally, the Germans answered Wilson's question about whether the German leaders were speaking for the people who had made the war. The present German government, they said, was formed "in agreement with the great majority of the Reichstag." That is, the Germans were insisting they already had a responsible parliamentary government and that they now had what the president had demanded they create.

Some of the effect the Germans hoped for dissipated when their submarines sank several Allied vessels at this critical moment. Of particular peril to the negotiations was the sinking of the passenger steamer *Leinster* on October 11, with the loss of 176 persons, mostly women and children, of the 700 passengers it carried.

Wilson and House got the details of the Second German Note on October 13, while they were dining together, and they met early the next morning to discuss Wilson's answer.[32] House wrote in his diary that they wanted to send a strong reply: "We fell back time and again on the theory I offered when the last note was written, that if Germany was beaten she would accept any terms. If she was not beaten, we did not wish to make any terms with her." Yet, House recorded, neither he nor Wilson wanted revenge, and he commented about the American outcry for vengeance, with Roosevelt, Lodge, and others calling for "the undesirable and the impossible." Wilson worried, too, that the Allied military and naval leaders might insist on armistice terms so exacting that the Germans would refuse to accept them.[33]

Wilson prepared the final draft of his Second Note on October 14.[34] The meeting in which Wilson drew it up took place in the afternoon, and just before that meeting, the British chargé gave Lansing the text of several telegrams the British government had sent the day before.[35] The main object of those telegrams, according to the British foreign secretary speaking to the British cabinet, was to "make it clear that it would be fatal to the interests of the Allies unless the armistice . . . was based upon such naval and military conditions as would prevent Germany from reopening the war in the event of a breakdown in the negotiations."[36]

The language of those British telegrams was abrupt. The British noted that they agreed with the Fourteen Points generally but disliked the points on freedom of the seas and German colonies. They insisted that armistice terms leave the Allies free to get appropriate peace terms and that the Allies and the United States needed to come to agreement on "doubtful points." Even more directly, one of the telegrams stated that the British government doubted that the Germans understood the Associated Powers would agree only to terms that would "render impossible any resumption of hostilities." The rough set of notes that Wilson took into the meeting echoed that warning.[37]

The final draft of Wilson's Second Note said that the conditions of an armistice must be left to the military advisers of the Allied and Associated Powers.[38] The United States could accept no arrangement that failed to provide "absolutely satisfactory safeguards and guarantees of the maintenance of the present military supremacy of the Armies of the United States and of the Allies in the field." Wilson also issued a stern warning to the Germans about their continuing "illegal and inhumane" practices, a reference not only to the torpedoing of the *Leinster* but also to the belief that much of the demolition the Germans were carrying out as they retreated from France and Belgium was not militarily justified.

Toward the end of his Second Note, Wilson returned to the subject of the German monarchy, quoting from his Fourth of July speech in which he had called for the destruction of autocracy. The German people, he wrote, could now alter the "power which has hitherto controlled the German Nation." Their doing so would be a condition necessary for making peace, and the process would "depend on the definiteness and the satisfactory character of the guarantees which can be given in this fundamental matter." That Wilson spoke here of proofs and guarantees suggests he did not envision a major upheaval in the German state. Proofs and guarantees would be necessary only if the basic form of government remained outwardly similar to its present form.[39]

So Wilson apparently heeded Allied warnings about the nature of the armistice. He told the British chargé that he did not think the German overtures were sincere, and he used House's phrase: "If the Germans are beaten, they will accept any terms; if they are not beaten we do not want them to accept any terms."[40] Against those words in the decoding of the chargé's report to London, one of the ranking members of the Foreign Office wrote, "This is somewhat cryptic."

Wilson also decided to send Colonel House to Europe.[41] Wilson wanted face-to-face representation in what were sure to be acrimonious debates with the Allies if the German overtures came to anything. House sailed almost immediately and would arrive at Brest on October 25.

The French and British leaders received Wilson's Second Note very well, although they continued to grouse about Wilson's monopolizing the negotiations.[42] They liked Wilson's Second Note because it was uncompromising. For the Germans, who had received Wilson's First Note with mixed feelings, the choices now before them were vexing.[43] The dominant German idea had been to use the armistice to withdraw to a defensible line and then negotiate peace from a stable position of relative strength. They might have lost the war, but perhaps they could still get acceptable peace terms covering western Europe while keeping a free hand in eastern Europe. Now, with conditions of armistice that would come from the Allied military advisers, and with Wilson's demand for various guarantees, such a program appeared impossible. When the Germans discussed what to do about the Second Wilson Note, the alternatives were not attractive: either drop the attempt to get an armistice and face the coming military storm or accept Wilson's proposals, knowing the peace would be unsatisfactory.

With the issue before them no longer war or peace, but a hopeless war or surrender, the German leaders met on October 17.[44] General Ludendorff, who earlier in a state of panic had demanded that Germany seek an armistice, had either recovered his nerve or was trying to escape the onus of surrender. "Before accepting the conditions of this [Second Wilson] note, which are too severe," said Ludendorff, "we should say to the enemy: Win such terms by fighting for them."

Yet Ludendorff kept running head-on into reality. The Germans did not have enough men to replace their losses on the Western Front. They could withdraw soldiers from the eastern occupation zones, but it would take three months to get them to the west, and the Germans had already stripped those forces of their best men for their spring offensive. Conscription offered no great hope, either. They could conscript more men, but the morale of draftees was low, if not revolutionary, and it took months to train new soldiers. Not only did Germany not have the men; it also lacked the supplies that would let the nation fight on. For example, the surrender of Bulgaria and the likely reentry of Rumania into the war as an Ally would cut off Rumanian oil, and Germany had only a six weeks' reserve of that precious commodity.

Ludendorff continued to recommend seeking an armistice, provided the Germans could get one that would let them carry out an orderly evacuation. He was more optimistic than his staff, the members of which thought the Allies would not grant Germany what Ludendorff wanted. In the end, the German leaders decided they had no choice but to keep up the negotiations with Wilson and continue to pursue an armistice.

The Germans sent their Third Note on October 20.[45] To send it, the German chancellor had to fight off both the German navy and Ludendorff, who, thoroughly out of touch with reality, was now talking about a war to the death. In their Third Note, the Germans maintained that the armistice must preserve the existing balance of power between the two armies. Likewise, the German government expressed its trust "that the President of the United States will approve of no demand which would be irreconcilable with the honor of the German people and with opening a way to a peace with justice."[46] In answer to Wilson's condemnation of demolitions carried out in the retreat, the Germans protested that what they were doing was militarily necessary. Hoping to appease Wilson, they did promise to order their submarines not to torpedo passenger ships. Finally, answering Wilson's comments about arbitrary power, the Germans declared that the new government represented the Reichstag, the same answer they had given in their Second Note.

The Germans had made their decision. They had come to realize that they would gain no military advantage from an armistice, but, regardless, they must get out of the war. Whatever they said in their Third Note, and however brave a face they tried to put on events, once they decided to continue negotiations, there was no turning back. The German public and the soldiers were all avidly following the correspondence between their government and Wilson. Both the public and the soldiers—and sailors, too, events would soon reveal—were showing more and more distaste for continuing a war that their government, by seeking an armistice, had confirmed was lost. The German rank and file now wanted, and would get, an end to hostilities.

The Third German Note did not remove all the diplomatic traps that might catch Wilson. The French ambassador to the United States warned the president that the Allied and Associated Powers must look at armistice conditions together; the United States must not act unilaterally.[47] Indeed, the Third German Note induced the French to tell Wilson that when he sought military advice, he must turn to Foch and the commanders of the Allied armies, not the Military Representatives.[48]

The Third German Note also caused the British to worry. The British foreign secretary pointed out that the Germans were trying to pretend that an undisturbed retreat to the German frontiers was all the Allies required.[49] An armistice made on that basis would give the Germans a breathing space in which to reorganize and time to create a defensible front. Peace discussions carried out in that setting could never get what the Allied nations wanted from the war.

Wilson learned the contents of the Third German Note on October 21. It was deftly drafted, and even Lansing believed Wilson could not deal with it easily.[50] He encouraged the president to lean on the advice of the military, and that evening Wilson met with Lansing, the secretaries of war and the navy, and the army's chief of staff.

The next day, Wilson presented the Third German Note, and indeed the whole problem of the negotiations, to his full cabinet.[51] Discussion centered on several questions. First and most important was whether Germany could be trusted. There was some feeling that it could not, but to the suggestion that no discussions take place until the Germans had retreated behind the Rhine, Wilson replied that such a delay was impossible. Another question was whether the armistice should provide assurances for an acceptable peace, and most of the cabinet members agreed that carefully drawn armistice terms could safeguard Allied and American interests.

Indeed, there was a feeling that the United States might gain a more desirable peace now than they could later. The American public was becoming less willing to compromise, the United States could not bear the financial strain of war for an indefinite period, and, most important, if the war continued, the "selfish aims" of the Allies would overwhelm Wilson's Fourteen Points. It is curious that the Allies at this same time were coming to the flatly contradictory conclusion that American influence would increase if the war continued for any great length of time.

Some of Wilson's cabinet members wanted to discuss matters with the Allies before answering the Third German Note. Others seemed more frightened of the Allies than of the Germans. The cabinet members were also concerned that the armistice not crush Germany militarily, because that would allow the Allies too free a hand in arranging postwar Europe. The real problem, in their view, was what would happen if the Allies refused to grant an armistice. Wilson had the solution to this problem: he would coerce the Allies. Wilson believed, too, that he could gain Allied acceptance of his Fourteen Points because the United States "will be master of the situation."[52] He assumed, he said, that when the Allies assented to the armistice, it would bind them morally to the Fourteen Points, a conclusion the Allies leaders might find both unpalatable and untenable.

The full cabinet took no part in the actual drafting of Wilson's Third Note.[53] In it, Wilson told the Germans that because they had accepted his Fourteen Points, because their spokesmen represented a majority in the Reichstag, and because they promised to cease inhumane practices in war, he would take up the question of armistice with the Allies. He would, he wrote, forward the German request to the Allies "with the suggestion that, if those Governments are disposed to effect peace upon the terms and principles indicated [the Fourteen Points], their military advisers and the military advisers of the United States" would be asked to draw up terms that would leave the Germans unable to renew hostilities. That armistice must give the Allied and Associated Governments the "unrestricted power" to enforce peace terms.

Wilson raised another matter. He explained that military safeguards were necessary because the German government was still unreformed.

The German people did not yet control the emperor, and the former leaders of Germany continued to lead the country. "The nations of the world do not and cannot trust the word of those who have hitherto been the masters of German policy." If the United States had to deal with the "military masters and monarchical autocrats" who had ruled the nation during the war, "it must demand, not peace negotiations, but surrender." Strong words, those, and yet at the cabinet meeting on October 22, Wilson had said that he feared Bolshevism in Germany. Germany needed to keep the emperor on the throne, he had said then, to block Bolshevism. Wilson's objections to arbitrary power are not without contradictions. Moreover, he was now forwarding the German request for an armistice to the Allies, and the emperor still ruled. Internal revolution and republican demands for William II's abdication had not yet reached major proportions, and Wilson apparently did not foresee a Germany without him, or at least some monarch.

Wilson's insistence on referring the question of precise armistice terms to the military is an enigmatic development in his thinking. The week before, repelled by the brutal and intransigent words of the military leaders, Wilson had shown himself little disposed to follow their lead.[54] A few days later, he said, to the contrary, that it would be best to get armistice terms from the military and naval leaders, although "the heads of the governments will probably have to modify them because the soldiers and sailors will make them too severe."[55] Then, on October 19, when Wilson was questioned about proposed terms for Turkey, he had said he could not judge military matters: "Such questions were purely for [the] military."[56]

Wilson's apparent abdication to the military leaders in his Third Note seems, therefore, the culmination of a continuously developing policy. His later actions make that conclusion less sure. Shortly after the Third Note went to the Germans, he began to send detailed instructions to the United States' military and naval experts in Paris. What is not clear is whether this was a reversal of his drift toward seeking military advice or whether he planned from the beginning to attempt to control the military as they prepared terms.

After dispatching the Third Wilson Note to Germany, the United States' State Department sent copies of it and the preceding correspondence to all the Allied countries—Belgium, Brazil, China, Cuba, France, Great Britain, Greece, Guatemala, Haiti, Honduras, Italy, Japan, Montenegro, Nicaragua, Panama, Portugal, Rumania, Russia (or certain representatives thereof), Serbia, and Siam—asking them to say whether they agreed to grant an armistice.[57] Wilson, thereby, agreed to the original German request. Nineteen days after the Germans sent him their First Note, Wilson was using his influence to bring about an armistice based on his Fourteen Points.

If Wilson's success is measured by the degree to which he was able to maintain his original intentions, he had done very well. He had managed to follow his own star despite loud and continuous criticism from Roosevelt, Lodge, and others who detested him and all he stood for. He had managed to exclude the Allies from the negotiations until he got complete German agreement to his Fourteen Points, and he had achieved this aim without tying his own hands. He had seemingly become more intransigent during his negotiations with Germany, but there was no way to measure how real and lasting that rigor was until House met with the Allies. The Allied leaders, of course, had made it clear that they had no intention of sacrificing their victory to any sort of Wilsonian meddling.[58] On the other hand, if the Allied governments rejected any reasonable opportunity for peace, the leaders would surely face an outcry from their overstrained populations, a fact that limited their freedom of decision.

Four days after Wilson sent his Third Note, the Germans responded that they awaited Allied proposals for an armistice.[59] The preparation of those proposals would take another ten days and would involve the complex interplay of British and French policy with the aims of the United States.

3

Great Britain
and the Armistice

reat Britain declared war in 1914 because of the immediate danger
that Germany might win Continental hegemony, but relations between the two nations had been deteriorating over the previous
decades. German naval competition angered the British, German colonial ambitions irritated them, and German commercial rivalry exasper-
ated them. Those matters, by themselves, would not have led to war between the two nations, but once war came, any termination of it had to
address those issues.

While Woodrow Wilson and the Germans were exchanging their notes,
the British were trying to work out a policy on the armistice that reconciled military, naval, and political ambitions. It was not a simple process.
Prime Minister David Lloyd George led only a minority Liberal Party
faction within a coalition government from which many of his own party
members had seceded, in effect, some months earlier. That left him scant
resources to deal with the Conservative (properly, at this time, Unionist)
majority in the coalition.[1] He could cajole, he could urge, but he could
not command. Now, perhaps as much from the situation in which he
found himself as from inclination, he was a political manipulator, not an
inspirational Moses. In October 1918, he used his very great political skills
to keep himself free from cabinet or parliamentary dictation.

Lloyd George had a brilliant mind and a consummate speaking style. Rising from obscure origins in Wales to become the leading radical politician before the war, he had been part of an intrigue that made him leader of the coalition government in 1916. He had ideals and held them strongly, but he did not communicate his hopes to his colleagues, and his faults left him open to snide criticism within the top circles of British political leadership. For example, a high-ranking official in the Foreign Office wrote that Lloyd George at the Conference of Prime Ministers "was really at his very worst . . .—a tricky attorney negotiating with an unsavoury county court could scarcely have been worse."[2]

When Lloyd George came back from Paris after the Conference of Prime Ministers, the British leaders had to decide what they really wanted from the war.[3] With talk centering on Wilson's Fourteen Points, discussion focused on two problems. First, how should the British government deal with the secret treaties they had signed during the war? Second, what relationship should Britain seek with the United States?

The British had come to regret the price they had paid in the secret treaties, especially the territory promised to Italy in the Treaty of London.[4] They had already told the Italians that a secondary agreement, St. Jean de Maurienne, giving Smyrna to Italy, was void, owing to that pact's not gaining Russian ratification before the 1917 Revolution.[5] The British leaders were equally unhappy over arrangements they had made with the French, particularly the Sykes-Picot Agreement of 1916 regulating their respective interests in the Middle East. Early in October, they told the French that the British government "thinks it right to point out that the general position has so much changed since that [Sykes-Picot] Agreement was entered into that its provisions did not in all aspects appear suitable to present conditions."[6] Yet however much the British might try to modify their commitments, they felt they had no alternative to standing behind the treaties and agreements they had signed.

Discussion about appropriate relations with the United States was tortuous. The British correctly assumed the United States was becoming more powerful as the war continued. At the beginning of October, Lloyd George was anti-American and, to some degree, anti-Wilsonian. In contrast, Sir Arthur Balfour, the foreign secretary, argued that the United States was absolutely necessary to shaping a peace that would suit Britain. Left to face France and Italy without American support, Great Britain would be overmatched. "It might be very important when we came to close grips with peace terms," Balfour told the cabinet, "for the United States and ourselves to work together." Therefore, the British should not tie themselves too tightly to the French.[7] Instead, they must cultivate, even court, the Americans.

Two other related problems concerned the British leaders. First, they worried about their own manpower.[8] The rifle strength of their army was steadily diminishing, and the only hope for substantially more men was to apply conscription to troubled Ireland, a solution that many British leaders feared would lead to an Irish uprising. Moreover, the manpower shortage affected not only battle strength, but also industrial production. Short of military manpower during these last, critical months, the British had ruthlessly drawn upon all possible reinforcements by revoking the exemptions to conscription previously given to industrial workers, and that would cause industrial production to diminish seriously in 1919. Therefore, to maintain essential war industries, the British now must withdraw men from the army and send them back to the factories, further reducing their rifle strength on the Western Front.[9]

Second, the leaders were concerned that popular support for granting an armistice was gathering strength. If the British leaders refused to end the war, given some sort of reasonable settlement, they would face serious political pressure.[10] With the politicians receiving frequent reports of growing political unrest within the nation, the situation appeared volatile.[11]

All these threads—secret treaties, relations with the United States, manpower, and public opinion—came together on October 13, when Lloyd George hosted a meeting at Danny, his country home, to discuss the Conference of Prime Ministers and British policy toward an armistice.[12] Two days before the Danny meeting, and just after his return from the Conference of Prime Ministers in Paris, Lloyd George had made a clear statement of policy. He had argued that because a resumption of hostilities was unlikely once an armistice took effect, it was "essential that the terms of the armistice should approximate as closely as possible to the conditions of peace which could be accepted."[13]

At the Danny meeting, Lloyd George contended that the Allies ought to invade Germany to provide that nation with a visible sign of its defeat. The foreign secretary argued that entering Germany was unnecessary, that the surrender of German territory—notably Posen, Silesia, and Alsace-Lorraine—would be a sufficiently visible sign of victory. He agreed, however, that the Allies should impose armistice terms that would make a renewal of hostilities impossible.[14]

The military leaders present at Danny, the chief of the Imperial General Staff and the first sea lord, both insisted on the need to disarm Germany on land and sea.[15] The chief of the Imperial General Staff noted that the Germans were short of supplies relative to the length of the front they were trying to maintain. Spreading the same quantity out along a shorter front line, which would happen automatically if the Allies asked only for the withdrawal of German forces from occupied territories, would improve the Germans' situation. To keep that from happening, he argued, the Allies should disarm the Germans. In response to this proposal from the chief of the Imperial General Staff, the politicians seemed to agree that the Allies must somehow make the armistice sufficiently disabling to prevent Germany's resuming the war under any circumstances.[16]

Possibly only as a rhetorical gesture, Lloyd George raised the question of whether it was desirable to have an armistice at all. If Britain made peace now, he suggested, the Germans might say in twenty years that they had made a mistake, and with better preparation and organization they might win the next war. "In a short time the Germans would say that these miserable democrats had taken charge and become panic-stricken, and the military would get in power again." The foreign secretary answered him, saying that peace, if it was conclusive, was desirable now, and he got general agreement.

What constituted a conclusive—and satisfactory—peace led the British leaders into discussing Wilson's Fourteen Points. The British leaders had no real objection to most of the Fourteen Points. Indeed, except for freedom of the seas, British and American interests were astonishingly parallel, particularly if the colonial settlement allowed British or Dominion occupation of the Turkish territory and the German colonies that British Imperial forces had captured during the war. Like any discussion of this nature, the meeting at Danny focused on those things with which the British leaders disagreed, and one politician appeared to speak for them all when he said he was happy to accept the Fourteen Points, "provided we could place our own interpretation on them."

The British leaders at Danny, like the Allied prime ministers at Paris before them, had to decide whether to wait to hear from President Wilson or to communicate their concerns to him directly. Concluding that it was better to tell the president their opinion immediately, they sent him several telegrams, the ones Wilson got on the fourteenth.[17] One warned the president that an armistice must make a renewal of hostilities impossible. Another discussed the Fourteen Points, the British stating they agreed with them in principle, but noting that the Allies had never discussed them and that the British, at least, would object to some possible interpretations "most strongly." The British stressed that any agreement must include mention of additional terms, such as reparations for the loss of ships, "on which, if full justice is to be done, we shall have to insist."

The day after the meeting at Danny, the secretary circulated the conclusions reached to the cabinet.[18] For several days after that, discussion about the armistice was subdued because politics were distracting Lloyd George and the other British leaders. With the end of the war in sight, they were making plans to call a general election, postponed because of the war and long overdue, and the prospect involved lengthy and delicate negotiations inside the governing coalition.[19] Equally important, the British leaders thought Wilson's Second Note was satisfactory.[20]

Lloyd George, like Winston Churchill a generation later, was at times too eager to compete with his generals as a strategist, but he depended, like most civilians, upon the advice of his military leaders. Two of the army leaders were critical to these decisions at the end of the war: Field Marshal Sir Douglas Haig, commander of the British armies in France, and General Sir Henry Wilson, chief of the Imperial General Staff. Sir Henry Wilson, a professional staff officer, had served in the field only briefly during his military career. With a tendency to dabble in intrigue, Sir Henry owed his high position in 1918 to quarrels between Haig and Lloyd George. Sir Henry got the appointment as chief of the Imperial General Staff after Lloyd George ousted one of Haig's supporters from the post. It was not that Sir Henry was a warm friend of Lloyd George or a supporter of Lloyd George's policies, for he was not; but Field Marshal Haig distrusted Sir Henry, and Lloyd George, by appointing Sir Henry to the senior staff position, weakened the military combination he faced.[21]

In October 1918, Sir Henry believed that President Wilson's program would bring Bolshevism to Germany, and Bolshevism frightened him more than the German army did.[22] Indeed, nothing about the American president pleased Sir Henry, and the president's direct negotiations with Germany were, he thought, "a disgraceful usurpation of power." At the same time, Sir Henry's bloodthirsty approach to the Irish question may have affected his thinking on the armistice. His roots lay in the Anglo-Irish gentry, and he loathed the Irish nationalist movement. In 1918, as part of his program for breaking the core of Irish resistance, he hoped to impose conscription on Ireland. With the end of the war in sight, the cabinet, calculating quite correctly that Great Britain had no need of a civil war in Ireland while the nation was still fighting Germany, had decided to hold up the imposition of conscription on Ireland, a decision that filled Sir Henry with despair.[23]

To the cabinet just after the Danny meeting, Sir Henry "pictured our army as tired, but willing and able to fight, the French Army as very tired and neither willing nor able to fight, and the Americans as unfit to fight."[24] True, the Germans were "in a bad way, but we are not in a position to take full advantage of their weakness." Sir Henry concluded there was no reason, given the current military situation, to suppose that the Germans were likely to surrender.

Field Marshal Sir Douglas Haig was the cabinet's other major source of military advice. Partly because of Lloyd George's hatred, great controversy has surrounded Haig ever since the war. Even Haig's death did not deter Lloyd George from brutally assaulting his reputation: "I thought Sir Douglas Haig intellectually and temperamentally unequal to the command of an Army of millions," Lloyd George wrote in his memoirs several years after the field marshal died.[25] For his part, Haig certainly disliked Lloyd George as much as Lloyd George disliked him: "The British Army has won the war in spite of L. G.," Haig wrote in his diary two weeks after the armistice.[26]

On October 17, Lloyd George ordered Haig to London to discuss armistice terms. A week earlier, Marshal Foch had sent Haig a copy of the proposals he had given the Conference of Prime Ministers. Haig was appalled and commented that Foch's program amounted to unconditional surrender.[27] A few days later, Haig spoke to Clemenceau and told him that Foch's "demands are too complicated. We ought to say 'hand over Metz and Strassburg as a preliminary sign of your good faith.' Then we can proceed at once to some peace terms."[28] Concerned about how far Foch had the power to commit the British army to his plans, Haig was reassured when Sir Henry told him the Allied naval leaders and the Military Representatives, not Foch, would draft the armistice terms.[29] Yet an undercurrent of unease about too-harsh armistice terms runs through Haig's diary during those days.

Late in the evening of October 18, Haig arrived in London, and the next morning he went to see Sir Henry.[30] Haig reported that the Allied attack launched two days earlier had met stiff opposition, and "the enemy was not ready for unconditional surrender." If the Allies tried to demand it, the Germans would refuse an armistice, "and the war would continue for at least another year." Sir Henry, who now was insisting on disarming the Germans and occupying all German territory up to the Rhine, remarked in his diary that Haig was far more lenient than he was.

What separated the two was not any real disagreement on the status of the war. Neither Haig nor Sir Henry thought Germany was ready to collapse. What separated them was Haig's belief that the Allies should propose moderate terms acceptable to the Germans and giving the Allies at least a partial victory, whereas Sir Henry, unwilling to compromise short of complete victory, preferred to wait until he could get exactly what he wanted. Perhaps it was only that Haig was closer to the bloody reality of war, and Sir Henry was closer to the broken promises of statecraft.

After talking together, the two walked to a special cabinet meeting, where each maintained his position.[31] When Lloyd George, no fonder of Haig now than he had ever been, asked the field marshal what terms the Allies should offer Germany, Haig's reply was lengthy for a man usually taciturn and inarticulate. He told the cabinet that his proposals for an armistice depended on the answers given to two questions. First, were the Germans so badly beaten that they would accept whatever terms the Allies chose to require? And second, if the Germans refused to sign the terms offered, could the Allies prevent them from destroying their communications as they retreated? To both those questions, Haig answered no. The German army, he said, was quite capable of withdrawing to the German frontiers and defending them.

Haig's opinions rested not only on his belief that Germany still had significant military strength, but also on a pessimistic evaluation of Allied military resources, an evaluation that echoed the comments Sir Henry had made to the cabinet several days earlier. The French army was "worn out" and had not been fighting recently. The Americans were "disorganized, ill-equipped, and ill-trained." Their army "had suffered severely through ignorance of modern war." The British army was doing very well, but it was fifty thousand men under strength. If the British army could get some rest, it would remain "the most formidable fighting force in the world," but morale was sure to decline as the number of effectives diminished. Haig's conclusion was that the French and American forces were incapable of taking the offensive in the immediate future. Expanding on this point in his diary, Haig commented that "the British alone might bring the enemy to his knees. But why expend more British lives—and for what?"

Because of Allied inability to force harsh terms on Germany without unduly prolonging the war, Haig recommended that the armistice require the Germans to withdraw their forces from Belgium, occupied France, and Alsace-Lorraine, and he estimated that it would take the Germans five months to evacuate those lands.[32] His other terms included only the return of French and Belgian railroad rolling stock, repatriation of deported citizens, and Allied occupation of Metz and Strasbourg. Haig thus put himself directly in opposition to the rigorous disarmament and evacuation Sir Henry demanded.

As moderate as Haig's terms were—compared with, for example, Foch's or Sir Henry's—they were by no means lenient, nor did they suggest that he was supporting a compromise peace. Secretary of State for War Alfred, Lord Milner found Haig's arguments "very reasonable."[33] He suggested adding the occupation of German territory on the left bank of the Rhine north of Koblenz as security for Allied claims, and the others agreed. With this proposal for, in effect, a lien on German territory, the discussion was entering new realms. Sir Henry added his voice to the chorus: "Once the 'cease fire' had sounded the War would never start again." Haig's terms, said Sir Henry, gave the Allies nothing with which to enforce their peace terms, and the Allies must get those guarantees in the armistice.

Lloyd George, echoing the pessimistic military evaluation both Sir Henry and Haig were giving, agreed with Haig on requiring terms less exacting than Sir Henry's. The Allies and the United States had not defeated Germany so completely that the German leaders would accept stringent proposals. He pointed out "the danger of losing a good bargain through asking too much. We knew exactly what we required, and if we obtained that we should be safe."

In his memoirs some years later, Lloyd George criticized Haig's statement, and other military advice, for being unduly pessimistic.[34] Haig's advice, Lloyd George wrote, was "extraordinary in view of the actual condition of the German Army." Lloyd George's explanation was that the military leaders were looking only at conditions on the Western Front and placing too little importance on the collapse of Germany's allies.[35] It is true, of course, that the British generals were poorly informed on conditions within Germany, but nobody else had any better information, and the final German collapse took the Germans themselves by surprise. Through all their discussions over terms of armistice, the Allied leaders assumed the Germans remained capable of stout resistance and believed the Germans could prolong the war for a considerable period, if they chose to do so.

The British admirals had no better information on conditions within Germany than the generals did, but from the beginning their terms were far harsher than Haig's. Halfway through the cabinet meeting on October 19, First Sea Lord Admiral Sir Rosslyn Wemyss joined the meeting, and discussion turned to naval terms. Wemyss had no way of knowing what people had said before he arrived. It would have dismayed him to have heard Lloyd George declare, as he had, that the armistice needed no naval terms. Both the Allies and Germany would continue to build ships during the armistice, Lloyd George had said, and if the armistice were broken off, Germany would only have gained a few submarines.

The first sea lord, the administrative head of the navy, had toiled with the Board of Admiralty to prepare naval armistice terms. On October 16, he wrote to Admiral Sir David Beatty, the dashing commander of the Grand Fleet at Scapa Flow, enclosing a memorandum on naval armistice terms he intended to submit to the cabinet.[36] His memorandum made two important additions to the terms that the military and naval committee had drafted at Versailles during the meeting of the Conference of Prime Ministers. First, in the interests of "international morality," Wemyss demanded not just the internment of sixty German submarines—what the military and naval committee at Versailles had proposed—but the surrender of all Germany's submarines. Second, instead of having enemy vessels simply withdraw to specified German bases, as the military and naval committee at Versailles had proposed, Wemyss would require the Germans to surrender a portion of their fleet to the Allies.

Admiral Beatty's response was an agonized scream protesting the failure to consult him.[37] Only a few days earlier he had written to a friend: "Germany is squealing for a cessation of hostilities. It is not to be thought of for a moment just when we are getting some of our own back."[38] Now, to Wemyss, Beatty listed ships that the Germans should surrender, including their fleet flagship, the *Baden,* their third and fourth battleship squadrons (which accounted for all their Dreadnoughts), all their battle cruisers, eight light cruisers, fifty destroyers, and all their submarines. He also proposed requiring the Germans to surrender the island of Heligoland.

After reading Beatty's list of demands, Wemyss wrote back trying to soothe him, a function he was to exercise frequently in the following few weeks.[39] Now, to the cabinet, Wemyss presented the Admiralty's terms, probably adding to them Beatty's list of ships.[40] Lloyd George appeared shocked by those demands. "This amounted to abject surrender," he said, and Admiral Wemyss agreed. The prime minister asked Haig what the effect on the army would be if the Allies proposed naval terms like those and Germany refused them. Haig answered that the effect would be bad.

Summing up the meeting, Lloyd George said that "only . . . a nation that was beaten to the dust" would accept terms like the ones Wemyss proposed. Sir Henry Wilson tentatively suggested that if the Germans came to realize they had lost the war, they might accept "almost any terms." Lloyd George disagreed. "Pride would overrule reason if the terms were too stiff," but they might accept Haig's terms, he thought. The great principle in regard to an armistice, Lloyd George said just before the meeting adjourned, was to include everything necessary. "In the event of peace negotiations breaking down, the enemy would then have to take the initiative to recover what he had given up, and not the Allies."

Two days later, just before noon on October 21, the cabinet met again.[41] It was a day full of pressing matters, not least among them an official Turkish request for an armistice. When the Allied leaders at the Conference of Prime Ministers had agreed on terms for the Ottoman Empire, they had left a problem: they had not settled who would receive the Turkish surrender.[42] Lacking specific instructions to the contrary, the senior officer in the area would take charge of negotiations with the Turks. When the Conference of Prime Ministers met, the senior naval officer in the Aegean was French, so the British had hastily transferred their commander-in-chief at Malta to the Aegean, where he outranked the French commander.[43] Prestige and possible postwar advantages hung on which nation received the Turkish surrender, and Clemenceau and Lloyd George exchanged bitter correspondence over the problem.[44] Now, Lloyd George proposed giving the British admiral in the Aegean—the cabinet simply ignored the French—the power to amend the terms, if necessary. If anyone at the Conference of Prime Ministers had dreamed of Allied solidarity on Near Eastern matters, that hope was ending here.

The foreign secretary, Sir Arthur Balfour, pointed out that the Turks were not asking for an armistice but, in fact, for peace terms. Even though, two weeks earlier, the Allied prime ministers had discussed and rejected giving the Turks full peace terms, Balfour now argued that the British should consider the Turkish request. Lloyd George cautiously associated himself with Balfour's proposal, a dangerous one because it meant circumventing the other Allies as well as the United States. Fortunately for Allied unity, the proposal died after the cabinet considered the ramifications of unilaterally preparing a separate peace for Turkey.

The cabinet did decide to negotiate the armistice unilaterally. Secretary of State for War Milner justified this action by reminding the cabinet of the French action in drawing up armistice terms for Bulgaria unilaterally.[45] The parallel fails, however, because the prime ministers had not previously and jointly approved armistice terms for Bulgaria, while they had agreed on terms for Turkey at the Conference of Prime Ministers earlier in the month.

British actions here were cavalier, but they saw that there was no hope of hiding what they were doing, so they agreed to inform the other nations of their decisions.[46] The French wasted no time: they protested this British arrogance almost immediately.[47] They also seem to have prepared to send out an officer senior to the British admiral who had just gone to the Aegean, thus continuing the game of musical admirals.[48]

In the meantime, Lloyd George sent Lord Milner to Paris with the mission of soothing Clemenceau.[49] The day Milner left for Paris, October 24, the French protested that the powers the British had accorded their admiral—to amend the terms without consultation—was a blow to the Anglo-French alliance.[50] In his conversations with Clemenceau, Milner got a far softer response. Clemenceau simply claimed that any occupation of Turkey should be a joint Anglo-French one, which the British were willing to grant.[51]

Why the French gave in so easily is hard to fathom. The basic British argument, of course, was sound: theirs were the dominant forces fighting the Ottoman Empire. Moreover, although the Mediterranean, through an earlier Anglo-French agreement, was a French naval preserve, the British usually had the greater strength in the Aegean area. On the diplomatic balance sheet, too, the British had allowed the French to name one of their generals as the commander-in-chief on the Western Front and another one to command the Army of the East. The point at issue, however, was giving the British admiral in the Aegean the power to amend, without consultation, the terms agreed to at Paris. It is entirely possible that Clemenceau, a practicing pragmatist, saw no reward in continuing a quarrel the French could not win.[52] Further discussion of Turkish matters would have to wait until the end of the month, when the Allied prime ministers once again gathered in Paris.

News of the Turkish overtures stimulated speculation at the October 21 cabinet meeting on the effect Turkey's withdrawal would have on military operations against Germany. Lloyd George suggested that the Allies might now demand sterner terms than Haig's if they could move their armies through the Black Sea and up the Danube. The cabinet, rather than making any decision, ordered Sir Henry to prepare a review of the situation in the east, working from the assumption that Turkey would surrender and that the Allies would have full access to the Black Sea and could get Rumanian help.

With those instructions, Sir Henry prepared an estimate.[53] He did it after dinner, with no detailed study and with little appreciation of transportation problems in that corner of Europe. His conclusion was that, with Turkey out of the war, the Allies could develop an attack through Rumania and up the Danube of fifty or sixty divisions: "This would knock out Austria and then we could move into Germany from south and west and defeat the Boch[e] armies on Boch[e] territory."[54] Clearly, this plan was not one that could be put into effect inside a few weeks, or even months.

The cabinet discussed the navy's terms a second time at the October 21 meeting.[55] Admiral Wemyss stood behind the crushing naval terms he had read two days earlier. Because the nation would not renew hostilities once the armistice was signed, Wemyss argued, "it was necessary that the terms of the armistice should approximate to what it was desired to obtain in the peace." Therefore, the Allies must not reduce the naval terms he was proposing: "To do so might mean that while we were victorious on shore, we should not reap the fruits of victory at sea."

Seconding these remarks in person was Admiral Beatty, who had left the Grand Fleet at Scapa Flow to rush down to London.[56] The main British object in the war, he said, was to destroy German militarism, which included not only militarism on land but also naval militarism. Beatty argued that "the terms of Armistice should be as nearly as possible the Terms of Peace." The naval terms must achieve one of Great Britain's major war aims by reducing Germany to a "second-rate Naval Power." It would achieve that end, said Beatty, by taking away from Germany the ships it would lose if it were to fight a naval battle with Great Britain. That was an optimistic evaluation, judging from the results of the one big naval battle of the war, Jutland in 1916. Nevertheless, Beatty proposed that the Allies force Germany to surrender all the ships he had listed earlier.

Meeting the objection that the real danger to England lay in Germany's submarines, not in Germany's surface battle fleet, Beatty claimed—quite correctly—that the menace of the German submarines depended on the force of the German fleet behind them. If the British required the surrender of submarines and not capital ships, the Germans could build submarines rapidly and soon become a threat again. Without the surface fleet, he said, submarines would be no menace in the future.

Extended discussion of these proposals got nowhere. Neither Beatty nor Wemyss really believed Germany would accept the terms they were proposing. These proposals astonished Haig, and Sir Henry endorsed them. The cabinet went to the heart of the situation and underlined the differences between what the various military and naval leaders were proposing. Haig was basing his recommendations on Germany's not being so badly beaten that it would accept what amounted to humiliating surrender, and the naval leaders were proposing terms that were "tantamount to unconditional surrender." If Germany was so badly off that it would accept those naval conditions, the Allies could ask for stronger military terms. If Germany could refuse the military conditions and fight on, there was no point in presenting harsh naval conditions.

Lloyd George tried to temporize. "It would be important," he said, "to consider the naval and military conditions together when the moment came." In the meantime, he asked that Beatty and the Board of Admiralty examine "what would be the minimum naval terms of an armistice which it would be possible for us to accept."

The British naval leaders were so desperately afraid the Allied leaders would act against their advice that they appealed over Lloyd George's head to Clemenceau, who on October 24 promised them that the British Admiralty would have direct representation at the coming interallied discussions on armistice terms.[57] On October 26, First Lord of the Admiralty Sir Eric Geddes, the political head of the navy, resubmitted to the cabinet precisely the same terms that Beatty and Wemyss had presented on October 21.[58] Whether the members of the Board of Admiralty had made the slightest effort to amend the naval terms according to Lloyd George's instructions is unclear.[59] The practical result was that the board ignored him.

Facing those resubmitted terms, Lloyd George expressed the fear that "the surrender of ships . . . would be so humiliating as to make an armistice impossible."[60] Geddes insisted that the British must not separate the terms of armistice from the terms of peace. Here the cabinet produced a formula and endorsed it:

> The naval conditions of the armistice should represent the admission of German defeat by sea in the same degree as the military conditions recognise the corresponding admission of German defeat by land.

At the cabinet on October 21, the British leaders, prompted by news of the Third German Note to Wilson, raised the subject of the president and his negotiations with Germany.[61] "Feeling was strong against the President," Haig wrote in his diary.[62] "He does not seem to realise our requirements." Sir Henry was more brusk. "My own opinion," he confided to his diary that evening, "is that unless L[loyd] G[eorge] and Tiger [Clemenceau] catch a hold, my . . . Cousin [Sir Henry's personal name for the president, to whom he was not related] will cart us all."[63] But the cabinet did nothing to intervene, which was probably wise.

The critical British cabinet meetings of October 19 and 21, the ones dealing with military and naval armistice terms, ended with no binding decisions concerning Germany. In his diary, Sir Henry summarized the results of discussion: Haig "weak in his terms of armistice. David Beatty excellent. Most of Cabinet including L. G. and Milner rather weak."[64]

From a later vantage point, it does appear that Haig's proposals gave adequate security. He believed that if hostilities resumed, his terms, which put the Allies on the German frontier, would leave the Allies in a stronger position than they had won in October.[65] They would also control northern France, from which Germany had drawn a large proportion of its war materials since 1914.

Adequate security, however, did not necessarily mean the British would gain the power to demand their war aims in the peace. With the Germans emplaced in strong defensive positions on the 1914 frontier and with the Rhine as a second German line of defense, the Allies would still face a tough opponent. For how long would British, or French, or American troops continue to throw themselves to bloody ruin against those German defenses to gain some point or other in the peace terms? Haig was asked whether the British could induce their army to fight again once the armistice was signed. He replied laconically that it "would depend entirely on the object for which we were fighting." In brief, Haig's terms gave adequate security, but were insufficient to ensure fulfillment of Britain's war aims, even though the members of the cabinet believed Haig's provisions included as much as the Allies could reasonably ask for. The Admiralty's terms seemed impossible, but they received strong emotional support.

On October 24, the British received the text of Wilson's Third Note.[66] Lloyd George was enthusiastic in praising the president. He thought the Third Note solved all the problems he and the cabinet had worried about: "If Germany meant peace she would accept [Wilson's demands], and the acceptance would be equivalent to a military surrender." To the cabinet, with great and unjustified optimism, he added, "The diplomatic wrangle was now over."

Satisfaction with Wilson's Third Note did not extend to Wilson's program. On the twenty-fifth, the British, still worrying that the Fourteen Points set limits they could not go beyond, discussed the president's program one more time.[67] Lloyd George suggested that when the Allies gathered in the coming meeting to decide armistice terms, the British should state that President Wilson's freedom of the seas did not bind them. They should also insist on the addition of several conditions not included. "Otherwise," he said, "the Germans would have a perfect right to assume that the Fourteen Points were the worst conditions that could be imposed on them."

The prime minister suggested that it would be useful if the Allies could agree on some sort of joint declaration.[68] Lloyd George thought that spelling out British objections in writing might offend the president. It would be better to handle the matter orally. First Lord of the Admiralty Geddes commented that when he had talked to the president earlier in the month, he had gotten the impression that Wilson no longer was eager to press for the freedom of the seas but would prefer to leave the declaration vague. Discussion was getting nowhere. The cabinet eventually told Lloyd George and Balfour, both of whom would represent Britain in the coming conversations, to reject the freedom of the seas and left the method of doing so to their discretion.

On October 25, Colonel House was just landing in France, and meetings on the armistice were clearly imminent. If talks among the British, French, Italians, and Colonel House were about to open, the British leaders did not yet have clear guidance about what ends they should seek. With an invitation from Clemenceau to begin meetings of the Supreme War Council in front of the cabinet, the secretary of the cabinet summed up the situation at this point: he wrote in his diary that the cabinet, "in a fog of confusion," decided to ask that the Supreme War Council meet the following Tuesday, October 29 (it was a Friday when he wrote), and to have the Allied Naval Council meet first.[69]

On Saturday, October 26, at the cabinet, Lloyd George went back to basics.[70] Did Great Britain really want an armistice? He reverted to the position he had taken at the Danny meeting: to teach the Germans a lesson, the Allies should fight until they stood on German soil and then dictate their terms. Lloyd George's position, if it was his real one, was a lonely one, but he waxed oratorical. The Germans had devastated France and were now trying to escape the consequences. Now that Britain "was in a position to put the lash on Germany's back she said, 'I give up.' The question arose whether we ought not to continue lashing her as she had lashed France." Balfour answered him with the same arguments he had used at Danny: Britain should make peace if it could get proper terms.

If the cabinet meeting was a debate between Balfour and Lloyd George, Balfour won. In the words of one participant, "Vengeance was too expensive in these days." The most eloquent statement of the majority opinion came from General Jan Christian Smuts, the South African member of the cabinet, who had written a long memorandum on that precise point two days earlier.[71] If the Allies let the war drag on, he wrote, they would win, but "the peace which will then be imposed on an utterly exhausted Europe will be an American peace. In another year of war the United States will have taken our place as the first military, diplomatic, and financial power of the world." The very fabric of civilization, Smuts claimed, was ripping under the strain of the war. Central Europe was fragmenting. "No League of Nations could hope to prevent a wild war dance of those so-called free nations in the future." For imperial self-interest, making peace now would be good, if the Germans would accept the necessary terms. Perhaps the Allied and Associated Powers had not achieved justice yet, but "the evil of continuing the war" was rapidly outweighing the good of a more complete victory. The British Empire needed to calculate its own self-interest and not sacrifice it to some fantasy.

Lloyd George got no support for continuing the war. It is probable that he was simply presenting the logical extreme of the argument that the Allies needed to impose exceedingly strict terms on Germany, even though he had already put forth the same savage proposal at Danny. To be sure, he had seemed to move toward Haig's terms in the two meetings on October 19 and 21.

One piece of evidence supports the supposition that Lloyd George was not expressing his true opinion when he suggested refusing to make an armistice until the Allies were on German soil. On October 24, the cabinet had agreed to phase out long-range plans for increasing munitions production.[72] Lloyd George had raised no objection, and if he had expected the war to last indefinitely, he would have wanted to increase production.

Here at the cabinet on October 26, the British leaders passed a resolution to guide Lloyd George and Balfour at the interallied sessions that were about to begin in Paris:[73]

> The Prime Minister and Mr. Balfour should in the forthcoming Conferences at Paris base their attitude on the question of an armistice on the assumption that the British Government desire a good peace if that is now attainable.

That formula gave no direction on what constituted a "good peace," although there was agreement on certain of its elements. Chief among them was that it must not allow Germany to enter the peace negotiations as an equal: the Allied and Associated Powers must have the power to dictate terms to a conquered Germany.

The British had reached complete agreement among themselves on opposing the freedom of the seas, their main objection to Wilson's peace program. They had also devised a formula that the naval terms should reflect as complete a victory as did the land terms, but in view of Lloyd George's reluctance to support severe naval terms, that formula might be an invitation to hair-splitting. Lloyd George and Balfour were still uninstructed on what general terms to seek. The cabinet had not ordered them to implement Haig's terms. Or Sir Henry's. Or the navy's. Or the military and naval committee's. Or Foch's.

If Lloyd George had planned to go to Paris with complete independence, he now had it. In a political exhibition of great skill, he had managed to keep his hands virtually free, at the cost of leaving his cabinet colleagues puzzled over precisely what they had decided and some of them resentful of the way he had manipulated them. Lloyd George got his free hand, but in the long run, he left no one happy.

4

France, Clemenceau, and Foch

In France, civil-military relations were more troubling than they were across the Channel. Prime Minister (properly President of the Council of Ministers) Georges Clemenceau, in his late seventies, sometime duelist, Communard and Dreyfusard, publisher and pamphleteer, called "the Tiger" by virtue of his political ferocity, had led France since 1917. Having twice seen Germany invade France, Clemenceau believed that his duty—and his destiny—lay in his preventing its ever occurring again.

Clemenceau ruled his cabinet with a firm hand, so that it played a less prominent role in airing policy on the armistice than the British cabinet did. In his cabinet, Clemenceau did not encourage strong or independent figures. Cunning men could prosper, but with the exception of Marshal Foch, who was a special case, Clemenceau brought no strong or independent person to the center of power. With the cabinet kept in line, armistice discussions in France focused on two men: Clemenceau and Foch.

During early October, the president of the Republic, Raymond Poincaré, also tried to play a role, but Clemenceau fought him off. Poor relations between those two stemmed less from principle than personality. They hated each other. A Lorrainer never reconciled to the Treaty of Frankfurt, Poincaré had been president of France since before the war. At the end of 1917, Poincaré called Clemenceau to office, not because of any fondness for the Tiger, but as a last alternative in desperate times.[1]

Clemenceau's problems with Poincaré reached feverish intensity even while the Conference of Prime Ministers was meeting. Just after the first news of the German request for an armistice arrived, Clemenceau met with President Poincaré, and, according to Poincaré, supported a less-than-rigorous position.[2] Clemenceau maintained that the Allies had to be "prudent and moderate." The president, still according to his own account, was "dumbfounded" by Clemenceau's words. He wanted to have the military leaders write the armistice conditions and leave Clemenceau and the cabinet only the task of approving them once written.[3] Whatever transpired at their meeting, Poincaré wrote to Clemenceau after it was over and accused him of "having hamstrung" the French soldiers during the German spring offensive six months earlier.[4]

Clemenceau, who usually exercised a talent for ignoring Poincaré, this time wrote back in fury, submitting his resignation.[5] Poincaré refused to accept it, and Clemenceau's aides and allies bent all their efforts to smoothing over the quarrel. Grudgingly, Clemenceau agreed not to resign, but he never forgave Poincaré. Relations between the two remained sour until the end of Clemenceau's ministry and even afterward.

If the animosity between Clemenceau and Poincaré rested on personalities, almost the same was true of relations between Clemenceau and Marshal Foch.[6] They had no real dispute over what terms the armistice should contain. During the Conference of Prime Ministers, Clemenceau deputized Foch to prepare terms, and he never made any real effort thereafter to amend the marshal's drafts. Both wanted terms that would mean an indisputable victory over Germany and a complete safeguarding of the peace to follow.

Ferdinand Foch had intense determination and moral courage and persevered in the face of reverses, but, of course, a general who lacked those qualities did not survive the test of the Great War. His mind was incisive and penetrating, but not subtle. Foch was conscientious, a devout Catholic, and, above all, a patriot.

Clemenceau distrusted Foch's clerical and conservative politics and disliked him personally. He had pushed for Foch's appointment as Allied commander-in-chief, but he exhibited a tinge of reluctance when he proposed it. Foch, for his part, never showed Clemenceau any noticeable gratitude. What focused hostility between the prime minister and the marshal in October 1918 was Foch's wanting control over the political aspects of the armistice negotiations. Clemenceau was entirely unwilling to cede him that power.

Except for that issue, the most important matter over which Foch and Clemenceau quarreled in October 1918 was Clemenceau's belief that Foch was not getting full value from newly arrived American soldiers. Clemenceau felt that the commander-in-chief of the American Expeditionary Forces (AEF), General John J. Pershing, was incompetent, and he wanted Foch either to make Pershing take effective action or to replace him.

The real center of this dispute, the evaluation of the AEF's performance, is a study in conflicting hopes. The Europeans wanted to shift the burden of fighting to American shoulders, and in the autumn of 1918, the American army was not doing well. Foch's chief of staff blamed American difficulties on inexperience, particularly staff inexperience, and Haig commented in October that the American supply system was so bad that starving men had to come back from the front lines to be fed.[7] Even if the AEF was not doing quite so badly as those comments suggest, it was not fighting as effectively as the Allies wanted, frustrating the European generals who were counting on using American soldiers to shield their own men from further losses. Time and experience would solve the problems of the American Expeditionary Forces, but every day that passed saw more Allied soldiers die to give the Americans that necessary experience, and the European leaders were convinced that their soldiers were dying unnecessarily because of American obstinacy.

When the United States had entered the war, the Allied leaders had concluded that the best way to use American soldiers was to absorb them individually or by small units into the existing European armies. American pride insisted on keeping the American effort separate and independent as much as possible. Because neither the British nor the French had allowed their own units to be absorbed wholesale into the army of the other, it is hard to see why they imagined the Americans would think differently. Still, Pershing's entire tenure was an effort to prevent his allies from stealing his army piecemeal, the so-called Amalgamation Controversy. The Americans won the point. Some American units did serve as regiments and divisions inside larger Allied formations, but most of the United States' soldiers were concentrated in the American Expeditionary Forces, although at the time of the First German Note, the AEF was organizationally a component of the French army.

Disturbed at the beginning of October that the Americans were bogged down, Clemenceau sent General Henri Mordacq to see Foch about the situation. General Mordacq, the chief of Clemenceau's military establishment in the Ministry of War (Clemenceau was war minister as well as prime minister), persuaded Foch to write Pershing that he should resume the attack at once.[8] Pershing was furious at Foch's letter. "The Marshal quite overstepped his bounds of authority in writing such a letter to me," Pershing stormed in his diary.[9] "His functions are strategical and he has no authority whatsoever to interfere in tactical questions. Any observations from him as to my way of carrying out the attack are all out of place."

On October 4, the American army resumed its offensive, but with disappointing results.[10] Mordacq learned that Pershing had hinted he wanted to be directly under Foch's command with an independent national force, instead of being organizationally under the French army.[11] If indeed that was the first Mordacq had heard of Pershing's wishes in that matter, he had been extraordinarily inattentive. Now, Mordacq strongly supported the American general's wish, perhaps hoping the change would inspire Pershing to greater efforts, but nothing was done immediately to carry out the reorganization. In the meantime, Clemenceau complained once again, this time to Poincaré, about Foch's failing to take effective action concerning Pershing.[12]

After the Conference of Prime Ministers, Clemenceau still felt Foch was not dealing properly with the American army.[13] Foch claimed in response that, on the contrary, he had put Pershing "face to face with reality, . . . [and] he asked of him now, 'No more promises, but some results.'" Foch added that he had told Pershing he would place him under his own direct orders, thus removing Pershing from the intermediate command of the French army and finally giving the United States' forces a status equal to the French and British armies. He published the order putting that change into effect on October 17.[14]

The members of the British cabinet, on October 21, came to much the same conclusion Clemenceau had reached: the American soldiers were good material, but the American staff was inexperienced and failing to get the best out of their men.[15] Lloyd George complained that the French criticized the Americans to the British, but not to the Americans' faces. "If only Marshal Foch could be induced to let President Wilson know the truth . . . , the President would insist on a better utilization of the American troops." When Lloyd George sent Lord Milner to see Clemenceau over Near Eastern matters, he also told Milner to persuade Clemenceau that "Foch should force Pershing to spread out the American Army over the French and over ours, as no one was getting full value for it now."[16]

All this concern during the first three weeks of October about using the United States' forces in the most effective fashion makes two points. First, the efforts to get the greatest possible value out of the American army underscore the proposition that neither the British nor the French believed an armistice was imminent. If it was, a major fight over the use of the American army was only wasted effort. Second, problems over the American army reinforced the distaste Foch and Clemenceau felt for each other.[17]

A decade later, when Clemenceau recounted his exchanges with Foch over the American army, he was at his most biting. Foch claimed, Clemenceau wrote, that he was pleased he had managed to stay as Pershing's friend through all this turmoil. Clemenceau commented: "In truth, France asked of the Americans, eminently combative people, something more than a parade of military amity among the great chiefs."[18] On the contrary, military amity among allies is not a useless quality, nor is it clear what more Foch might have done so long as Pershing enjoyed the confidence of President Wilson.

This dispute over how to use the American forces in the most effective way possible was never resolved. It came to an end only with the armistice, although the quarrel certainly played a role in the poor relations that existed between the commander-in-chief and the prime minister. Of greater effect, however, was the falling out the two had when Foch tried to include himself in political decisions, and Clemenceau felt obliged to block him from access to that power. For a week after the Conference of Prime Ministers adjourned, while President Wilson was still monopolizing negotiations, Foch apparently did nothing about the armistice. On October 16, two days after Wilson's Second Note—the one that said the terms of armistice must be left to the military advisers—Foch wrote to Clemenceau.[19]

Foch was sure that no armistice was likely soon, but he worried that when final decisions on armistice terms became necessary, the politicians might use the Military Representatives to the Supreme War Council for military advice. On the contrary, Foch wrote, "the only military advisers qualified to negotiate the conditions of an armistice are the commanders-in-chief." Perhaps because Haig was unsympathetic to French claims, Foch went on to argue that even the advice of the commanders-in-chief was insufficient: "In what concerns the theater of France and Belgium, I consider that it is the Marshal Commander-in-Chief of the Allied Armies who after an understanding [*entente*] with the Commanders-in-Chief of the French, British, and American Armies and the Chief of the General Staff of the Belgian Army acts as the adviser of the government."[20] Thus, the commanders-in-chief of the Allied armies and the AEF would not fetter him, because he was obliged only to come to an "understanding"— his own word—with them, not to be bound in any manner by their wishes.

In his letter of October 16, Foch also asked for direct liaison with the Ministry of Foreign Affairs. As an example of the reasons for which he needed that contact, Foch discussed the Rhineland. He wanted an armistice to provide for taking the Rhineland as "security for reparations exactable for the damage [*dégâts*] committed in allied countries." But, he noted to Clemenceau, the issue did not end there. Would the occupation continue after the Germans had paid reparations, or would the left bank of the Rhine be subject to some other political future? "Will we annex all or part of this country, or will we endeavor to create autonomous, independent neutral States, forming buffers?" he asked. Having to deal with matters like those, he wrote Clemenceau, he needed continuous and close contact with a high-ranking member of the Ministry of Foreign Affairs.

If Clemenceau gave Foch that liaison officer, it would make the marshal dominant in the armistice negotiations. At the least, it would diminish the prime minister's authority, which stemmed in part from his power to balance demands from various sources and to pit one agency against another. Clemenceau would never agree to Foch's request.

Clemenceau did not answer Foch immediately, perhaps because Wilson's Second Note led him to believe the Germans would drop their armistice request. The Third German Note of October 20 showed that the subject was still very much alive. In the meantime, two days after his first letter, Foch had written to Clemenceau again, this time ostensibly to warn him of the moderate views that Field Marshal Haig held on armistice terms.[21] Foch hoped to goad Clemenceau into giving him dominance in the armistice negotiations by pointing out that if Haig and the British gained an equal voice, they would ask for less than the French wanted. If Clemenceau gave Foch the power to act independently, Foch believed he could suppress Haig's views, for Haig was nominally his subordinate in the military chain of command.

It could not happen that way. Foch was assuming he could stifle British wishes through his military authority, when all that his attempt to choke off Haig could possibly gain was ill feelings. Haig would never abdicate his responsibility to advise his own government simply because Foch ignored him.

In any event, Clemenceau would never give control over the negotiations to the generals as a group or to Foch as an individual.[22] When Clemenceau answered Foch on October 23, he did it in a letter that was little more than brutal.[23] He began by agreeing that the political leaders ought to consult the military. But, he said, the military would give only technical advice, and the Allied governmental leaders would make final decisions, accepting whatever part of that advice they chose to. The political leaders would naturally consult the commanders-in-chief in the field, and Clemenceau added that the political leaders should hear from the admirals, too.

Clemenceau thus refused Foch's request for direct liaison with the foreign ministry. To underline his rejection of Foch's proposals, Clemenceau appended a letter from Stephen Pichon, his minister of foreign affairs, who was regarded in military circles as a nonentity. For Clemenceau to append any letter from Pichon to a general was a studied insult. Pichon's letter stated that the minister of foreign affairs was responsible to the government, while Foch, who owed his appointment to the Supreme War Council, was not. Foch was furious.[24] He insisted his ideas were entirely reasonable and a claim Clemenceau had made, a declaration that diplomats and generals worked in separate spheres, was absurd: "War, like peace," Foch said later, "is not a double thing, but *one.*"[25]

Nevertheless, Clemenceau kept Foch from acting independently during the armistice negotiations. What Foch did in the next weeks, he did on Clemenceau's orders. Clemenceau had settled, in his own favor, the question of who in France would command the armistice negotiations.[26] On October 24, Clemenceau invited Foch to meet with him, and Foch came docilely. In their meeting that afternoon, Clemenceau and Foch, with the commander of the French army and several staff officers also in attendance, worked on armistice conditions.[27] Wilson's Third Note had said he was sending his correspondence to the Allies

> with the suggestion that, if those Governments are disposed to effect peace upon the terms and principles indicated [the Fourteen Points], their military advisers and the military advisers of the United States be asked to submit to the Governments . . . the necessary terms of such an armistice as will fully protect the interests of the peoples involved and ensure to the Associated Governments the unrestricted power to safeguard and enforce the details of the peace to which the German Government has agreed, provided they deem such an armistice possible from the military point of view.

Wilson's proposal thus had two steps. First, the Allies had to agree to the American program or reject it. Then, if the statesmen agreed to Wilson's Fourteen Points, they would solicit armistice terms from their military advisers. From a strictly technical point of view, Wilson's note left those military advisers free to warn against an armistice if they believed one would fail to give the Associated governments "unrestricted power to safeguard and enforce the details of the peace." In practice, that decision, too, was political, not military.

At the meeting on the twenty-fourth, Clemenceau did not ask the question of whether the Allies should grant an armistice. Yet, as Foch's chief of staff wrote later, nothing Marshal Foch ever said gave the slightest indication that he opposed an armistice as long as it contained proper safeguards.[28] For his part, Clemenceau's summoning of Foch to polish a draft of terms implies his agreement, even if tentative, to the idea of an armistice. Like Foch, Clemenceau believed that an armistice, so long as it contained adequate safeguards, was entirely desirable.[29] His approval did not extend to Wilson's peace program, but that was a matter to be dealt with separately.[30]

On October 24, Clemenceau gave Foch two general instructions. First, while the armistice remained in force, it had to guarantee the safety of the Allied armies. Second, if the armistice broke down, the Germans must not gain a better position than they had when they first signed the document.[31] On these matters, Clemenceau's thoughts exactly paralleled Foch's.

At this meeting, Clemenceau and Foch adopted Foch's draft of October 8 almost whole.[32] The only major change made was to substitute bridgeheads on the middle Rhine for the bridgeheads on the upper Rhine proposed in Foch's earlier draft, with Strasbourg included in both texts.[33] Foch later explained the change to bridgeheads over the middle Rhine as simply one of expediency. On October 8, Allied forces had been too far from the Rhine in the north to demand bridgeheads there, but by October 24, Allied forces were nearer to that great river.[34]

His explanation was not altogether candid. There was a great difference in the effect those new bridgeheads—Köln, Mainz, and Koblenz—would have on the strategic situation compared with the effect of bridgeheads on the upper Rhine. The bridgeheads proposed earlier led nowhere. These new bridgeheads lay in a direct line from France to Berlin, controlled the industry and commerce of western Germany, and sat astride the railroad communications between northern France, Belgium, and Germany.

Clemenceau ordered Foch to summon the Allied commanders-in-chief to meet the next day at Foch's headquarters, Senlis, a town about thirty miles north of Paris. Foch would show them the draft just agreed to and ask them if they had any objections. That action, Clemenceau believed, would keep the other military leaders from making problems over Foch's terms in front of the Supreme War Council when it met.[35] That is, Clemenceau was not asking Foch to get the Allied commanders to approve the document, so long as Foch felt they were unlikely to raise major objections.

Foch already knew their views. The day before, October 23, he and General Pershing had eaten lunch together. Pershing, to this time, had spent little mental energy on the problems of an armistice. Even when he went to meet with Foch on October 23, he had no definite plans, nor had Washington given him any guidance.[36] At that lunch with Foch, he discovered that his views were largely those of the marshal, and he told Foch so. Foch, therefore, could reasonably expect Pershing's support at the forthcoming Senlis meeting.[37] Haig would be another matter.

Field Marshal Haig, believing Germany was still strong and Allied strength depleted, thought Germany would accept only moderate terms. Haig was so convinced of his analysis that he drafted a savage letter to Foch on October 23. After having studied the October 8 draft of terms, Haig wrote, "I should be glad to know whether you are of opinion that the enemy will accept those terms or whether you merely put them forward to prevent an armistice from taking place."[38] Perhaps Haig thought this sentence was too strong, because he deleted it when he actually sent the letter two days later. In both drafts of the letter, Haig echoed the testimony he had given the British cabinet. The German army was beaten, but it had not yet disintegrated. It could withdraw to shorter lines and hold them indefinitely. At the same time, the Allied armies were not well off. The French army was tired, the British army was under strength, and the American army lacked experience. It had "suffered severely through ignorance of modern war," and it would be some time before it could become "a serious fighting force."

With his letter drafted but not yet sent, Haig met with Foch on the morning of October 24, just before Foch's afternoon meeting with Clemenceau.[39] Over lunch with Foch and Foch's chief of staff, Haig gave them the gist of his letter and ended by reaffirming the mild provisions he had supported in front of the British cabinet a few days earlier. Foch retorted that the Allies and the United States needed to occupy the left bank and the bridgeheads. That action would put Germany in a weaker position than if the German army were straddling the river. For technical military reasons, Haig disagreed, and in his diary he described Foch's argument as "political and not military."

The meeting was fruitless on another subject, too. Foch had just given command of Haig's Second Army to the Belgians, and Haig wanted it back.[40] Foch refused, which led Haig to comment in his diary that Foch "is suffering from a swollen head and thinks himself another Napoleon!"[41] Eventually, the two agreed to a formula that let both sides save face. Under it, Foch promised to return the Second Army to Haig's command when it crossed the line of the Scheldt. But Allied unity had not prospered during this altercation.

Early on the morning of October 25, Foch sent messages to the Allied commanders asking them to meet in his headquarters at Senlis that afternoon at four. He did not intend the meeting to be a conference of equals. In the same fashion that a battalion commander hears the views of his company officers before an attack, Foch prepared to listen to the Allied commanders.[42]

When the various commanders-in-chief assembled, Foch opened the Senlis Conference with the statement that the Allied Governments had entrusted him with the mission of drawing up the main lines of an armistice with Germany.[43] "The French Government," he said, "had asked him, with approval of the Allied and Associated Governments, to take up the question of armistice terms with the Commanders-in-Chief." That was not precisely a truthful start, for the Allied and Associated governments had issued no such request. In an attempt to set ground rules, General Philippe Pétain, commander-in-chief of the French armies, interjected here that terms of peace were not the military's concern; "their duty was to only outline the conditions of an armistice which would make the resumption of hostilities impossible." It is likely that Pétain and Foch had agreed beforehand on what each would say.

Haig made the first substantive contribution, repeating the statements he had made on October 19 and 21 to the British cabinet and, the day before, to Foch. The German army was beaten, but its forces had not yet disintegrated. "In his opinion," Haig said, "that army was still capable of withdrawing to a shorter front and of making a very effective stand there against equal or even superior forces. On the other hand, the Allied Armies were pretty well exhausted." The British army was short of men and so was the French, and the American army was not doing well.[44]

Haig concluded that conditions did not warrant the Allies' trying to impose a severe armistice on Germany, and he proposed the same terms he had given the British cabinet on October 19. The armistice needed to include only German evacuation of Alsace-Lorraine and invaded Belgium and France, Allied occupation of Metz and Strasbourg, restitution of French and Belgian rolling stock, and repatriation of the inhabitants of invaded territories. Those terms would place the Allies on the German frontier if hostilities resumed.

Haig claimed that the Allies would face a more favorable military situation if the Germans kept part of their army on the left bank than if the Germans entrenched all their forces on the far side of the Rhine. Judging that question is not easy. If the German army sat astride the Rhine, the Allies could pinch off and destroy whatever part the Germans kept on the left bank. Haig here—as he had dealt with the Western Front for the past three years—had his eye fixed on destroying German divisions and corps. Given World War I technology, however, the Allies and the AEF would find it extremely difficult to force the line of the Rhine thereafter.

Under either Haig's plan or Foch's, the Germans would lose the resources of the Rhineland, in Haig's plan after the Allies had smashed whatever German forces remained on the left bank, in Foch's plan through an immediate occupation of the region. Eventually, the loss of Rhenish raw materials and industrial capacity would diminish German powers of resistance.

If hostilities should resume after an armistice was signed, Haig's plan would have a greater immediate effect on the rifle strength of the German army, and Haig's plan would very likely cause larger German (and Allied-American) military casualties immediately than Foch's plan would. Foch's plan would have a greater immediate effect on the industrial strength of Germany. Moreover, with Foch's bridgeheads, the Allied and American forces would not have to force the line of the Rhine. Yet entrenched on the other side of those bridgeheads would be the entire German army, not whatever smaller part would be left after Haig's plan had caused the destruction of the forces left in the Rhineland. On balance, Foch's plan, which took the industrial resources of the Rhineland from Germany and which gave the Allied and American forces bridgeheads over the Rhine, seems militarily stronger, but the choice is not absolutely clear.

Those considerations do not appear in the formal records of the Senlis Conference. Foch confined himself to arguing with Haig over Haig's assessment of the military situation. The German army was not disintegrating, Foch said, but it had been beaten constantly for three months. It had lost a quarter of a million prisoners since July 15. He agreed with Haig that the Allied armies were not fresh, "but victorious armies are never fresh." Foch concluded that the military situation was good, and "we must push it."

At Pershing's urging, Pétain spoke next, presenting, although he never openly said so to Pershing and Haig, the draft terms that Clemenceau and Foch had prepared the day before. Pétain presented himself as simply a military technician. He emphasized that peace terms were not his concern, but that the armistice should provide guarantees that would let the Allies and the United States get what they wanted in the peace. The armistice should provide for resuming hostilities under favorable conditions, too, if that action became necessary. For the Allies and the United States to occupy the entire left bank and control bridgeheads on the right bank, Pétain said, would meet both requirements. He added, correctly, that the occupation of Alsace and Lorraine was militarily useless. More important was requiring the surrender of railroad rolling stock, which would limit the mobility of the German army and cripple its supply system.[45]

Pershing spoke last, saying, "If the German Government was really sincere in its desire to end the war, then neither the German Government nor the German people should object to strict conditions regarding an armistice."[46] This specious reasoning passed without comment. Agreeing with Pétain that the armistice should provide a guarantee against a resumption of hostilities and give the Allies a clear edge if fighting resumed, Pershing added that the enemy had done such damage during the war that the Allies should not tilt toward leniency. He added that the military situation favored the Allies. Pershing proposed that the Germans evacuate Belgium, France, and all other foreign territory within thirty days. The Allies would occupy Alsace and Lorraine, and the Germans would withdraw all their forces east of the Rhine, with the Allies and the United States occupying any necessary bridgeheads. The United States should get the right of unrestricted transportation of soldiers and material across the seas. Germany must repatriate all foreigners, return French and Belgian rolling stock, and surrender all submarines and submarine bases "to the control of a neutral power."

Thus, in outline, Pershing's terms nearly duplicated Foch's.[47] In view of what Pershing will do five days later, it is important to note that neither at this meeting nor privately in his diary did Pershing question whether an armistice was desirable. In fact, in his first remarks at the Senlis

Conference, he specifically noted President Wilson's instructions that the military leaders draw up terms "provided they deem it possible to give an armistice." He raised no objection to granting one here, nor did his report to Washington on the events at Senlis suggest any reservations.[48]

After Pershing's presentation, the Senlis Conference closed quickly. Foch presented no views of his own, nor did he ask the generals to vote or to make any other gesture toward consensus. He had heard their opinions. Foch asked Haig if the field marshal wanted to modify his views in light of what Pétain and Pershing had said, and when Haig declined to do so, Foch adjourned the meeting, requesting that the generals give him their views in writing.

When Haig reflected on the Senlis Conference that evening, he still felt no need to change his opinion.[49] He had just received a report that the Germans had no fresh divisions and that the internal situation of the country was serious. Under those circumstances, harsh terms would be an error, he thought, for they might stimulate a Bolshevik uprising. That, in turn, would probably cause the German government to fall, and the threat of Bolshevism would bring the military party back to power. To Haig, that chain of reasoning suggested the need for moderation in the terms, which suited him. Meditating on Foch's and Pétain's insistence on occupying the left bank, Haig decided that the French were simply trying to get control over the Rhineland as well as Alsace-Lorraine.

When Foch returned to Paris, he made some slight changes to the draft he and Clemenceau had agreed to on October 24, and he gave this new document to Clemenceau on the twenty-sixth.[50] "After having consulted the commanders-in-chief," Foch wrote, "I have the honor to make known to you the military conditions according to which an armistice could be made capable of protecting in an absolute manner the interests of the peoples concerned and of assuring the Associated Governments the unlimited power to safeguard and impose the details of the peace." First, Foch required the immediate evacuation of Belgium, France, Alsace-Lorraine, and Luxembourg, and the repatriation of their inhabitants. To force the Germans to abandon part of their military material, Foch proposed that the evacuation take place very quickly, with Belgium, Alsace-Lorraine, and Luxembourg cleared within fourteen days. The Germans must surrender at least twenty-five hundred heavy cannon, twenty-five hundred light cannon, three thousand trench mortars, and thirty thousand machine guns, numbers that Foch explained would constitute about one-third of Germany's artillery and one-half of its machine guns.[51]

Foch included all that in his first clause. His second clause directed the Germans to evacuate the left bank of the Rhine. The Allies would establish bridgeheads, with a thirty-kilometer radius, at Köln, Mainz, and Koblenz, and the Germans must evacuate a neutral zone on the right bank, forty kilometers deep, from the Netherlands to Switzerland. The Germans must have their forces across the Rhine twenty-two days after signing the armistice. The Germans would get three more days to withdraw beyond the neutral zone. With the problems of moving millions of men, particularly when those men would have to pass through the bottlenecks that the scarcity of bridges over the Rhine created, it would be almost impossible for the Germans to meet those time limits.

His third clause forbade the Germans' destroying anything as they withdrew. The fourth demanded the surrender of 5,000 locomotives and 150,000 railroad cars.[52] The Germans could not possibly meet that requirement because they needed the railway equipment in question to fulfill the time limits for evacuation.

Foch's fifth clause required that the Germans give the Allied armies the locations of all delayed-action mines, a sensible request. The sixth clause stated that the Allies would maintain the blockade to guarantee the execution of the armistice. Foch's last clause said that the Allied and Associated Powers and Germany would make an agreement concerning the return of prisoners of war. That ended the military clauses.

Foch's draft will become substantially the military terms of the armistice agreement, although a number of painful days separated it from eventual ratification. It differed from his October 8 draft only in detail and in the selection of bridgeheads. This October 25 draft did narrow the time limits, and it set specific numbers of weapons and railroad equipment for the Germans to surrender, but his October 8 draft had assumed the surrender of large quantities of both. Although his terms required some disarmament, Foch's proposal, unlike the Salonika Armistice with Bulgaria or the proposed armistice for Turkey, required no enemy demobilization. It depended for its force on the occupation of the Rhineland and on the chaos that rapid withdrawal must cause the German army.

Foch's draft had some major omissions. There was no reference to air power, nothing about German forces in Russia or Africa, and no mention of economic provisions. All those items would appear in the final armistice. He did suggest briefly some naval terms, but his proposals would not satisfy the British Admiralty.[53]

In sum, then, Foch's first draft, prepared hurriedly early in October and possibly prepared under the assumption that the German overtures would come to nothing, was still the heart of the draft military document. Clemenceau hurried to give Foch's report legitimacy by disseminating it widely.[54]

Yet these proposals are similar to the ones that had caused Douglas Haig on October 23 to question whether Foch really wanted an armistice. If Haig could carry along the British politicians, and if the British could get the support of the United States for proposals that were more moderate, then the French might find it difficult to get Foch's terms ratified without significant amendment. The French, of course, would resist a lenient armistice. Foch's terms gave them the Rhineland, for the moment, and Alsace-Lorraine, as well as making Germany defenseless against any other claims the French might make in the future. Clemenceau, Foch, Poincaré, the Chamber of Deputies—all would fight any lessening of these draft armistice conditions.

With Foch's terms, the French had a document that promised them a proportion of their war aims. Perhaps they might gain even more if they could block President Wilson's peace program. To do so, the French made overtures to the British, suggesting that they create a solid front against Wilson. Exactly where the initiative for that proposal came from is unclear. The focus of it, the counsellor of the French embassy in London, Aimé-Joseph de Fleuriau, had behind him at least the French ambassador in London, Paul Cambon, and Paul's brother, Jules, who was undersecretary of state in the Ministry of Foreign Affairs.

The overture began when de Fleuriau spoke with the assistant undersecretary of state in the British foreign ministry, Sir Eyre Crowe, a man more powerful than his title suggests.[55] De Fleuriau claimed that his colleagues at the French foreign ministry worried about the Germans' manipulating the Fourteen Points. He feared, also, that other conditions, covering matters on which the Fourteen Points were silent, might escape attention. "The wording of President Wilson's pronouncement was vague," Crowe quoted de Fleuriau as saying, "and generally most unsatisfactory." De Fleuriau proposed stating jointly that the Fourteen Points were necessary and wise, but required precise definitions, which they did not have at present. There needed to be "a definite understanding among the Allies of what is the proper interpretation of the President's pronouncement."

Framed in diplomatic language, there it was: an offer to make a solid front against the Fourteen Points, Wilson, and the United States. De Fleuriau said that the prime ministers should discuss the matter at one of their conferences. No sense of urgency showed here. Like other people, de Fleuriau assumed that a cease-fire was still months away. What he proposed now was that the French and British should each name technical experts to go over the Fourteen Points. Crowe reported all this, strongly endorsing de Fleuriau's proposal. De Fleuriau had made at least one convert to his program of making common cause against the United States.

As the memorandum of the conversation and Crowe's endorsement worked their way through the Foreign Office hierarchy, they collected a number of minutes. The first person who read them noted that French policy was "to detach us from the US and bring us into the European fold." The author of that minute suggested temporizing. The foreign secretary, Balfour, was even colder to the proposal. He suggested sending the memorandum to the cabinet for decision, but only after Colonel House arrived in Europe. At that time, Balfour wrote, there might be some advantage in discussing the matter with France. "But France despises Italy, and Italy hates France," and thus it might be difficult to create a common European front even if both the French and British saw advantages in doing so.[56]

On October 28, the French moved one level higher in their contacts with the British. This time, the French ambassador in London, Paul Cambon, spoke with Undersecretary of State for Foreign Affairs Lord Robert Cecil.[57] Cambon said that Clemenceau was not sufficiently concerned with peace terms, and he suggested that Lloyd George might suffer from the same problem. "He was therefore afraid," Cecil wrote, "that no accurate consideration would be given to the eventual terms of peace." What Cambon wanted was for the Allies to come to "an agreement as to their [peace] demands before the armistice was concluded." Cecil told Cambon he agreed with him and proposed redrafting the Fourteen Points "in a more precise and specific form so as to make them satisfactory to ourselves." Cambon quickly agreed, but then Cecil poured cold water on the enterprise by saying that it was up to Balfour and Lloyd George to declare the government's policy on such a matter.

Again before November 11, the French would hint at creating an Anglo-French bloc to confront Wilson's Fourteen Points, but each time they met the same British response: a temporizing based on the British conclusion that they had as much to lose as to gain from following the French lead. The same theme would recur, for both nations, during the interval between the armistice and the gathering of the peace conference and during the peace conference itself, with the same conclusion each time.

There was tacit agreement that the Allied leaders would assemble as a Supreme War Council as soon as House reached Europe. On October 24, with House's arrival expected within twenty-four hours, the British ambassador in Paris telegraphed London that Clemenceau was anxious for the prime ministers to come to Paris as soon as possible.[58] The next day, Lloyd George, after receiving the support of the cabinet, wrote back asking that Clemenceau arrange for the leaders to assemble on the following Tuesday, October 29.[59] He told Clemenceau he was telegraphing the Italian prime minister to that effect and asked Clemenceau to telegraph him, too. He also asked Clemenceau to invite Colonel House to attend (this was the proper protocol). Lloyd George added that the Allied Naval Council should meet before the twenty-ninth so that the Supreme War Council might get its advice immediately.

There was a momentary problem when Italian prime minister Vittorio Orlando, pleading the serious illness of both his wife and daughter, wired back that he could not attend a Supreme War Council until at least November 1.[60] Lloyd George replied to Orlando that it was impossible to postpone the meeting. The conversations in Paris must begin on October 28, he wrote, subtracting a day from the proposal he had sent Clemenceau, but discussions the first day would concern only the Western Front.[61] He assured the Italians that the Supreme War Council would make no decisions affecting Italian interests before the arrival of at least the Italian foreign minister, if Orlando could not be present. That assurance was cold comfort. Orlando telegraphed Lloyd George that he would make every effort to attend, and in the meantime asked him to accept Foreign Minister Baron Sidney Sonnino as his representative.[62]

Clemenceau took immediate advantage of the situation. He encouraged Lloyd George to come to Paris on the evening of October 27, "as there is a great deal to be settled here and a good deal you ought to know before there is any regular meeting of governments."[63] As it turned out, however, there was little time for private Anglo-French conversations, because Lloyd George arrived in Paris only on the evening of the twenty-eighth, and Sonnino arrived on the morning of the twenty-ninth.[64]

The decisive meetings started on the twenty-ninth. The main problems the French had had in determining their policy on the armistice had come in the arena of civil-military relations. Clemenceau had won that fight. He was the unchallenged leader and spokesman for French interests. He had muzzled Foch, although Foch's willingness to accept defeat probably hinged on Clemenceau's not denying what the marshal thought was necessary in the armistice document. The generally poor personal relations between Clemenceau and Foch, and between Clemenceau and

Poincaré, did not damage French prospects in the armistice, but in the longer run, they might prove troublesome. That the French diplomats had failed to bring about an Anglo-French accord affected French interests far more immediately.

Now, in the last days of October, the Allied leaders prepared to meet and make decisions on the armistice. Central to those decisions was Colonel House, who had just arrived in Europe.

5

The Fourteen Points, House, and the Allied Prime Ministers

Charged with persuading the Allies to accept the Fourteen Points, Colonel House landed at Brest on October 25, and late that evening, he arrived in Paris. During the next several days, he spoke with American advisers and with individual Allied leaders. House and the Allied leaders began to meet informally as a group beginning on October 29, but not until the thirty-first did the full, formal Supreme War Council meet.

By the time of House's arrival, the military situation looked extremely good for the Allies and the United States. Bulgaria had already surrendered, Turkey was about to surrender, and even an Italian offensive launched, finally, against disintegrating Austria-Hungary was going well. On the Western Front, Allied and American forces continued to advance, while inside Germany, General Ludendorff resigned on October 26.

House's initial ideas on procedure were naïve. He wanted to consult the commanders-in-chief and the Military Representatives to the Supreme War Council on military measures and then ask the Germans to send their military leaders to receive terms.[1] He would grant a truce, which would last until the Germans accepted Allied peace terms or until it was clear that no agreement was possible. That is, though he was carrying the Wilsonian peace program, he did not yet see the connection between armistice terms and preliminary peace terms. He did not even realize, at first, that the military clauses of the armistice necessarily had political overtones. His only requirement was that armistice terms prevent the

Germans from fighting again, and he saw his mission of getting the Allied leaders to agree to the Fourteen Points as a separate enterprise.

About the only guidance Wilson had offered House before he left was: "I have not given you any instructions because I feel you will know what to do."[2] In view of the importance of House's mission not only to Wilson but also to the United States, that was not adequate. Even Colonel House, never easily daunted by responsibility, appeared uneasy about the situation. The catchy phrase House had coined before leaving the United States—"If Germany was beaten, she would accept any terms. If she was not beaten we did not wish to make any terms with her"—was of little help.

House had one other item in mind. He knew, obviously, that a peace conference would follow an armistice, and he wanted to be the United States' chief delegate.[3] Some of his actions during the armistice negotiations suggest subtle efforts to keep Wilson at home.[4] If Wilson did not attend, House was the logical person to head the United States' peace delegation; Wilson favored him over the other obvious contender for the post, Secretary of State Lansing. In House's favor, too, was his having headed the Inquiry, the United States' technical commission that had worked on policy for the coming conference, and his having represented the United States in Europe at previous diplomatic meetings.

On October 26, House had his first contact with the European leaders. He had lunch with Field Marshal Haig and Lord Milner, a very successful lunch, House believed.[5] He wrote in his diary that both Haig and Milner were moderate in what they wanted to demand of Germany, Haig not believing that the Allied military situation was sufficiently overpowering to compel the Germans to surrender.

Later that afternoon, House talked to Clemenceau. Before his arrival in France, House had written Wilson that if Clemenceau continued to cooperate with the United States as he had in 1917, it would shorten negotiations.[6] Now, he saw the Tiger face to face. "He received me with open arms," House wrote in his diary.[7] Clemenceau spent some time denigrating the British to House, and he took advantage of House's presence to complain of Pershing's failings. He also gave House a copy of Foch's terms drawn up after the Senlis Conference. "Clemenceau expressed his belief," House wrote in his diary, "which was also that of Marshal Foch, that Germany was so badly beaten that she would accept any terms offered." House added reflectively, "Haig does not agree with this conclusion and neither does [General] Bliss."[8]

The next morning, October 27, House had a long conference with General Tasker Bliss, the American military representative to the Supreme War Council.[9] Bliss, after his graduation from West Point, had served more often in staff positions than in line commands, ultimately rising to become chief of staff for the United States Army in 1917 before being appointed to the Military Representatives when that body was created. Bliss knew the Allied political and military leaders at least as well as any other American did, and the Allied leaders held him in high regard.[10] The military hierarchy in Washington also thought well of him, and although he was not close to General Pershing, they worked together effectively enough.[11]

In his conversation with House, General Bliss, who loathed both militarism and armaments races, pushed hard for disarmament, proposing that armistice terms simply demand the disarmament of the German forces with no other provisions. What concerned Bliss was that, in his view, Foch's terms multiplied irritating conditions but left the German army's organization intact and allowed the Germans to keep a great deal of equipment. With Germany disarmed and demobilized, Bliss believed, the Allies could enforce all their war aims and go on to demobilize themselves at the same time.

The next morning, Bliss gave House a written draft embodying his proposal to disarm Germany.[12] Foch's plan of partial disarmament, Bliss argued, "accompanied by [the] imposition of certain conditions which apparently foreshadow (and will be regarded by the enemy as foreshadowing) certain of the peace terms," left Germany with strong military resources. If the Germans would accept terms like Foch's, Bliss believed that they would accept demobilization. Therefore, the Allies and the United States should demand disarmament and demobilization. Then they could tell the Germans that Allied and American war aims must be fulfilled. The Germans might protest, but with their forces demobilized, ultimately they "must submit to whatever the associated powers finally agree upon."

There is the elegance of simplicity to Bliss's proposal, but House never promoted it. Bliss did receive support from General Mordacq and others.[13] He also showed a copy of his proposal to Lord Milner and Sir Henry Wilson, prompting Sir Henry to remark in his diary that he thought Bliss was more extreme than anyone else in Paris.[14] Milner was at his most diplomatic, telling the American general that his only hesitation about accepting disarmament was his fear that it would lay Germany open to Bolshevism.[15] "It seemed to me," Bliss wrote later to the United States' secretary of war, "that the army was quite as likely to become revolutionary as any other element in the German Empire. And a large German army, armed and with the German people behind it, might be more dangerous to the Allies than an unarmed revolution." Nevertheless, Milner gave Bliss's disarmament plan no support, and with neither House nor the British behind it, it died swiftly.

Bliss's plan, if imposed and supervised, might have prevented the situation that disturbed the peace conference the following spring, when claims arose that the Allies had to protect themselves against the Germans' resuming hostilities. Under Bliss's plan, Germany, lacking both arms and army, would threaten no one, but whether the new German republic could have survived without an army is another matter. Support from the army was crucial in the nation's overcoming the future Spartacist uprising and other disorders, which, even if the revolutionaries had no great popular support, might have grown into unquenchable fires if the army had not suppressed them.

Possibly one reason for House's turning away from Bliss's terms was a telegram from President Wilson.[16] Wilson ordered House to throw "our whole weight" behind any plan that would prevent Germany's renewing hostilities, "but which will be as moderate and reasonable as possible within those limits, because it is certain that too much success or security on the part of the Allies will make a genuine peace settlement difficult if not impossible." President Wilson did not want the Allies to have an entirely free hand in dealing with Germany, for he feared that they would put demands on that nation that would destroy hopes for future peace in Europe. The president concluded enigmatically that "foresight is better than immediate advantage."[17] But Wilson could not escape a contradiction: any armistice able to prevent Germany's renewing hostilities could not be "moderate and reasonable."

House, if he set himself against severe terms, would be flying in the face of strong French feelings, and possibly British ones, too. That could jeopardize his main mission. He dared not lose sight of his primary goal, which was to get the Allied leaders to agree to Wilson's Fourteen Points. To help get that agreement, House set Frank Cobb, the veteran editor of the *New York World,* and Walter Lippmann, the secretary of the Inquiry, the task of preparing a commentary on the Fourteen Points.[18] If Wilson approved the document, House expected to use it in his negotiations. As

House noted, "The Fourteen Points are considered vague and I am constantly asked to interpret them."

The Cobb-Lippmann Memorandum did not tighten up definitions in the Fourteen Points. If anything, it introduced a further lessening to whatever precision the Fourteen Points had.[19] Discussion of the Fourteen Points in chapter 2 showed that many of them, like Point Three on removing economic barriers, contained qualifying phrases that reduced their force. What the Cobb-Lippmann Memorandum did was to make explicit the amendments Wilson himself had issued over the past year and, in some cases, to introduce further qualifications.

On the critically important Point Two, the freedom of the seas, Cobb and Lippmann assumed the establishment of a League of Nations and then said that freedom of the seas would become an issue only if the league remained neutral in some dispute. If the league took sides against an "outlaw nation," then "complete non-intercourse is intended." If the league did not take sides, the rights of neutrals would be maintained.[20]

The adjustment of colonial claims, Point Five, would involve only German colonies, a practical but limited view. In a vein that would not satisfy the British Dominions, many of which had hopes of annexing German territories, Cobb and Lippmann stressed that the interests of the population involved must be the main consideration. "A colonial power," the Cobb-Lippmann Memorandum read, "acts not as the owner of its colonies, but as trustees for the natives and for the interests of the society of nations."

On Russia, Point Six, the Cobb-Lippmann Memorandum maintained that the victorious nations should make no effort to restore the territory of the old Russian Empire. The Allies should recognize the new Baltic nations, Poland, and possibly Ukraine. The peace conference should ask what remained, Great Russia and Siberia, to create "a government sufficiently representative" to speak for the Russian heartland. The memorandum did not suggest to whom the peace conference might send such a message. Finally, the memorandum demanded the evacuation of the German troops still present in Russia. Exactly that stipulation would cause anxious discussion in the Supreme War Council a few days later.

When the memorandum discussed Belgium, it touched on the dangerous question of reparations and indemnities. Declaring that Belgium must be restored, Cobb and Lippmann distinguished between the German invasion of Belgium, which was a violation of international law because Germany had guaranteed Belgian neutrality, and the invasion of France, which was an act of war, not a violation of international law. That distinction would sharply limit French claims. The memorandum did pledge the return of Alsace and Lorraine to France, although it opposed the additional French claim for the Saar.

When Cobb and Lippmann discussed Italian questions, Point Nine of the Fourteen Points, they avoided dealing with the conflicting claims of the Yugoslav Committee, the Kingdom of Serbia, and Italy, and they tried to strike a compromise. What they proposed was accepting the Treaty of London but placing any ethnically non-Italian districts annexed by the Italian monarchy under a special governmental regime. That arrangement would allow Italy to get its strategic frontier, and it would protect minorities from persecution.

In sum, the Cobb-Lippmann Memorandum avoided some of the predictable objections to the Fourteen Points by redefining and blurring their statements. By and large, Cobb and Lippmann accepted the secret treaties. They approved British and Japanese annexation of German colonies. Not only did they accept the Treaty of London, but when they dealt with Point Twelve on the Ottoman Empire, they raised no objections to the Sykes-Picot Agreement. They also agreed to all the Belgian financial claims against Germany and accepted part of the French claims.

The only statements left in the original Fourteen Points that could cause serious controversy with the French and British concerned the freedom of the seas and French claims for the Saar. The implied denial of reparations claims also might cause problems. Trouble might well come over French ambitions in the Rhineland, but neither the Fourteen Points nor the Cobb-Lippmann Memorandum mentioned that territory. Italian hopes for gains in the Balkans were another focus for likely controversy, but on that subject, the French and British might very well side with the United States.

House cabled the Cobb-Lippmann Memorandum in its entirety to Wilson on October 29.[21] The next day, the president cabled back, too quickly for him to have studied the memorandum in detail: "Analysis of fourteen points satisfactory interpretation of principles involved but details of application mentioned should be regarded as merely illustrative suggestions and reserved for peace conference."[22] House now had an approved gloss on the Fourteen Points, one that had the effect of making them even less rigorous than they were in their original presentation.[23]

During those first days after his arrival in Paris, House talked with the British about the freedom of the seas. Despite rumors that the French and Americans had held private talks on the subject, the British showed no sign of relenting in their adamant refusal even to consider the topic.[24] Sir William Wiseman, who had worked closely with House in the United States and who was now in Paris, told House that the British cabinet would never accept freedom of the seas, and they also wanted reparations for losses at sea.[25]

In response, House threatened Wiseman that the British would make the whole world their enemies if they continued in that vein. He added that the United States and other countries were no more willing to submit to Great Britain's controlling the seas than they had been willing to submit to Germany's dominating the Continent. He warned Wiseman that if Britain challenged the United States, the United States would build a navy bigger than Britain's.[26] Faced with so strong a threat, the British chose to confront it rather than surrender to what they saw as an even greater menace to their vital naval supremacy than a building competition with the United States. What House said may have angered the British, but it did not lessen their resolve. House's efforts to reach a private agreement with the British over the freedom of the seas failed.

On October 29, just before the prime ministers and Colonel House met as a group for the first time, Lloyd George and House had lunch together. Lloyd George was at that moment coming under increasing pressure from the English press to support harsh armistice terms, and he seemed to be trying to steer a middle course. At least, that was the impression House got during his lunch with the British prime minister.[27]

The only information about this meeting comes from House's reports to Wilson, which can be misleading. The first problem in using House's reports is a mechanical one. There was always the possibility of clerical errors in coding or decoding, but, more important, the messages, as circulated, contained only a paraphrase of the decoded text. The intention was to prevent a third party from comparing the decoded message against an intercept of the transmission and so gaining a key to the code, but a paraphrase might not present exactly what the sender intended.[28] The second problem in using House's cables as a source for what happened in Paris lies in the circumstances of the moment. House was trying to influence the president on several subjects, and he sent messages calculated to affect Wilson, not necessarily to report the full proceedings of the day.

Incidentally, House assumed that his cables to Wilson were secure, and the two had even taken the precaution of arranging a private code to use for especially sensitive messages. In fact, the British had broken the

American diplomatic codes some time before the Paris meeting, and they were reading the regular telegrams House and Wilson sent each other in the standard Department of State codes. Sir Henry Wilson remarked in his diary that the British had been reading all the cables between House, Lansing, and Wilson, "& they are the most amazing reading."[29] By the end of the Paris meetings, the British had broken the special code and were reading those messages, also.[30] It would be sensible to assume that the British could read all the ordinary diplomatic correspondence from before the time of House's arrival, but that it took them several days (or more precisely, several messages) to break the private code series. It is strange that the United States' officials had no concerns over the security of their communications until December, when they decided to begin sending cables from different points of origin and to break up their sequence, both elementary precautions.[31]

At their lunch on October 29, Lloyd George lectured House, telling him that if the Allies agreed to give Germany armistice terms, the Germans, without specific notice to the contrary, would assume the Allies had accepted the Fourteen Points. Great Britain, however, could not agree to the freedom of the seas without qualifications. According to House's report, which may have reflected wishful thinking on his part, Lloyd George did relent some.[32] With some hesitation, Lloyd George said that if freedom of the seas formed part of a larger agreement on the League of Nations, then the British might consent to the concept. Nevertheless, Lloyd George refused to accept the point as it stood. "If freedom of the seas was a condition of Peace," Lloyd George told House, "Great Britain could not agree to it." There was one bright spot to the conversation, which House failed to note: when Lloyd George voiced objections against only Point Two, he was tacitly agreeing to the other thirteen.

During this discussion, Lloyd George offered German East Africa to the United States. He also suggested that the Australians get German Oceana, the Union of South Africa take over German Southwest Africa, and Britain assume a protectorate over Palestine. He added that Arabia might become autonomous, and France might get Syria. That is, Lloyd George was sounding out House on the territorial arrangements the British contemplated making, with the one novelty of giving East Africa to the United States. House guessed his intentions, which were not difficult to grasp, and remained noncommittal.

At three that afternoon, the first meeting of the Allied prime ministers and House took place.[33] The leaders settled procedural questions without great difficulty. They decided to send their conclusions, whatever they might be, to Wilson and ask him to tell the Germans to request an armistice from the Allies. At this point, none of the Allied leaders contemplated flatly refusing the German request, although, for one reason or another, some of them might hope to postpone action.

Then they discussed which of the smaller Allied nations, if any, should have representation at the Supreme War Council's discussions of an armistice. Because more than a score of nations were at war with Germany, the leaders of the large nations thought they would accomplish nothing if all of the small nations had representation. The leaders of the Great Powers tried to find some formula that would let them include only the few nations they wished to include, but they found no satisfactory one. The Chinese, who had sent labor battalions to the Western Front, would not get representation. The Belgians, who had asked for representation, and the Japanese, who were involved in colonial matters covered in the Fourteen Points, would both get representation, but only at times the leaders of the Great Powers thought appropriate. To deal with all the nations except Belgium, Japan, and China, the leaders adopted a vague formula: those nations that had "made great sacrifices" could participate, "if they demanded it." The leaders expected to admit Serbia and Greece intermittently under this formula.[34]

What was happening here was the same situation that had already arisen during the war, one that would occur again when the peace conference met. Efficiency demanded that the leaders keep the number of participants small. Self-interest operated, also, to exclude persons who might object to the arrangements being made.

In discussing procedure, Clemenceau minimized the role Marshal Foch would play. Foch was the commander-in-chief only for the Western Front, Clemenceau said, and the armistice would have to encompass other theaters of war and other questions, like naval and diplomatic ones. The Allied leaders, he said, should consider Foch's opinions along with those of other experts. Because Clemenceau objected to none of Foch's terms, what he was probably doing here was, first, dissociating himself from any objections the leaders of the other nations might make to Foch's provisions and, equally important to him, keeping the reins of power firmly in his own hands, not Foch's.

These matters, important as they were, only served as a preface to the main subject of debate on the twenty-ninth: the Fourteen Points. Lloyd George opened the discussion by repeating the statement he had made to House at lunch. If the Allies accepted the idea of an armistice now, he said, and made no definite statement to the contrary, "they would be committed to President Wilson's peace terms." The American minutes are more complete here than the British. According to them, Lloyd George went on to say:

> The question is: do we or do we not accept the whole of P[resident] W[ilson]'s 14 points. I am going to put quite clearly the points which I do not accept. Should we make it clear to the German Government that we are not going in on the 14 terms of peace?

The American minutes make Lloyd George's statement read as a direct challenge to House, which it was. Clemenceau picked up Lloyd George's lead and asked blandly if the British had ever been consulted officially on the Fourteen Points. The French had not been, he said, and he asked whether the British believed they were committed to them.

Suddenly, the situation was falling apart. Perhaps frightened by the crevasse opening beneath him, Lloyd George began to hedge. Public opinion in Great Britain—and whatever his personal feelings, Lloyd George was always conscious of public opinion—would never allow him to ignore the Fourteen Points totally. Lloyd George answered Clemenceau that the British were uncommitted now, but to grant an armistice without comment would bind them to the Wilsonian program. Clemenceau agreed and asked for a reading of the document.

The first point, open covenants, caused a minor flurry, but after House read the Cobb-Lippmann explanation, which quoted Wilson's agreement to private talks, the Allies raised no objections.[35] It was over the second point, freedom of the seas, that the storm broke. House may have thought that Lloyd George had been groping toward some sort of agreement at lunch. In fact, Lloyd George was reconnoitering House's position. The British cabinet, in one of its few definite decisions, had instructed Lloyd George to reject the freedom of the seas, and Lloyd George believed British public opinion strongly backed that action.[36] Now, he flatly refused to accept the freedom of the seas. He did grant the possibility of discussion, which was by no means a promise of agreement, after the League of Nations was a working entity, provided Germany did not participate in those hypothetical future discussions. Clemenceau and Italian Foreign Minister Sidney Sonnino supported Lloyd George with barbed irony.

House lost his deft touch. "The President," House told the Allied leaders,

> would have no alternative but to tell the enemy that his conditions were not accepted by his Allies. The question would then arise whether America would not have to take up these questions direct with Germany and Austria.[37]

There it was. House was playing his highest trump early. Clemenceau asked whether House meant that the United States would make a separate peace, and House answered that it might. His threat did not move Lloyd George. The secretary, Hankey, recounted the passage-at-arms in his diary that evening:[38]

> Clemenceau—Do you mean that you would make a separate peace? House—It might amount to that—it depends on how far your criticisms go. LLG—We shall be very sorry if you go out—but we shall fight on. Sensation.

In the less elliptical language of the minutes, Lloyd George said that whatever happened, the British could never agree to the freedom of the seas: "If the United States of America was to make a separate peace, we should deeply regret it, but, nevertheless, should be prepared to go on fighting." Clemenceau interrupted Lloyd George to agree with him.

House had expected his threat to be decisive.[39] No evidence, other than House's diary, which is not trustworthy on the point, corroborates the threat's having any effect at all.[40] Lloyd George had expected House to make it, although he believed, incorrectly, that freedom of the seas was House's project, not Wilson's, and that eventually House would back down. Working from a wrong assumption, Lloyd George had been prepared to call what he thought was House's bluff.

He also subtly offered House a deal. First, having rejected the freedom of the seas, he slid over to another criticism of the Fourteen Points. In them and in Wilson's other speeches, he said, there was no explicit mention of indemnities, and an explicit statement was necessary. But after raising those objections, Lloyd George said that, except for those two matters, he had no disagreement with any of the other Fourteen Points. He would be happy to accept them if reparations were included and Point Two struck. Thus, Lloyd George was telling House that he would support him against what were sure to be a chorus of French and Italian objections to the Fourteen Points, if House would only drop the freedom of the seas and agree to reparations. Given the alternatives looming before House, Lloyd George was making an attractive offer.

Instead of taking the offer, House made a bad situation worse. He proposed that the British, French, and Italians meet without him and agree on their exceptions to the Fourteen Points. The American minutes have House adding sourly, "You may be in such a disagreement that there will be no need for an armistice." The British foreign secretary, Balfour, saved House from himself. Concerned at the turn events were taking, Balfour cautioned the leaders against letting the Germans cause dissent among the Associated governments, and the leaders went on with the reading of the Fourteen Points.

Lloyd George became conciliatory, reinforcing his implicit offer of support. When Point Three, the removal of economic barriers, was read, Lloyd George took it on himself to stress the "so far as possible" phrase. He even added that he "had no particular objection to any of the other clauses. They were wide enough to allow us to place our own interpretation on them."

Here, the Italian delegate interjected that Point Nine on Italy's frontiers was unsatisfactory, but House ignored him to agree with Lloyd George that the Fourteen Points were "couched in very broad terms." Somewhat later in the meeting, Lloyd George carried that idea to its logical conclusion. If Germany accepted Foch's military conditions, the British prime minister said, "the Allies could interpret President Wilson's Fourteen Points as they wished," which was not what Wilson had in mind.

No further discussion of the Fourteen Points took place at this first meeting, other than some desultory remarks on the League of Nations. Lloyd George amended House's poisonous suggestion that the Allies meet and draft their common objections to the Fourteen Points. Instead, he proposed that each nation draw up its objections to the points and let the Allied leaders discuss them one at a time the next day. The Allied leaders agreed to follow that less perilous course.

Colonel House, perhaps glad to move to a new subject, suggested that they look at specific terms of armistice. Lloyd George thereupon read a draft of the Allied Naval Council's terms. The British Admiralty dominated the Allied Naval Council, and its draft naval terms were essentially those that Admirals Wemyss and Beatty had presented to the British cabinet.[41] To the cabinet, Beatty had demanded that "the Terms of Armistice should be as nearly as possible the Terms of Peace." He had proposed forcing Germany to surrender its Dreadnoughts and battle cruisers, eight light cruisers, fifty of its most modern destroyers, and all of its submarines. The cabinet, frightened of those proposals and equally frightened of offending the powerful forces that supported the navy, had ordered Beatty and Wemyss to decide upon the minimum terms possible.

No thought of moderating their terms crossed either Beatty's or Wemyss's mind in the days that followed, and Wemyss had gone to the Allied Naval Council without the slightest doubt that his views would prevail. "I . . . look forward to a unanimous resolution to put before the Supreme War Council," he wrote Admiral Beatty.[42] "The First Lord [of the Admiralty, Sir Eric Geddes,] accompanies me . . . and will back me up at the final business." Wemyss was right: no softening of conditions took place before the Allied Naval Council met. Wemyss persisted in supporting the basic theme. The terms of armistice must be the terms they wanted in the peace.[43]

Wemyss and Geddes refused to give any ground at all. Wemyss met informally with French naval chief-of-staff F. F. J. de Bon on the morning of October 28 and found that Admiral de Bon supported "very much our way of thinking."[44] With the French backing the British when the naval leaders met that afternoon, they had little to discuss.[45] French minister of marine Georges Leygues, who served as chairman of the meeting, presented the British draft, with various minor French amendments attached as a result of the morning meeting.

Before they examined specific terms, Geddes warned that the naval leaders must guard against the Fourteen Points limiting the use of naval power or barring reparation claims for losses at sea. When the naval leaders discussed the surrender of German vessels, they reached quick agreement on requiring the Germans to surrender all their submarines. Estimates of the number of seaworthy German submarines varied between 150 and 160, and the naval leaders decided to recommend that the armistice terms require Germany to surrender 160 submarines. Setting that specific number "would, in practice, achieve what was desired and at the same time might not be so mortifying to Germany" as a demand to surrender all submarines.

They agreed, also, that the armistice must reduce the number of Germany's capital ships. "So far as Naval material was concerned," the conclusion of the report read, "the terms of the Armistice would in all probability be substantially the terms of the eventual Peace." The British were particularly concerned about German battle cruisers, and the naval leaders decided to demand the surrender of the German flagship, ten battleships, six battle cruisers, eight light cruisers, and fifty modern destroyers—Beatty's list of the week before. Those vessels would "be held in trust for final disposal at a Conference of the Allied and United States of America Representatives."

Over maintenance of the blockade and access to enemy ports, they had no debate. They discussed sweeping German mines and dismantling German fortifications on the North Sea and the Baltic so that the Allies could force the Baltic passage if they chose to do so later. Then the naval leaders agreed to the same general principles for Austria-Hungary, although they set no figures for the surrender of Austro-Hungarian surface ships and submarines.

Not everything went according to British dictation. The British wanted to require the surrender of Heligoland in the armistice. The other naval leaders blocked it, claiming that occupying the island would give the Allied and Associated Powers little advantage. The United States' representatives objected to a suggestion on how the surrendered vessels should be handled.[46] But except for those matters and some technical details, the draft of naval armistice terms that the Allied Naval Council approved duplicated the proposals Wemyss had presented to the British cabinet. "The naval terms," Admiral Wemyss noted in a memorandum to himself, "are stiff—but not more than they should be nor more than we deserve and is good for Europe."[47]

The next day, the Allied Naval Council met again and made minor changes in their preliminary work.[48] They decided not to require the surrender of the German flagship because it would be unnecessarily humiliating. The American representative, pleading a lack of instructions from Washington, refused to accept the clause that left final disposal of the surrendered vessels to a conference between the Allies and the United States.[49]

Jealous of naval prerogatives, or concerned about losing control of essential matters, First Lord of the Admiralty Geddes raised objections to Marshal Foch's having included naval provisions in his draft military terms. Whether Geddes was acting with Lloyd George's knowledge here is uncertain, but possible. It would do Lloyd George no harm in his meetings with Clemenceau to have had Foch's terms criticized, especially if Geddes could induce the French naval leaders to concur in a British protest. The French naval delegates claimed they had no knowledge of Foch's terms, and perhaps prompted by interservice rivalry, Leygues promised to bring the matter to Clemenceau's attention.[50]

When Lloyd George read the draft naval terms to the Allied leaders and House on October 29, he conceded that they were harsh, but he insisted at this presentation that British public opinion demanded their imposition on Germany.[51] House asked what would happen to the surrendered ships. Lloyd George answered that the Allies might divide them, to which Clemenceau, possibly for House's benefit, commented that such a division appeared to contradict Wilson's Point Four, the reduction of armaments.

Then the Allied leaders and House adjourned for the day. The Fourteen Points were still in doubt, although their outright rejection no longer seemed likely. The Allied leaders and House were uneasy over the effect of combining Foch's terms and those of the Allied Naval Council, but no one worried enough about them at this moment to mount a direct challenge.[52] On the other hand, no one was predicting yet that Germany would sign an armistice containing terms like those. Foch was still talking about "if" the Germans accepted the conditions.[53]

To free themselves from the Italians, Lloyd George, House, and Clemenceau agreed to meet by themselves on the morning of October 30.[54] It is probable that House met with Clemenceau and came to a major understanding with him before Lloyd George arrived at the meeting.[55] House needed support for the Fourteen Points. Clemenceau needed House's support for the occupation of the left bank of the Rhine, which Lloyd George opposed. If Clemenceau could obtain House's backing, he would present a Franco-American front that might overwhelm British objections. For House to agree to the occupation of the left bank would violate Wilson's instruction to seek moderation, but it would be easier to explain agreement to that occupation than to explain Allied rejection of the Fourteen Points. Clemenceau was lukewarm—at best—toward Wilson's program, but because of all the qualifying phrases, the Fourteen Points were endurable and a worthwhile exchange for the Rhineland. Thus, each leader had something to get and something to give, and they seem to have struck a deal.[56]

After this probable meeting with Clemenceau, House sensibly left Clemenceau's inner office and posted himself outside the door to wait for Lloyd George's arrival. When the British prime minister appeared, he handed House a draft of an answer he proposed the Allies send Wilson concerning the Fourteen Points.[57] Considering what his document might have contained, Lloyd George's draft was generous. The Allied leaders, it read, were willing to tell Germany they would make peace on the basis of the Fourteen Points, with two exceptions. One was the freedom of the seas clause, which was "open to various interpretations some of which they [the Allies] could not accept." Therefore, the Allies reserved "complete freedom on this subject." The second exception concerned the failure of the Fourteen Points to mention Germany's financial responsibilities: reparations. The evacuation and restoration of invaded territories must be understood to mean that Germany would make compensation "for all damage done to the civilian population of the Allies, and their property."

House should probably have agreed to that text immediately, because it gave far more than it kept. Nevertheless, it was still a denial of Point Two. "I told Lloyd George before we went into Clemenceau's room," House wrote in his diary, "that I was afraid his attitude at yesterday's meeting had lifted the floodgates; Clemenceau [and] Sonnino would have elaborate memoranda to submit containing their reservations."

When the meeting of Lloyd George, House, and Clemenceau began, the French prime minister did suggest that he had a long memorandum against the Fourteen Points. House reported to Wilson that he immediately told Clemenceau and Lloyd George that the Italians, who had not been invited to this meeting, were undoubtedly also preparing objections to the president's program. House repeated his threat of the day before, or one very close to it. If the Allied governments did not accept Wilson's program, "it would doubtless be necessary for the President to go to Congress and to place before that body exactly what Italy, France, and Great Britain were fighting for and to place the responsibility upon Congress for the further continuation of the war by the United States."[58]

Only the afternoon before, House had menaced the Allies with a separate peace to no effect, and this new threat—that Wilson would appeal to public opinion—was no more likely to move the Allied leaders, who believed they were already responding to their own publics' concerns. What seems probable is that House and Clemenceau had already agreed that they would go through this bit of playacting, and then Clemenceau would accept the Fourteen Points. House telegraphed to President Wilson that when he made his threat, "[Lloyd] George and Clemenceau looked at each other significantly." Clemenceau dropped his objections to the Fourteen Points and agreed to Lloyd George's draft, the one making reservations only over the freedom of the seas and reparations. House advised Wilson to accept it.[59]

With Lloyd George's draft adopted—provisionally, of course, because all of this discussion was taking place in the absence of the Italians—and with exceptions to the Fourteen Points limited to only two subjects, the three men turned to specific armistice terms. Lloyd George, as expected, opposed the occupation of the left bank, but when House supported Clemenceau, he yielded. Clemenceau "gave us his word of honor that France would withdraw after the peace conditions had been fulfilled," House telegraphed to Wilson. "I am inclined to sympathize with the position taken by Clemenceau."[60]

Both House and Lloyd George, however, held out against making the armistice conditions too severe.[61] House worried that harsh terms might foster Bolshevism in Germany. The danger, of course, lay not just in encouraging revolution in that nation, but in the chance that Bolshevism might spread to Allied nations. Clemenceau denied that there was any danger of Bolshevism in France, Lloyd George was less optimistic about England, and both allied leaders agreed that in Italy anything might happen.

By the end of this meeting on the morning of October 30, House seemed to have won agreement to the Fourteen Points, with two exceptions. Clemenceau had gained the left bank but was meeting resistance to other harsh military terms. It also seemed likely that the Allied leaders would revise the naval terms, because, according to House's diary, the three men agreed that the Allied Naval Council was asking for too much. The leaders might reduce naval terms, House thought, to a demand for the surrender of only battle cruisers and submarines.[62]

Before the three adjourned, they briefly considered other matters, among them where the eventual peace conference might meet. Clemenceau wanted Versailles, to which Lloyd George said that he and House wanted Geneva.[63] That issue was not trivial. The host nation of an international conference provides support functions, such as the secretariat, so the host nation gets a diplomatic edge. Equally important in this case was whether the conference would be held in a neutral nation or in a nation that had been at war with Germany, for that choice would set the tone of the peace conference. At this meeting on October 30, the three leaders made no final decision on a site.

Finally, the three established their agenda for the coming days. They decided to discuss the Ottoman Empire and Austria-Hungary that afternoon and return to German questions only after they disposed of those matters. Then they adjourned until the afternoon, when the Italians would be present.

Neither the Ottoman Empire nor Austria-Hungary was a subject the Allied leaders and House could dispose of easily. Turkish questions had already produced fierce acrimony between the British and French, and the situation had not improved markedly since the Conference of Prime Ministers early in the month. At that time, the British and French had fought over who would control the forces advancing on Constantinople. The conclusion was that British general Milne would command that operation but remain, for form's sake, under the nominal overall command of Franchet d'Esperey. Milne's army had gone by forced marches and was now on the Ottoman Empire's Balkan frontiers, only a few miles from Constantinople.[64] In the separate theater of Palestine, British forces had turned the Turkish flank.

The British had sent their admiral commanding in the Aegean the authority to make an armistice with Turkey and had instructed him, in effect, to operate unilaterally.[65] The French sent their admiral in the area instructions to intrude into the negotiations, but the British admiral refused to deal with him.[66] After Clemenceau and Lloyd George exchanged bitter letters over each others' intentions, Clemenceau finally agreed to order the French admiral to "'accommodate' himself" to the British.[67]

On the afternoon of October 30, when Lloyd George told the assembled Allied leaders that Turkish representatives were meeting with the British at Mudros and were about to sign an armistice, the dispute broke out anew.[68] The French foreign minister immediately objected to the British authorities' having excluded a French admiral from the negotiations. The Turkish armistice negotiations, he charged, had, in consequence, "failed to partake of an allied character." In response, Lloyd George noted smoothly that he had simply followed the precedent the French had set with the Bulgarian armistice, when they had failed to consult either the British or the Italians. In any event, he added, most of the forces operating against the Ottoman Empire were British.

Clemenceau and Lloyd George continued to bicker over the matter, each raising such points as national dignity and precedence. Lloyd George at one point protested the French "lack of generosity." The argument continued, with Lloyd George eventually warning that if the French kept challenging British power to make an armistice on behalf of the Allies, he would protest Foch's powers on the Western Front. The French finally accepted the British position, and the matter was closed, at least insofar as it concerned who would sign the armistice with the Ottoman Empire. The French ambassador in London called the entire argument puerile, and House described it as a "childish waste of time."[69]

As Lloyd George forecast, Turkish representatives signed the Mudros Armistice that same evening, and it went into effect at noon the following day, October 31.[70] The second of Germany's allies had fallen. Through the Mudros Armistice, the Straits were opened and the Allies obtained use of Turkey's waters and ports, thus allowing Allied forces to move through the Black Sea to the Danube. The armistice required the Turks to demobilize their army, surrender their warships, and allow occupation of any strategic point the Allies named. The Allies gained control of Caucasia and required the surrender of Turkish forces in the Hejaz, Assis, Yemen, Syria, and Mesopotamia. General Maurice, commenting on the document later, called the Mudros Armistice one of the most complete victories the British had ever won.[71]

Another and quite different matter came up unexpectedly on the afternoon of October 30. With no warning, the Allied leaders suddenly had to deal with another matter, the episode that has become known as "the Pershing Letter." What General Pershing did was present a formal recommendation to the Supreme War Council in which he seemed to oppose granting an armistice to Germany.

Pershing, early in October, had paid no particular attention to talk of an armistice. The first mention of an armistice in his diary—a diary that is elliptical and unrevealing, to be sure—did not come until the middle of October. At the Senlis Conference, Pershing had raised no objections to granting an armistice, nor did his subsequent report to Washington show any hesitation on the matter.[72] At Senlis, he had presented terms that included German evacuation of Allied territory and Alsace-Lorraine, Allied occupation of bridgeheads over the Rhine, continued unrestricted transportation of United States troops to Europe, surrender of all submarines and submarine bases to a neutral power, and return of French and Belgian rolling stock. Thus, at the Senlis Conference, Pershing had been slightly more moderate than Pétain, who had demanded very strict time limits on German evacuation and the surrender of military material, and much more exacting than Haig.

On October 27, the secretary of war sent Pershing Wilson's observations, article by article, on the American general's Senlis proposals.[73] Wilson suggested strengthening Pershing's first article, the evacuation of German territory, by requiring the surrender of some German heavy guns.

But from then on, Wilson was less rigorous than Pershing. The president thought the occupation of Alsace and Lorraine unnecessary, and he opposed occupying the Rhineland or holding bridgeheads over the Rhine. He believed that the only naval condition necessary was the internment of German submarines in a neutral port. "In general," the telegram from the secretary of war to Pershing read, "the President feels that the terms of the armistice should be rigid enough to secure us against renewal of hostilities by Germany but not humiliating beyond that necessity as such terms would throw the advantage to the military party in Germany."[74] The secretary of war's telegram dismayed Pershing, but it did not close the subject. The telegram ended with the statement that President Wilson "is relying on your counsel and advice. . . . He will be glad to have you feel entirely free to bring to his attention any consideration he may have overlooked."[75]

Pershing believed that his own terms, or ones of the same order, would ratify military victory, and that Wilson's terms would serve as little more than an inconvenience to Germany. Therefore, on October 30, in an attempt to block adoption of Wilson's terms, Pershing wrote a letter to the Supreme War Council opposing the Allies' granting any armistice at all to Germany at that time, or at least opposing their granting one on less than very severe conditions.[76]

Pershing began his letter with an analysis of the military situation, which he concluded was very favorable. "An armistice," he wrote, "would revivify the low spirits of the German army and enable it to reorganize and resist later on, and deprive the Allies of the full measure of victory by failing to press their present advantage to its complete military end." Once the Allies and the United States gave Germany an armistice, they would lose the initiative and find it hard to resume hostilities. "It is the experience of history," Pershing pontificated, "that victorious armies are prone to overestimate the enemy's strength and too eagerly seek an opportunity for peace." He concluded:

> I believe the complete victory can only be obtained by continuing the war until we force unconditional surrender from Germany, but if the Allied Governments decide to grant an armistice, the terms should be so rigid that under no circumstances could Germany again take up arms.

Pershing's final words make his intention clear. He wanted to prevent the Allies from approving terms like President Wilson's or Haig's. His argument was not directed against granting any armistice at all, only against granting a moderate one. He was happy with his own provisions or the French ones, but he feared Wilson's.

When Pershing's letter arrived at the Supreme War Council, the immediate reaction on the part of not only House, but also Clemenceau and Lloyd George, was irritation. Indeed, now that House had agreed to the occupation of the Rhineland, lenient armistice terms were most unlikely, and Pershing's battle, fought because he knew only Wilson's position and was ignorant of the negotiations, was a struggle against a phantom. The Allied leaders would never agree to Wilson's conception of an armistice, and Pershing might have left well enough alone.

In the event, the Allied leaders turned on the general. In the margin of his own copy of the memorandum, House scribbled: "I read it and handed it first to Clemenceau who read it carefully [Clemenceau both read and spoke English] and gave it back with the one word 'theatrical'—I handed it to [Lloyd] George who returned it saying 'Politics.'" In his diary, House added that "everyone believes it is a political document and a clear announcement of his intention to become a candidate for the Presidency in 1920."[77] House went on to note in his diary a detailed assessment of Pershing's qualifications.

House's first move in dealing with Pershing's letter was to write Pershing, asking him if the other Allied generals shared his views.[78] Pershing sent an aide to see House, instructing him to tell House that Pershing had no idea whether the other generals shared his views because they had never discussed his proposal.[79] Pershing was dissimulating here. To the copy of the Supreme War Council letter he sent to Washington, Pershing appended a separate section saying that he believed Foch would agree with his views and Haig disagree. In Pershing's defense, however, it should be noted that House did not ask him for his opinions about what the other generals thought, but for facts.[80]

When his aide returned and reported, Pershing decided to amplify his explanation in a letter to House.[81] The reasons for which he had submitted his views to the Supreme War Council, he wrote, were "purely military." He added that he had ordered one of his officers to take a copy of his letter to Foch that afternoon, and he promised to report Foch's reaction to House. "I feel very confident," Pershing concluded, "that unless the terms are made rigid, very rigid, that no armistice should be granted now." About this new letter, House commented in his diary that Pershing had made "further explanation which indeed does not explain at all."[82]

Pershing's last effort came later that same evening, when he wrote to House once again.[83] He told him that Foch's terms were "in practical agreement with my views," and he repeated his objections to granting an armistice. But, he wrote, if the Allies and the United States did decide to grant one, then Marshal Foch's terms

> seem to be such as would protect very completely the interests of the Allies and of the peoples concerned and would insure to the associated governments such a position as would enable them to impose upon Germany the details of a peace which would be satisfactory to the Allied Governments.

The Pershing letter created no further interallied stir, and Pershing and House composed their differences. For various reasons, not least among them that Pershing was a likely contender for the presidential nomination in 1920, House was ready to be charitable. Indeed, he thought enough of Pershing's judgment that on November 1 he summoned him from his headquarters to discuss operations against Austria.[84] The two men drove the ten miles from Versailles to Paris together. "We had a heart to heart talk," House wrote in his diary, "and agreed we would not allow mischief makers to cause trouble between us."[85] Pershing, according to House, apologized for not consulting the colonel before submitting his letter to the Supreme War Council. "He said he was wrong and was sorry," House wrote. "I found he had submitted it [the letter] to the War Department at Washington—a fact which I did not know and which modifies the matter." It modified the matter only if House was looking for a way out, but House was certain the letter should be forgiven and forgotten. That evening, November 2, he cabled the president that he and Pershing had settled the affair in a satisfactory manner.[86]

It was not that simple. Pershing's letter had caused anguished cries in Washington. Secretary of War Newton D. Baker had sent it to Wilson immediately.[87] "General March [the chief of staff]," Secretary Baker wrote in his covering letter, "read the enclosed with amazement and frank expressions of distress." Baker added that March believed politics was motivating Pershing. Pershing, Baker charged, was disobeying Wilson's orders and contradicting his own words at the Senlis Conference.

Wilson made no sudden move. He cabled House simply to have the Supreme War Council refer Pershing's letter to Washington.[88] House's assurance on November 2 that the matter was settled closed the issue for him. Baker, who was not receiving copies of that correspondence, was ignorant of what had transpired between House and Pershing and was incubating a long letter dressing Pershing down, which he submitted in draft to Wilson on November 5.[89] Baker's draft letter was far less peremptory than one Clemenceau might have written to a French general in similar circumstances, but it would have done no one any good to send it. Wilson saw that and sent it back to Baker, advising him not to send it and telling him that House had reported the matter was closed.[90]

So ended the Pershing affair, fitfully, and with rumors that would continue to haunt the general's reputation. Pershing's letter to the Supreme War Council had no other effect—or, to be precise, the effect he hoped to gain had already happened. By October 30, there was no chance the Allied leaders and House would approve moderate armistice terms. Foch, in fact, had responded to Pershing's letter by saying he could not tell the Germans, if they sent him a flag of truce, that he would accept nothing but unconditional surrender. He did promise, though, that while his conditions "might not bear the name of unconditional surrender," they would "approximate to that."[91]

At the meeting on October 30, the Allied leaders and House, after they dealt with Pershing's letter, turned to the Fourteen Points again.[92] Lloyd George read the letter that House and Clemenceau had accepted that morning in the absence of the Italians. Now, in the afternoon, the Italians were present. Italian foreign minister Sonnino immediately leaped in with a draft of Italian objections to Point Nine on Italy's frontiers. Lloyd George interposed, with some sophistry, that Germany alone was under consideration and that the leaders should hold back comments on the Fourteen Points having to do with Austria-Hungary until that nation came under discussion. Sonnino argued that unless the Allies made reservations against the Fourteen Points as they drafted the German armistice, the Fourteen Points would bind them on every other subject.

Lloyd George maintained that reservations concerning Austria-Hungary were not germane. He added that he planned to propose a new procedure concerning Austria-Hungary by which the Allies would deal with the Dual Monarchy directly, not indirectly through the United States as in the case of Germany. That proposal should have made House uneasy, but he raised no objection. Lloyd George's suggestion did not pacify Sonnino, who insisted on reading the full text of Italian objections to Point Nine, but Clemenceau took a hand and stated that the Allies should not insert the Italian reservation in communications to Wilson concerning Germany. After Sonnino had once again declared that he would not accept Lloyd George's draft letter with its two reservations, the prime ministers and House adopted Lloyd George's original and unamended draft statement on the Fourteen Points as the text for their response to Wilson.[93]

Thus, by the end of this second day of meetings, House had gained Allied approval of the Fourteen Points—to a degree. The Allied leaders believed they had settled the matter gracefully, with reparations protected and with a reservation against the freedom of the seas. Italian objections still hung heavy in the air, but by implication the Italians had accepted everything other than Point Nine.

To get this agreement, House had sacrificed the Rhineland, although it could be argued that the French were apt to get that territory eventually anyway, one way or another. The British got relief from freedom of the seas, and everyone got reparations. At this moment, therefore, the great majority of the Fourteen Points were still substantially intact, with difficulties over their interpretation postponed to some better time.

As events turned out, however, the Allied leaders and House had not yet settled the matter of the Fourteen Points—the political basis of the preliminary peace. President Wilson would refuse to accept the Allied statement on the freedom of the seas. That would push House into further discussions with the British; but at the close of the meeting on October 30, the Allied leaders and House thought they had reached a comfortable agreement.

For the next several days, they concentrated on how to deal with Austria-Hungary. With Austria-Hungary collapsing both militarily and internally, dealing with the Dual Monarchy was no easy matter.

6

The Austro-Hungarian Armistice

Drafting armistice terms for Austria-Hungary led the prime ministers and House down some unexpected byways. They had to deal with a disintegrating empire as national group after national group in the territory of Austria-Hungary announced its independence, set up a provisional government, and declared the previous regime irrelevant. The Allied leaders and House also had to take into account longstanding quarrels between Allies, particularly between Italy and Serbia/Yugoslavia. Finally, in drawing up military and naval clauses for the Austro-Hungarians, the leaders had to decide whether to follow the model of the Bulgarian armistice or to adapt the clauses they were preparing for Germany.

Early in October, the Austro-Hungarians, like the Germans, appealed to President Wilson to arrange an armistice.[1] Wilson let them dangle for almost two weeks and then wrote them that Point Ten of the Fourteen Points, which promised "autonomous development" to the nationalities of the Dual Monarchy, no longer applied.[2] Nothing but independence, he said, would satisfy those national minorities now. Wilson did imply that a Dual Monarchy could continue to exist, though shorn of vast tracts of territory, and he believed that other clauses of the Fourteen Points would protect its inhabitants from a vengeful peace.

Faced with the prospect of major surgery, the Austro-Hungarians hesitated before replying, but dissolution proceeded regardless. Attempts at creating a Habsburg-dominated government over Austria and Hungary failed miserably. When the emperor issued a manifesto federalizing the Dual Monarchy, the various nationalities ignored it. On October 15, the Poles announced their independence. A Czech provisional government had already gotten recognition from the Allies and the United States.[3] On the twentieth, the Hungarian Parliament demanded control over Hungarian units in the army, which it received. This accelerating internal chaos and the collapse of the army, added to the rapid advance of an Italian offensive launched on the twenty-fourth, drove Emperor Charles on the twenty-sixth to notify the Germans that Austria-Hungary was leaving the war. The government leaders of the Dual Monarchy thereupon told President Wilson they accepted his new statement on the future of Austria-Hungary and wanted an immediate armistice, although whether those government leaders now spoke for anything more than the Germanic provinces of Austria was uncertain.[4]

Adding complexity to the Austro-Hungarian question was the Treaty of London (1915) and the problem posed by that treaty's allotting ethnically Slav territory to Italy. Drawing boundaries for the western Balkans must cause bitter quarrels between the Italians and Serbians, and how that predictable Italian-Serbian dispute turned out would depend on which side France, Great Britain, and the United States supported.

The Serbs thought the Allies had treated them shabbily throughout the war. In fact, the Allies had been singularly ready to sell out Serbian interests in any number of negotiations. To begin with, the Serbs felt strongly that the Allies had betrayed them in the Treaty of London, one of the clauses of which was that signatories would not reveal the contents of the treaty to non-signatory Allies, a category that included Serbia. Although the Serbs did learn the details of the treaty very quickly—it is nearly impossible to keep a secret held in four capitals—they could do little about it. Also in 1915, in negotiations aimed at bringing Bulgaria into the war on the Allied side, the Allies showed they were ready to give away other Serbian hopes. Those blandishments to Bulgaria ended in nothing when the Bulgarians joined the Central Powers, but in similar and more successful negotiations with the Rumanians in 1916, the Allies gave Rumania other territory the Serbians had hoped to incorporate into an enlarged Serb nation.

With a more successful army, the Serbs might have fared better, but when the Central Powers turned their full attention to the destruction of Serbia, that nation collapsed rapidly. In the autumn of 1915, first Belgrade and then Niš fell to the Central Powers; the Serbian army fought its way southward over the mountains during the winter and eventually joined other Allied forces. Although the Serbs established a government-in-exile at Corfu in 1916, Serbia was thereafter an army without a country.

Nor were the exiles united. Under a 1917 pact, the Yugoslav Committee and the leaders-in-exile of the Kingdom of Serbia did manage to cooperate, but reluctantly. The problem was that the Serbian premier wanted to annex other Slav territory to Serbia, while the Yugoslav Committee wanted to incorporate Serbia into a greater pan-Slav nation.

The Italians certainly posed a threat to Slav ambitions, but Italian policy on Serbia/Yugoslavia was not monolithic.[5] Vittorio Orlando, whose prime ministership was an accident of Italian politics, was flexible. Early in 1918, he met with Yugoslavian leaders in an attempt to reach some sort of accommodation, one result of his overtures being the gathering labeled the Congress of Oppressed Nationalities. In April 1918, this congress produced the Pact of Rome, which set no specific territorial boundaries but did recognize the legitimacy of Yugoslav aspirations. Orlando was a moderate compared to Foreign Minister Sidney Sonnino, the architect of Italy's entry into the war. Sonnino was unbendingly anti-Serbian and anti-Yugoslavian, and he devoted herculean efforts to trying to keep any Yugoslavian program from getting official recognition from any Allied government.[6]

When the Italians finally launched their offensive against a crumbling Austria-Hungary in October 1918, the French claimed the Italians had attacked only after they saw Austria-Hungary was already defeated, a judgment that roused "intense indignation" in Italy.[7] Clemenceau, at the Conference of Prime Ministers early in the month, had tried to spur the Italians into taking the offensive, but by the time they did attack, he no longer wanted it. As he explained the situation to the president of France, "He expected to have to oppose the unreasonable demands of the Italians and did not wish a success to encourage them."[8]

When the Allied leaders and House met to prepare terms for Austria-Hungary on the afternoon of October 30, Lloyd George suggested settling armistice terms with Austria-Hungary before dealing further with Germany.[9] For Austria-Hungary, he proposed avoiding President Wilson as an intermediary, in contrast to the procedure the Allies expected to follow for Germany. House accepted Lloyd George's proposal, and why he did so is a mystery. If the Allied leaders followed the British prime minister's plan, neither Wilson nor the Austro-Hungarians would receive assurances that the Fourteen Points would guide the Austro-Hungarian peace settlement. House tried to explain his strategy to Wilson. "The direct approach," he cabled the president, "has the advantage of avoiding political discussion respecting Italian and other claims before capitulation of Austria."[10] House had gone to Europe precisely to make certain that the Fourteen Points directed the settlement of matters like those "Italian and other claims." House's assent to Lloyd George's proposal here was a lapse.

With House silent and no one else objecting to Lloyd George's plan, the British prime minister noted the advantages an immediate armistice with Austria-Hungary would bring the Allies, among them the chance to mount an attack against Germany's southeastern frontiers. As the basis for an Austro-Hungarian armistice, Lloyd George introduced a draft of military terms Sir Henry Wilson had drawn up that morning.[11] The prime ministers and House referred Sir Henry's draft to an ad hoc committee composed of the Military Representatives and the military leaders who happened to be at hand, ordering them to report back the next day.[12]

The Allied Naval Council had already prepared naval terms for Austria-Hungary consciously using as a model the principles they were proposing for Germany: the surrender of warships and submarines.[13] The Allied Naval Council's draft required the Austro-Hungarians to surrender six battleships, four light cruisers, nine destroyers, one minelayer, six Danube monitors, and fifteen submarines.[14] The Austro-Hungarians would disarm and disable all remaining ships under Allied direction. The Allied blockade would continue, and other clauses would force Austria-Hungary to give full access to the Adriatic and the Danube and allow the Allies to occupy the Austro-Hungarian naval base at Pola.

When the prime ministers and House looked at these draft naval terms, they decided the provisions were far too severe.[15] Clemenceau proposed that the Allied leaders tell the admirals "to demand what was necessary and nothing else," and he added sourly that "the naval men have acted as if there were no land army." Lloyd George, in words that would have given the British admirals pause, added: "I think the naval terms to Austria and also to Germany go beyond the necessity of the situation."

To consider the response of the prime ministers and House to their draft, the Allied Naval Council met on October 30.[16] The chairman, French minister of marine Leygues, who had presented the naval draft to the prime ministers and House, was not entirely candid when he reported back to the naval leaders. The political leaders, he said, had "generally approved in principle" the naval terms for Austria-Hungary, but they desired "some minor modifications." First Lord of the Admiralty Sir Eric Geddes ended that deception when he said the prime ministers and House wanted to know if the surrender of all the vessels demanded was necessary for naval security.

French naval chief-of-staff de Bon was furious. The Allied Naval Council, he said, had given its recommendation after careful consideration, and the prime ministers now wanted to change the terms. The members of the Allied Naval Council should refuse to amend their recommendations, for if they did change their terms, it would look as if "they had no settled convictions," and any proposals they made in the "future would equally be susceptible of similar revision." If Admiral de Bon suffered from misapprehensions about who ran the French government, Clemenceau could have enlightened him.

Geddes suggested that the Allied Naval Council make no changes in their formal proposal. Instead, the members should separately advise their governments on how much they might safely reduce the number of ships surrendered. They speedily adopted that resolution, an evil one if the naval leaders wished to have the power that only a united front could give them. To carry it out, they adjourned their formal session. The admirals, now without the civilian ministers, reconvened to consider what advice they would separately give their civilian leaders. It was a pointless maneuver, because once the naval leaders had agreed they would not support their draft proposal, the document became prey to the politicians. Nevertheless, de Bon, now having calmed down, suggested the surrender of only four Austro-Hungarian battleships, not six, and three light cruisers, not four. American admiral William S. Benson wanted to reduce the number still further, but de Bon, echoing the British slogan, argued that the "Armistice terms . . . would probably also be the Peace Terms." Austria must not come out of the war almost as strong as when the war began, he declared. The admirals agreed to de Bon's figures and adjourned.[17]

Up to this time, the Allied prime ministers and House had met informally in small "conferences." On the afternoon of October 31, the full, formal Supreme War Council met for the first time.[18] In the morning, the prime ministers and House had discussed military and naval terms for Austria-Hungary, but owing to the absence of a secretary, they were confused over precisely what they had agreed to.[19] Now, the large and unwieldy formal meeting had to deal with Austria-Hungary in an open arena.

The Supreme War Council went through the draft military terms for Austria-Hungary that the ad hoc military committee had recommended. The first clauses required the demobilization of the Austro-Hungarian army down to twenty prewar divisions and the surrender of half of the army's total equipment and artillery. Those requirements caused no controversy.

Potentially the most controversial element of the draft armistice terms for Austria-Hungary was an occupation zone duplicating the territory the Treaty of London gave Italy.[20] House might well raise objections to this de facto implementation of the Treaty of London. He did not do so. The original draft of the document, discussed informally that morning, had specifically cited the Treaty of London.[21] House had objected to mentioning the Treaty of London by name, and this amended draft omitted the name, although it described the same line by citing geographical landmarks. That removed House's objection.

Italian insistence on that zone, which included much ethnically Slav territory, predictably would cause a confrontation between the Italians and the Serbians, and the Serbians had a representative at this formal meeting of the Supreme War Council, Milenko Vesnić. The Serbian representative to the Supreme War Council proposed having the armistice text read simply, "All Yugo-Slav territories should be evacuated." That phrase would do double duty. It would recognize the legitimacy of Yugoslav claims, and it would reduce the likelihood that the other nations would support the Treaty of London without amendment.

Clemenceau tried to conciliate Vesnić by observing that armistice terms were not peace terms: "Our conditions of armistice did not prejudice our terms of peace." But, of course, they did, which Vesnić understood very well. Lloyd George tried to buy Vesnić off with the suggestion that Serbian troops—the Allied leaders other than Vesnić carefully avoided using the word "Yugoslav"—might occupy Bosnia and Herzegovina. Vesnić retorted that his concern lay not with just Bosnia and Herzegovina, but with "the whole Yugo-Slav territory," and he stated that if anything other than a temporary military occupation were contemplated, he would object formally. The prime ministers and House made no comment on that statement, and they adopted the clause as it stood.

With demobilization, the surrender of equipment, and an occupation zone agreed to, the Supreme War Council adopted the remainder of the draft military clauses with no significant discussion or changes. The clauses covered details like repatriation of prisoners and care for the wounded.

More important was the requirement that all German troops had to leave Austro-Hungarian territory within fifteen days or face internment. Finally, the Allies could occupy strategic points, and they also acquired the right of movement through Austria-Hungary, which would let them attack Germany through Austria.

With military terms tentatively approved, the Supreme War Council turned to the naval terms. Geddes read them, making the substitution of four battleships for six, whereupon Lloyd George asked why the number could not be further reduced to three. An Italian admiral, who was representing his nation at the Supreme War Council, said he thought the surrender of three Dreadnoughts was enough. Then he made a bad mistake: he went on to remark that "Italy might be content with two big ships to replace those which had been sunk by the Austrians."

Here the greed that lay beneath the surface of debate came glaringly into view. In animated discussion, Lloyd George suggested that instead of debating the distribution of the ships, the leaders confine their comments to the question of how many ships the Austro-Hungarians should deliver to Allied control. The Allies must be moderate, Lloyd George said. "We wished Austria to accept our conditions. Our military conditions were very severe and must be so. If, on the other hand, we imposed naval conditions of equal severity we run the risk of compelling the Austrians to continue the war." Eventually, the Supreme War Council decided to require the surrender of three battleships, three light cruisers, nine destroyers, twelve torpedo boats, six Danube monitors, and fifteen submarines. Even if the Supreme War Council had slightly eased the terms of the Allied Naval Council's first draft, Austria-Hungary would keep few naval resources.

When they came to the clause demanding the maintenance of the blockade, Vesnić objected. A large number of merchant ships based in the Adriatic belonged to Yugoslavs, he claimed. Those people had supported the Allied cause since the beginning of the war, and he proposed relaxing the blockade for "merchant shipping blockaded in the Adriatic belonging to Austrian Yugo-Slav subjects."[22]

Vesnić's proposal would create a subgroup out of the citizens and property of the old empire. Out of total enemy property and citizenry, it would subtract that which was Yugoslavian, in most cases a subjective identification. If the major Allied nations intended to end the oppression of Slavs in the Austro-Hungarian Empire, then treating those persons as enemies after the war was surely wrong. But from the Italian point of view, Italy

had suffered terrible wounds so that the nation might make certain specified and unspecified gains at the end of a victorious war. Now, with victory, persons of ambiguous status proposed eroding Italian profits.

Clemenceau opposed any Italian claims beyond a strict fulfillment of
the Treaty of London. In response to Vesnić's proposal, he commented
that "the Yugo-Slavs might be regarded as an Associated Power." That was
precisely the declaration that the Allies had avoided making because it
was a direct affront to Italy. Vesnić saw his chance. He "begged that this
should now be done, and that the brothers of the Serbs should be
recognised as associated in the same way as the Serbs themselves." Pi-
ously, Balfour explained to Vesnić that he favored the idea, but the question of naming Yugoslavia as an Associated Power was a question separate from the ones set for discussion at this particular meeting. The British
and French leaders concurred in referring the question of recognizing
Yugoslavia to a meeting of their foreign minsters the next morning.

Now, at the Supreme War Council, Orlando turned Vesnić's argument
against the Serbian leader. He agreed that the victorious nations might
make exceptions to the blockade, and then he went on to claim that there
was no reason to limit those exceptions to the Yugoslavs. A great many
Italian ships, he said, lay in harbor at Fiume. They should obtain similar
freedom from the blockade. Orlando, of course, was counting many of
the same ships Vesnić was. The difference was that the Italians hoped to
occupy Fiume, though the Treaty of London had not granted them that
port, and if they did occupy Fiume, they could manipulate any ownership claim to Italian advantage.

In fact, because historical Serbia was a land-locked nation, all Austrian
ships in the Adriatic could become prey to this Italian claim if the Italians
could keep the British and French and the Americans from recognizing
Yugoslavia as an Associated Power. Vesnić should have avoided raising
this issue in the first place. Now, presumably sensing that the Supreme
War Council was likely to accept the Italian proposal, he tried to recover
by demanding that any exception must apply to "Yugo-Slav shipping."
But, of course, no Yugoslav shipping existed until the Allies and the United
States recognized the new nation.

Sonnino responded coldly: "It appeared to him very difficult to make
distinctions among Yugo-Slavs. Some of them were Austrian and
Austrophile." Here, the gauntlet was dropped, but Vesnić, wisely, refused
to pick it up. He said that he did not wish to pursue the subject, only to
register his protest. With that, the Supreme War Council adopted a clause

allowing an interallied commission to make exceptions to the blockade, and the Supreme War Council approved the rest of the amended naval terms.

The naval terms the Supreme War Council adopted for Austria-Hungary were the amended ones of the Allied Naval Council. The military terms derived from an English draft that Sir Henry Wilson had originally sketched out and that an ad hoc committee had amended. In brief, the Austro-Hungarian army must demobilize the greater part of its men and surrender a large quantity of arms and equipment. The Allies, which for all practical purposes meant the Italian army, would occupy Austro-Hungarian territory that was identical with gains promised to Italy in the Treaty of London. The blockade would remain in force. The Allies and the United States obtained the right of transit across Austria, which would let them develop an attack against Germany's vulnerable southeastern frontiers and make the German military position untenable. Finally, the Allies and the United States would take the most powerful part of the Austro-Hungarian fleet. If the Austro-Hungarians accepted these terms, it was an overwhelming Allied victory. The Allied leaders and House immediately sent the document to the Italian army command for presentation to Austro-Hungarian envoys.

House approved the turn events had taken. "Fortunately," he cabled Washington, "I was able [to prevent] discussion of the political questions. I regard this feature as most favorable."[23]

The Serbians had no reason to rejoice. Other than their having had the opportunity to express opinions at the Supreme War Council, the day had been an unrelieved disaster for them. The Italians had prevented their gaining anything of moment and had probably won the right to put a claim on large portions of Austro-Hungarian shipping in the Adriatic.

The situation of Serbia did not improve the next morning, when the foreign ministers of Great Britain, France, and Italy discussed recognizing Yugoslavia.[24] Sonnino argued that recognizing Yugoslavia after sending armistice terms to Austria-Hungary would let the Austrians avoid the responsibility of executing those terms. Although it was not a very logical argument, Pichon supported it.[25] Balfour agreed to wait until the Austrian reply came in, asking Sonnino if the Italians would agree to recognize Yugoslavia then. Sonnino answered that he would do so "if the Yugo-Slavs too were ready to comply with the armistice conditions." An ambiguous reply, it required that an ally suffer the restrictions put on an enemy, and Balfour thought the Italians might not stand behind even that statement. Nevertheless, outnumbered two to one, he agreed to postpone the recognition of Yugoslavia until some later time.

Any sighs of relief from House and the Allied leaders for having completed the navigation of Yugoslav/Serbian issues were premature. Suddenly, the Allied leaders and House had to face an entirely unexpected problem involving Yugoslavia and Italy directly. On November 1, they learned that Slavs in the Austrian navy had just gained control of the Austrian battle fleet.

A new faction was involved, a third one. Weary of the political bickering between Serbia and the Yugoslav Committee, leaders of the Croats and Slovenes had proclaimed an independent revolutionary government, the Narodno Vijece or (Yugoslav) National Council, in Zagreb, Croatia. On October 29, the National Council declared independence for all Croats, Slovenes, and Serbs who previously were Austro-Hungarian subjects.[26] On the thirty-first, Emperor Charles, who was presiding over the dissolution of his empire, recognized this National Council and transferred the Austro-Hungarian battle fleet to its ownership.[27]

An event without parallel in military history, that transfer made unwelcome news in Paris. The National Council at Zagreb, the new owner of the fleet, was an untested revolutionary group, whether nationalist or radical no one knew. Indeed, there was confusion over what group, precisely, had control of the fleet.

Clemenceau broke the news at a small meeting on the morning of November 1, and that afternoon he brought up the subject again.[28] He read a telegram to President Wilson from Zagreb, in which the National Council requested the president to help put the ships under the protection of the United States or any Allied navy "not interested in our national problems."[29] Now, at the Supreme War Council, the Italians started from the assumption that Yugoslavian control of the fleet was unacceptable, and the British, French, and Americans did not really want to debate the question at all. They would have preferred to postpone having to choose between Yugoslav and Italian ambitions, but because of Emperor Charles's action, they could not wait.

Sonnino declared that the transfer was simply "a new Austrian trick." Armistice terms had already gone to the Italian high command, and the Allied leaders "could not now accept any declarations to the effect that this or that thing had been yielded to someone else." Sonnino's angry response was not just dismay at seeing the spoils of victory melt away. The Italians truly saw Yugoslavian possession of those ships as a threat to Italian security.

The British and French were not united on how to deal with the matter. This time, Clemenceau supported the Italians, arguing that the National Committee should deliver the Austro-Hungarian fleet to the Allies collectively. Lloyd George, however, stated that the Allies would make a mistake if they sent the Yugoslavs a message "revealing any sort of illwill." The Allies and the United States were going to present severe conditions to the Germans, and if the German leaders refused to accept those terms, the Allies and the United States would need everyone's help to impose them on Germany. The Yugoslavs could help an attack on Germany coming from the south.

To encourage the Yugoslavs, Lloyd George proposed that the Supreme War Council ask President Wilson to invite the ships to sail to Corfu, where they would be put under the orders of the Allied commander-in-chief for the Mediterranean, a French admiral. If the fleet sailed, Lloyd George said, all was well. If it did not, the armistice conditions the Supreme War Council had already sent to Austria-Hungary would cover the situation. Lloyd George's proposal did not really meet Italian objections, and the leaders reached no agreement, deferring the problem to the next day.

In the meantime, on House's suggestion, the United States' ambassador in France called in Ante Trumbić, the president of the Yugoslav Committee and the just-appointed representative of the National Council at Zagreb, to discuss the matter.[30] Trumbić told the ambassador that the Yugoslavs, who controlled the ships, hated the Italians more than they hated Austrians. He promised they would fire on any Italian ships that entered Yugoslav-controlled waters.

House received instructions from Wilson on the subject, although perhaps too late to affect his actions.[31] Regardless of when he received the president's orders, he did not follow them. Wilson ordered "the most liberal possible concurrence in transfer of actual armed force to Czecho-Slovak and Jugo-Slav local authorities as the best proof of our utter good faith towards them." He instructed House to "keep hands off the pieces of Austria-Hungary and reduce outside intervention to minimum. This is the time to win the confidence of the population there and the peace of Europe pivots there."

On November 2, the three Allied prime minsters and House met without the Serbians and worked out a temporary settlement along the lines Lloyd George had suggested the afternoon before.[32] The prime ministers and House signed and sent a message ordering the ships to sail to Corfu under a white flag—not, be it noted, a flag of the National Council or the tricolor of nascent Yugoslavia.[33] The Slav-controlled fleet would now presumably sail to Corfu, where the Slavs could be betrayed at leisure.[34]

The other matter still unsettled was how to exploit the surrender of Austria-Hungary by launching an attack against Germany's southeastern frontiers. On the morning of November 2, the Allied leaders met with their military advisers.[35] The severity of the terms the Allies and the United States could impose on Germany depended, to a degree, on what they could do to exploit the Austro-Hungarian surrender. It was, of course, not certain that the Austro-Hungarian leaders would accept the armistice terms just sent them. Once they received the terms—whether they had gotten them yet was unknown—they had forty-eight hours to answer, so the Allied leaders could not expect the situation to clear up for several days. In those circumstances, the prime ministers and House asked their military leaders for advice on what to do in any of three possible futures: if the Austro-Hungarians refused to sign the armistice; if the Austro-Hungarians signed it, but their internal situation was so chaotic that they could not carry out the provisions agreed to; or if the Austro-Hungarians both accepted the terms and carried them out.[36]

On November 3, the situation became clearer. That day, at the Villa Giusti near Padua, Austro-Hungarian envoys signed the armistice. Signature of the Villa Giusti Armistice dispelled one uncertainty, but, of course, the Allies and the Americans did not yet know whether the Austro-Hungarians could or would carry out the terms they had just signed.[37]

Foch and the chief of staff of the French army had already drawn up rough plans for an attack on Germany through the Tyrol and Bohemia.[38] The other generals agreed to what had begun as a French plan, and the day that the Austrians signed the Villa Giusti Armistice, a small group met to flesh out the details.[39] For operations against southeastern Germany—the Bavarian Offensive—this small military committee put together a plan that had Allied forces move concentrically against Munich. One army of ten Italian divisions would strike north from the Inn River Valley; those divisions would concentrate around Innsbruck within twenty-two days. Because of the terrain and the available railroads, a second force was the more important one. That second group, organized as two armies, would contain twenty to thirty divisions and move westward from a line between Salzburg and Linz. Twenty of the thirty divisions could concentrate in twenty-four to twenty-eight days, the generals thought, and the other ten divisions could concentrate in thirty to thirty-

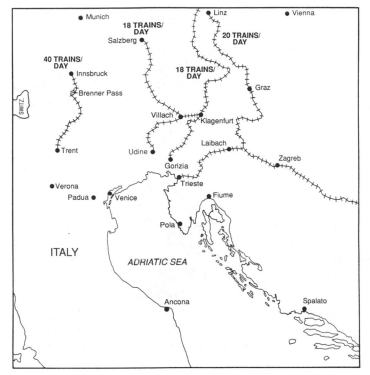

Proposed Bavarian Offensive

five days. Twenty-five of those divisions would be Italian, and the three British and two French divisions then operating in Italy would join the Salzburg-Linz group.[40]

The Allies stood to make enormous gains from this attack. The Bavarian Offensive might smash through the thin military defenses that were all the Germans could create on their southeastern border. Moreover, Bavarian separatism was increasing, and a successful assault might begin the dissolution of the German Empire.

But implementing this planned forty-division attack on south Germany involved many more problems than the small military committee comprehended. World War I armies moved on railroads, and an Allied division in 1918 needed about sixty trains for men and equipment, plus another ten or so for its ammunition supply. Corps and army headquarters, heavy corps artillery, and other units required additional trains. Thus, moving ten divisions with corps and army establishments north to Innsbruck would require seven to eight hundred forty-car trains, and once in the forward area, the men would need daily supplies, further burdening the railroad network.

Italian forces moving to Innsbruck had to use the Trent–Brenner Pass–Innsbruck railroad line, which had a maximum capacity of only forty trains per day. The generals believed that if they could move four or five of those ten divisions 140 kilometers by road, they could reduce the number of trains they needed, but because the roads were of uncertain condition, they expected delays. One hazard their report did not note was the calendar. Planning for mid-November, the generals laid down a timetable for moving large numbers of men and trains through the Brenner Pass into the Alps, and the weather would certainly turn against them soon.

The military committee planned for the second, larger group of soldiers, the one that would assemble on the Salzburg-Linz line, to use three railroad routes. One went through Villach to Salzburg, another through Klagenfurt to Linz, and the last from Trieste to Laibach and then north. The three routes, the military committee members calculated, would allow the passage of fifty-six trains per day.[41]

The whole plan savors of an indecent optimism. The Allies had not collected the locomotives and rolling stock necessary for all those trains, and that material might not exist. The weather would turn bad any day, and neither trains nor marching men move in an Alpine blizzard. The final shortcoming of the plan was that it made no allowance for the Germans' opposing the concentration by attacking the railroads in the mountains and passes.[42] In sum, the signing of the Austro-Hungarian armistice at Villa Giusti created the potential for an offensive against south Germany. Its realization, however, required Allied planners to take full account of possible German actions and the geography of the area. They did not do so.

Whatever the plan's shortcomings, Foch presented it to the prime ministers and House on the morning of November 4.[43] Lloyd George asked whether the Allies could use Franchet d'Esperey's Army of the East, then in the middle of the Balkans, against Germany. He suggested shipping the Army of the East to Trieste, or perhaps moving it there over the roads, and then having it go north from Istria. The Italians immediately suspected a deep plot behind this sensible-sounding proposal. The Army of the East included not only British and French components but also Serbian ones, and the Italians feared the presence of Serbian army units in the area they were preparing to contest with Yugoslavia/Serbia.[44] Therefore, they began to raise difficulties. The British, French, and Americans ultimately accepted what amounted to an Italian veto on the immediate use of the Army of the East for the attack on Germany, although the Supreme War Council ordered Foch to work out how to use it eventually.

In the days just before the Austro-Hungarian acceptance of the Villa Giusti Armistice, the dissolution of the Dual Monarchy accelerated.[45] In Prague on October 28, the executive committee of the Czech National Council took over administration of the government.[46] At the same time, the Kingdom of Serbia, the Yugoslav Committee, and the National Council at Zagreb were trying to work out their differences, although they did not finally succeed until December 1, when they proclaimed the formation of the Kingdom of Serbs, Croats, and Slovenes, or, more familiarly, Yugoslavia.[47] On October 28, the Hungarian National Council appointed a government in Budapest, and on October 30, the nonmonarchist German-Austrian National Council declared that it alone had the authority to speak for the German-Austrian peoples.[48]

Emperor Charles simply faded from the scene.[49] On November 11, he renounced his claims over the government of Austria, although he did not formally abdicate, and on the thirteenth, he issued substantially the same proclamation in Hungary. On November 12 and 16, respectively, the two nations declared they were republics, thus in effect abdicating Charles, whatever his wishes.

As it turned out, the Hungarians required a separate armistice protocol.[50] On November 1, they, like Trotsky before them, tried to declare peace unilaterally, but the Allies refused to accept it. On November 7, Franchet d'Esperey met in Belgrade with the new Hungarian premier to talk about how to apply the Villa Giusti Armistice to Hungary.[51] The Hungarians wanted to have their nation recognized as something other than a part of defeated Austria-Hungary, and they had a certain amount of justice and historical precedent behind their claim. The Allies had recognized Poland and Czechoslovakia, and except for the Italians, they might give similar recognition to Yugoslavia. There was thus no logical reason why this new Hungary—or, for that matter, the Republic of Austria—should carry the sins of the Dual Monarchy on its shoulders. The Hungarian delegates failed utterly.[52] They did succeed in one respect, however. One clause of the Austro-Hungarian armistice seemed to leave Hungarian territory open to annexation by Rumania and Czechoslovakia, and Franchet d'Esperey agreed to delete that clause, although later events proved the Hungarians would not retain their historic boundaries.

To deal with the Hungarians over details of the armistice, Franchet d'Esperey deputized a French general and the Serbian chief of staff to act for the Allies, perhaps including the Serb as a deliberate affront to the Italians. Both sides signed the Allied-Hungarian arrangement, the Military Convention of Belgrade, on November 13.[53] It applied relevant clauses of the Villa Giusti Armistice to Hungary.

The most striking characteristic of the Villa Giusti Armistice and the Belgrade Convention was how casually they were prepared compared to the discussions the Allies and the United States had over terms for Germany. Another conspicuous point is how easily the Italians got their Treaty of London claims. At the same time, debate over the terms for Austria-Hungary had revealed deep divisions in Allied ranks. No one who had heard the angry words that passed between the Italians and the Serbians/Yugoslavians could expect any sort of easy settlement of their differences, and those passions promised to continue troubling the peace of Europe.

However important the French and British and Americans at Paris thought their actions relative to Austria-Hungary were, they still kept their gaze focused on Germany. Even several days before the Austrians signed the Villa Giusti Armistice, the situation on the Western Front appeared very promising, and while the Allied prime ministers and House drew up terms for the Dual Monarchy and planned the offensive against Bavaria, they were putting together terms to impose on Germany.

7

The Allies, House, and the Terms for Germany

By the morning of November 1, the Allied leaders and House appeared to have strong justification for optimism. The Turks had signed the Mudros Armistice the day before, Austro-Hungarian envoys were about to receive Allied terms, and the prime ministers and House believed they had come to agreement over the Fourteen Points. The Allied leaders and House did still need to polish final terms for Germany, an effort that would include drafting economic terms as well as clauses for the Eastern Front, and, of course, they faced serious disagreements over naval terms. More serious was the possibility of a potential unraveling of their agreement over the Fourteen Points.

At a meeting of the Allied leaders and House on the morning on November 1, military terms for Germany came under detailed scrutiny.[1] Marshal Foch and his chief of staff, General Maxime Weygand, were the only military leaders present. The day before, House had asked Foch the critical question: was it better to make an armistice or to continue the war?[2] Foch had answered him bluntly:

> I do not make war for the purpose of making war but for the purpose of getting results. If the Germans sign an armistice with the conditions recognized as necessary to guarantee to us the results, I am satisfied. No one has the right to prolong the bloodshed longer.

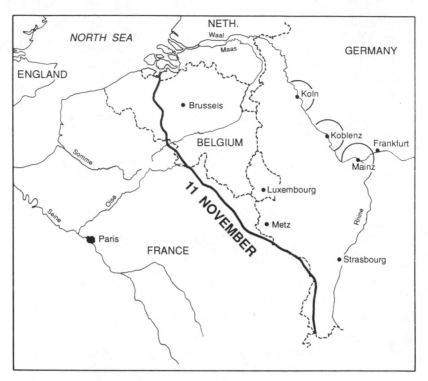

Western Front, Showing Proposed Bridgeheads and Situation on November 11, 1918

That had been the morning before. To the full Supreme War Council the afternoon before, Foch had given a rosy appraisal of the military situation. Since midsummer, he said, the Allies had forced the Germans back: "An army which for three months had been compelled to retreat, to suffer losses without being able to react, was a beaten army."[3] Winter was coming, but the Allies could physically keep pressing the attack, and their morale was high, though the Germans were still resisting them tenaciously.

Now, on the morning of November 1, the prime ministers and House in a small meeting examined the military terms for Germany, clause by clause.[4] With minor changes, these were the draft terms that Foch had given Clemenceau after the Senlis Conference. Foch's first article demanded the evacuation of Belgium, France, Alsace, Lorraine, and Luxembourg within fourteen days. The Germans had to abandon military material in the area evacuated and surrender twenty-five hundred heavy guns, twenty-five hundred light guns, three thousand trench mortars, and thirty thousand machine guns. At Foch's suggestion, the prime ministers and House added two thousand airplanes to the material Germany must surrender.

The second article was the one that could cause the most contention if either House or Lloyd George objected. It demanded the evacuation of the left bank of the Rhine and the establishment of Allied and American bridgeheads with a thirty-kilometer radius on the right bank at Köln, Mainz, and Koblenz. In addition, the Germans must create a demilitarized zone forty kilometers deep stretching along the right bank from the Netherlands to Gersheim and thirty kilometers deep from Gersheim to Switzerland.[5] All German forces had to cross the Rhine twenty-one days after the signing of the armistice, and they would get only three more days to evacuate the neutral zone.

On a map, Lloyd George charted Foch's proposals. Mannheim, he noted, was inside the occupied zone, and the Mainz bridgehead reached to within two miles of Frankfurt, so the Allies would control all the major cities of western Germany. Lloyd George asked Foch whether he could set up bridgeheads that avoided the occupation of those cities.

When Foch replied that he needed to occupy those cities because they were transportation hubs, Lloyd George took the opportunity to put forth Haig's ideas. Haig claimed, Lloyd George said, that with the Germans thrown out of Belgium, France, Alsace-Lorraine, and Luxembourg, the Allies had everything they needed for the peace conference. If the peace negotiations broke down, "it would not be necessary for you to attack but for the enemy to do so." Foch responded that the principle he had used as a guide in drawing up terms was that the enemy must not get "a better position than he now occupied." The Allies must be able to "destroy" Germany if peace negotiations broke down. Because the Germans based their defensive system on the Rhine, Foch declared, the armistice had to give the Allies control of that river.[6]

Here House interjected that, although he opposed taking more than necessary from Germany, he favored leaving judgments about what was militarily necessary to Foch. House's continuing to support the French Rhineland proposals flies in the face of Wilson's instructions, but it is perfectly compatible with the theory that House had traded Clemenceau support on the Rhine for French support of the Fourteen Points.

Lloyd George was not setting himself flatly against Foch's terms; he was only quoting his own general, whom he was not necessarily backing. If House sided with Lloyd George, the British prime minister's comments might develop into opposition. As it was, Lloyd George remained uncommitted, and he persevered for a time with Haig's arguments. Haig, he said, did not believe that the Allies and the United States had broken the German army. The Allies and the United States were forcing the Germans back, but they had neither vanquished their enemies nor stampeded them into any sort of disorganized rout. Haig believed, Lloyd George said, that if the Allies occupied the line of the Rhine and the bridgeheads, the Germans would withdraw from their present 400-kilometer front to one of 245 kilometers. To hold that shortened front against Allied assaults, the Germans would need seventy fewer divisions than they required at present, and they could maintain their new line indefinitely.

The real question, Lloyd George said, was whether Germany was so thoroughly beaten that it must accept Marshal Foch's terms. Foch answered that it was not. Lloyd George then asked Foch if the Allies could prevent Germany's taking up a new defensive position. Again Foch said no, the Allies could not.

With Foch's words, the meeting suddenly took on a new tone. Foch was admitting that he had drawn up terms the Germans would refuse, and with that refusal in hand, he would continue the war into 1919. That is, here on November 1, Foch—and Clemenceau, too, as discussion would demonstrate—foresaw the offer of those terms, Germany's refusal of them, and then continued Allied and American attacks compelling Germany to accept the terms some time in 1919. House, through his support of the French Rhineland proposals, backed this French plan indirectly.

Lloyd George finally gave in to the majority and agreed to require the occupation of the left bank and the bridgeheads, even though it would mean that at first the Germans must reject the terms. What Clemenceau, Lloyd George, and House did here on November 1 was refuse the German request for an armistice. They expected the war to continue, and if events had gone the way they calculated, gaining the French terms would cost the lives of countless thousands of Allied, American, and German soldiers.

By this time, Foch's terms had become the mildest terms the Supreme War Council were willing to grant. If the Germans were ready to reject even those terms, the Allied leaders had no reason to stay their ambitions. Once the prime ministers and House concluded that the Germans would refuse Foch's provisions, they had no reason to seek balance or moderation. The armistice document being crafted therefore became a wish list of items. Whether the prime ministers and House expected to make immediate use of the draft armistice or not, they went on to complete it, and they approved Foch's draft without much amendment. With the Rhenish terms agreed to, the other military clauses did not pose major problems.

Naturally, some ambiguity appeared in all this. On the one hand, the Allied leaders and House believed the Germans would refuse the armistice terms. On the other, they continued to hope that, despite all logic, the Germans would sign them. The coming battle over naval terms will take place because some of the leaders wanted at least one show of generosity to lure the Germans into accepting the document.

The prime ministers and House had already addressed the naval terms recommended by the Allied Naval Council, first on October 29 and then again on the thirtieth, when Clemenceau had quipped, "They have not asked for the Kaiser's trousers, but that is about all."[7] At the latter meeting, the leaders did agree unanimously to continue the blockade and to require the Germans to surrender their submarines. Those two principles were never questioned again in the Supreme War Council.

The question on November 1 was how to treat the German surface warships. The Allied leaders and House had three main choices: they could require the Germans to withdraw their warships to German ports; they could require internment of those vessels—that is, place them under Allied or neutral guard in a German, neutral, or Allied port; or they might require the outright surrender of the ships. Of course, different types of warships—battleships or destroyers—might receive different treatment. Thus, the prime ministers and House really had many more than three choices open to them. In discussions over the next several days, the leaders moved different types of warship from category to category, and slight changes of wording could make a great difference in the fate of the German High Seas Fleet.

Here on November 1, First Lord of the Admiralty Sir Eric Geddes urged acceptance of the Allied Naval Council's terms concerning the German warships.[8] He presented three arguments to support his position, but none of them was very persuasive. First, he advanced the same argument the British admirals had offered earlier: the Germans must surrender a large number of ships, the precise number being a total the British admirals estimated that the Germans would have lost if they had fought the British in an all-out battle. Geddes's second rationale was that to fulfill President Wilson's conditions and not put the Germans in a better position than they now had, the Allies must reduce the German battle fleet.

His third justification was that the Germans had more and better battle cruisers than the British, and if the terms did not force the Germans to surrender them, the British must start to build battle cruisers. This last argument might be a good one for surrendering battle cruisers, but it seems irrelevant to a demand for battleships, light cruisers, and destroyers.

The French leaders never wholly understood the role of sea power. This charge, frequently made against them at the time of World War I and earlier, is no less true for repetition. Now, on November 1, Foch showed no reluctance about sacrificing the British Admiralty's desires. Submarines, he said, had menaced Allied supply lines, and for that reason, the Allies should seize them. Battle cruisers, not to speak of the other capital ships, were another matter. The Allied and Associated Powers should not continue the war just to obtain surrender of these vessels.

On this question, the French and British simply did not understand each other. Foch did not comprehend the British admirals' point of view, and the British naval leaders could not understand why he failed to do so. Geddes rebutted Foch, saying that if the British fleet had not blocked the German fleet in harbor, the Germans would have shut off Allied commerce and prevented American soldiers from coming to Europe. Precisely because the British Grand Fleet had succeeded, Geddes claimed, Foch did not understand how much it had done. To fail to secure the surrender of the German ships now, he said, would leave the navies facing each other "in the same state of tension as that of two armies opposed to each other in battle array in trenches."

Foch answered that although he opposed requiring surrender of the vessels, he supported shutting the German fleet up in designated ports. For example, he said, the Allies might restrict the German fleet to the Baltic. Geddes rejected that plan at once. It would close the Baltic to the Allies, and the British fleet would still have to stay at full war strength to stand watch over the Germans.

Then Foch received help from an unexpected source: Lloyd George turned on his admirals. The Allied Naval Council's terms, he said, were "rather excessive." Declaring that he agreed with Foch about the German battleships, he proposed sending the naval terms back to the Allied Naval Council with orders to redraft them to require the surrender of only the battle cruisers, some light cruisers, and the submarines. The Allies and the United States could intern the battleships in neutral ports.

With the British fleet overwhelmingly superior to the Germans in battleships, Lloyd George's proposal made sense. If the Allies and the

United States made the Germans intern their battleships in neutral ports with only skeleton crews aboard, that was far better than having those warships battle-ready, with steam up, at the other end of the Kiel Canal, which might be the effect of Foch's proposal. Lloyd George's plan would leave the German ships in no position to threaten the Allies, and internment might appear more lenient to the Germans than surrender.

The British admirals felt Lloyd George was betraying them and their nation. Instead of demanding the surrender of the larger and more effective portion of the German fleet—as the admirals were insisting—Lloyd George was proposing internment of a part of it as a supplement to the surrender of submarines and battle cruisers. The Allied leaders and House, however, accepted Lloyd George's proposal and referred the naval terms back to the Allied Naval Council. Now, Lloyd George would have to square off against his admirals.[9]

Having dealt with naval terms for the moment, the prime ministers and House adjourned. House's report to Wilson of the morning's activities was neither complete nor truthful.[10] "We made satisfactory progress this morning regarding terms for German armistice," he wrote. "Both Clemenceau and [Lloyd] George now [as] moderate as Foch will permit." That does not describe the various factions very well. "They realize that the terms [are] somewhat harsher than is necessary to fulfill your conditions regarding the making of it impossible for Germany to renew hostilities." The only mention of Wilson's terms that morning had been a passing remark in which Geddes had used them to justify the surrender of German warships. "We are modifying the naval program in the interest of commerce." Whatever interests the leaders were modifying the naval terms in favor of, commerce was not among them. House was being less than candid with Wilson, even though he could expect the negotiations to outdistance any response Wilson might make.

House could avoid having to pick sides in the dispute over naval terms. He faced a far more serious problem when President Wilson refused to accept the compromise on the Fourteen Points that he had reached with Lloyd George and Clemenceau on October 30. House had agreed to Lloyd George's letter, which said that because the freedom of the seas was open to unacceptable interpretations, the Allies reserved complete freedom on the subject. House had also agreed to another Allied reservation that required Germany to make compensation for damage done.

On the twenty-ninth, before Wilson had any inkling that House would compromise, he had cabled House to tell him that there "can be no real difficulty about peace terms and interpretations of fourteen points if the Entente statesmen will be perfectly frank with us and have no selfish aims of their own which would in any case alienate us from them altogether."[11] That was absurd. Naturally, the Allied leaders had selfish aims. They served their own nations, not the United States. In his cable, Wilson went on to analyze the situation: the British needed the friendship of the United States, and the other nations needed the United States to check Britain. That was a shrewd assessment, but Wilson failed to see that it was incomplete. While it might describe the general situation, it did not mean that pressure from the United States could drive any nation, whether Great Britain or a Continental country, to deny its national imperatives. Nevertheless, he ignored that problem. "If it is the purpose of the Allied statesmen to nullify my influence," Wilson told House, "force the purpose boldly to the surface and let me speak of it to the world as I shall."[12]

To obtain additional leverage for forcing Allied acceptance of the Fourteen Points, House telegraphed Wilson several days later, suggesting that he slow down the transportation of soldiers to Europe and begin diminishing shipments of money and supplies.[13] If Wilson followed his advice, it would put pressure on the Allies only very slowly, however. Not until the Allies began to suspect what was happening would House's strategy have any effect, which suggests that he anticipated prolonged negotiations.

It was on the thirtieth that House and the Allied prime ministers had reached their compromise. That same day, Wilson, who had no way of knowing what was happening, sent House his strictest instructions yet:[14]

> I feel it my solemn duty to authorize you to say I cannot consent to take part in the negotiations of a peace which does not include freedom of the seas because we are pledged to fight not only to do away with Prussian militarism but with militarism everywhere. Neither could I participate in a settlement which did not include [the] league of nations because peace would be without any guarantee except universal armament which would be intolerable. I hope I shall not be obliged to make this decision public.

It is odd that Wilson raised no objection to Lloyd George's having included a reservation allowing virtually unlimited financial claims against Germany; instead, Wilson saved his wrath for the British denial of freedom of the seas. House received that cable during the discussion of Austro-Hungarian terms. Wilson's cable was "intemperate," House wrote in his diary.[15] He dashed off a quick response to soothe the president.[16] "Everything is changing for the better since yesterday," he told him, "and I hope you will not insist upon my using your cable." That was an odd request, almost an impertinent one, because it admitted implicitly that House had failed to keep the Allies from rejecting one or more of the president's main principles. House went on to promise he would not "embarrass" the president or "compromise" his peace program, and he concluded by cautioning the president that "it is exceedingly important that nothing be said or done at this time which may in any way halt the armistice which will save thousands of lives. Negotiations are now proceeding satisfactorily." In effect, House was telling the president that he had not gained support for all of the president's peace program, but an armistice was the greater good. House may have made a correct judgment on this point, but it was not really his decision to make.

When Wilson received the actual text of the compromise House and the Allied prime ministers had reached, his attitude appeared to soften slightly.[17] With cables crossing each other, Wilson sent still another to House: "I fully and sympathetically recognize the exceptional position and necessities of Great Britain with regard to the use of the seas for defence both at home and throughout the Empire."[18] He added that he also realized that freedom of the seas required "careful definition" and contained a number of questions "about which there is need of the freest discussion and the most liberal interchange of views."

Then he dropped his bomb: "I am not clear that the reply of the Allies quoted in your [regular series number] 12 [of October 30] definitely accepts the principle of the freedom of the seas and means to reserve only the freest discussion of definitions and limitations." He ordered House to insist that the Allies accept the principle, adding that the Allies and the United States did not need to discuss the freedom of the seas with Germany, and he insisted that he did not intend to abolish the use of the blockade. If the Allies refused to accept the principle, he would go before Congress, which "confidentially will have no sympathy with spending American lives for British naval control," he told House. "I cannot recede from the position taken in my [private code series] 5 [of October 30]," Wilson said, "though of course I depend on you to insist at the right time and in the right way."

Wilson then spelled out the core of his program: "Terms one, two, three, and fourteen are the essentially American terms in the programme and I cannot change what our troops are fighting for or consent to end with only European arrangements of peace." Wilson concluded his cable on a warm note. Although he usually gave praise sparingly, he told House that "I am proud of the way you are handling things."[19]

For a time, only House knew officially of Wilson's refusal to accept this compromise, but the British, if not other nations, had broken the United States' diplomatic codes. They were reading all the ordinary cables between Wilson and House that went through standard diplomatic channels. At some point during these Paris negotiations, the British learned to read the "private code series."[20] The possibility that the British knew the details of Wilson's instructions to House and House's reports to Wilson must be borne in mind.

When the full Supreme War Council met on the afternoon of November 1, House was mulling over the president's refusal to accept the compromise.[21] Apparently, he had said nothing to the Allied prime ministers about the matter yet, because Clemenceau read to the large meeting the letter to Wilson that he and Lloyd George had approved two mornings before. When Clemenceau finished, the Belgian representative immediately objected to Points Three and Five of the Fourteen Points. His objection to Point Three, the reduction of trade barriers, opened a new door, for none of the Allies had mentioned it earlier. The Belgian representative claimed that his nation would have to maintain a high tariff wall to keep out German goods while it rebuilt its own war-ravaged factories. He also objected to Point Five on colonial questions: "Belgium would maintain her rights to the integrity of her colonial possessions." The Belgian colonial regime in the African Congo, the personal property of the Belgian monarch until 1908, had scandalized the civilized world, but the other colonial powers would object, too, if the peace conference tried to discuss any colonies other than Germany's.

Instead of soothing the Belgians, as he might have, Lloyd George egged them on against Point Three. His actions make sense if he was reading intercepted House-Wilson correspondence. Perhaps he was looking for a bargaining point with House, hoping to make him more tractable on the freedom of the seas or some other subject. He asked House to explain what Point Three meant. House responded that "he had not his notes with him, but that he was ready to explain in detail to any who might wish to have explanations, President Wilson's Fourteen Points." Lloyd George continued to press House to explain Point Three. Did Wilson mean that no nation was to have preferential tariffs? House said evasively that he "was unable to reply at once as he had not his notes with him."

Vesnic´ and Orlando joined in, Orlando declaring, as he had two days before, that he wanted to place his objection to Point Nine on record. Lloyd George thereupon proposed separating Points Nine through Twelve from the answer to Germany because they dealt with matters that did not concern Germany. That would certainly have disposed of any hope House might have had, if indeed it was his plan, of arguing later that an answer to Germany accepting the Fourteen Points bound the Allies when they made peace with other enemy nations.

Another few moments, and even with House's elusiveness the Fourteen Points might have been in real trouble. Clemenceau saved the situation. As the presiding officer, he changed the subject to Foch's military terms. Thereafter, the chief Allied leaders would draw the Fourteen Points back into the small meetings and keep them from the Belgian representative, Vesnic´, and the open arena. The leaders might use the threat of returning the Fourteen Points to the lion's den of the full Supreme War Council to keep House in line, but for the moment, the document was safe from the smaller nations. No clearer evidence of an arrangement between House and Clemenceau exists than this incident on the afternoon of November 1.

House had no leisure to bask in Clemenceau's support. Because of Wilson's orders on October 31, he had to press the British for positive agreement to Point Two, not just the amiable evasion he had accepted on October 30, and the freedom of the seas continued to poison Anglo-American relations. Uncertainty existed on both sides over precisely what the phrase meant. The American admiral, William S. Sims, is reported to have said he did not care what the Supreme War Council did about freedom of the seas "so long as they did not interfere with mixed bathing."[22] That such a story circulated shows something about the nature of the issue.

House worked through intermediaries trying to cajole or force Lloyd George into accepting the freedom of the seas. On November 1, he spoke at length with Lord Reading, the British ambassador to the United States, who was then in Paris, and then he talked to Sir William Wiseman.[23] House and Wiseman shared a close friendship as well as a professional relationship, but House's statements to Wiseman, if he said what he recorded in his diary, were far from cordial. Unless Lloyd George relented on the freedom of the seas, House told Wiseman, "all hope of Anglo-Saxon unity would be at an end."

The next day, House had lunch with the British press magnate, Lord Northcliffe.[24] Northcliffe had once been close to Lloyd George, but their alliance had deteriorated badly in recent months.[25] House asked Northcliffe for help in influencing Lloyd George, and House claimed that at the end of their conversation Northcliffe offered to use his publications in whatever way House wanted.

For House to deal with Northcliffe behind Lloyd George's back was unwise. House ought to have realized that Northcliffe, a proponent of the harshest terms possible for Germany, would never join any campaign to limit Britain's sea power, even to discomfort Lloyd George.[26] House was miscalculating badly, and Lloyd George could be bitterly vindictive. Fortunately for relations between House and Lloyd George, House refrained from asking Northcliffe to become actively involved.

Lloyd George was handling an extraordinary number of problems at one time in Paris. He was writing armistice terms, trying to rein in his admirals, dealing with a minor cabinet blowup, negotiating with House, and making plans for an impending general election. Election plans required extremely delicate agreements with his political allies, and at the critical moment of the armistice negotiations, the prime minister had to write the leader of the Unionists a detailed letter laying out the possible bases for continuing their wartime coalition.[27] Lloyd George, who generally knew precisely what public opinion would allow, was, at the time of the negotiations over the freedom of the seas, even more conscious than usual of the constraints that public opinion fixed on him.

By November 3, debate on the freedom of the seas seemed entirely deadlocked. In private discussions with House, the British refused to accept even the principle. House went as far as cabling Wilson to suggest postponing the question until the president could come to Europe and meet face to face with the Allied leaders.[28] That confessed defeat, and it would omit the freedom of the seas from any preliminary arrangement.

That afternoon, Sunday, the debate came to a climax.[29] To the Allied leaders, House read Wilson's cable of October 31 (number 6 in the private code series), censoring it to remove the threats. In that cable, Wilson had written that he "fully and sympathetically recognized the exceptional position and necessities of Great Britain." In response, now on November 3, Lloyd George reiterated his earlier statement, which, he said, "provided for free discussion." That, he said, was as far as he would go. House begged Lloyd George to accept only the principle. Lloyd George refused, because, he said, in the public mind the freedom of the seas had come to mean abandoning the blockade. To that, Colonel House said he "only wished to get the principle accepted."

The United States' minutes have Clemenceau interject here: "I do not see any reason for not accepting the principle." Lloyd George refused again. If he did accept it, he said, "it would mean that in a week's time a new Prime Minister would be here who would say he could not accept the principle."[30] British public opinion, he declared, flatly opposed his accepting it. What happened next is clearer in the United States' minutes than in the British:

> H[ouse]—I strongly advised the President to accept the reservations of the Allies. I wish (turning to L G) you will write something I can send him.
>
> L[loyd] G[eorge]—Will he like something of this kind: "We are quite willing to discuss the freedom of the seas and its application."
>
> C[lemenceau]—The new conditions of naval warfare make it necessary that the international law on this subject be reviewed.
>
> L[loyd] G[eorge]—Yes, it is obvious that the regulations of maritime commerce have to be revised.

That passage-at-arms, in which Lloyd George conceded virtually nothing, was the climax of the debate. After the meeting, Lloyd George confirmed his statement to House in a formal letter. The key sentence of that letter read that the British "were quite willing to discuss the freedom of the seas in the light of the new conditions that have arisen in the course of the present war."[31]

On that slender framework, House based a claim to diplomatic victory. In his report to Wilson, House gave the impression that, through deft pressure and adroit diplomacy, he had forced Lloyd George to accede to American wishes.[32] He gave Wilson an edited report of the meeting and quoted Lloyd George's letter. "If I do not hear from you to the contrary," he wrote the president, "I shall assume that you accept the situation as it now is. This I strongly advise. Any other decision would cause serious friction and delay."

When Wilson received this cable from House, he surrendered without a struggle. He cabled House simply: "I accept the situation."[33] House crowed in his diary that he had won a great victory.[34] "This has been a red letter day," he recorded. "I brought Lloyd George to terms regarding the 'freedom of the seas.'" He added: "I feel that I have won a distinct victory and consequently I am happy tonight. The British seemed to me so wholly in the wrong that I have been confident they would eventually give way." House never admitted to himself that the British gave away very little. On October 30, Lloyd George had refused to accept the freedom of the seas, although he seems to have hinted that he might be willing to discuss the issue after the League of Nations had proved itself. Now, on November 3, Lloyd George did agree to discuss the matter, but he certainly gave no promise of accepting anything at all.

Lloyd George, writing later on the struggle over Point Two, said that House and Wilson finally came to understand the depth of British feeling over the freedom of the seas.[35] The result was complete British liberty on the subject. In fact, Lloyd George stated that rather than House maneuvering the British into accepting the freedom of the seas, Lloyd George had forced House, and through him, Wilson, to accept the British position.

The British refused to compromise over Point Two because they sincerely believed they owed the coming victory largely to their sea power. The British leaders believed—and the British public believed—that any attempt to shackle it was evil. The diplomats did discuss freedom of the seas at the coming peace conference, but nothing came of the discussion, and the issue died for a time, to reappear fitfully in the 1920s.

In this same afternoon meeting on November 3, there was some debate over the rest of the Fourteen Points, but nothing meaningful happened. House noted that the clauses requiring restoration of France and Belgium interacted with Point Three, lowering economic barriers, to which the Belgians had objected. The French and Belgians, he said, had the right to protect themselves for five or ten years against German imports. In the course of the session, Lloyd George asked that the qualifying phrase in Point Three, "so far as possible," be moved to the beginning of the clause to emphasize it, and House promised to make that suggestion to Wilson.[36] The Belgian representative wanted to add a phrase guaranteeing German responsibility for indirect war damages. Lloyd George opposed this proposal because it might lead the Germans to worry that the Allies were preparing to levy impossibly large claims. House opposed it, too, and he noted cynically, echoing any number of people who had already made the observation, that the Fourteen Points "would be subject to our own interpretation."

No further significant discussion of the Fourteen Points occurred. The Allies had agreed to them, subject to two reservations, one on the freedom of the seas and the other on reparations, and that is what Wilson would tell the Germans.

In the meantime, the Allied leaders and House had met as the formal Supreme War Council on the afternoon of November 1 to look at Foch's military terms, which they had approved that morning.[37] According to the procedure the Supreme War Council followed, this occasion was the first formal reading, designed to discover errors, omissions, and any interallied discord that previous small meetings had not shown. If they found a problem, they would withdraw the controversial item into the smaller sessions and deal with it before the second and final reading. There were no problems with Foch's terms, and the leaders made no significant changes in them.

Then the Supreme War Council turned to the subject of financial clauses for the armistice. Although the Allied leaders and House had agreed to a general reservation on October 30 making Germany liable for reparations, Clemenceau wanted specific mention in the text of the armistice of "restitution of stolen goods" and "reparation for damage done [*reparation des dommages*]."[38] Lloyd George agreed to demand restitution of stolen goods, but reparation, he said, was a question for the peace conference. House made the sensible observation that carrying out terms like those would take a very long time and "the armistice would never come to an end."

With the issues of reparations and restitution still unsettled, the members of the Supreme War Council asked their economic advisers to prepare draft terms on financial matters for their next meeting. On November 2, the Allied leaders and House discussed the financial clauses that had now gone through the hands of the financial experts.[39] Again, Clemenceau raised the subject of reparations. The French public, he claimed, would not understand the armistice's lacking any mention of reparations. He proposed adding the phrase *reparation des dommages* "without any commentary." He met some objection, but he persisted, and the leaders finally added *reparation des dommages*, with even House joining in the general chorus of approval. At the end of the meeting, the French finance minister proposed prefacing all the financial clauses with the phrase "all future claims or demands of the Allies being reserved." Those words covered a great deal, but no one commented on them, and the leaders accepted that proposal, too. In view of Wilson's narrow interpretation of what payments were just—Point Seven spoke of the "restoration" of Belgium, and Point Eight said that the invaded portions of

France should be "restored"—and considering the grief that reparations caused in Europe over the next decade, it is surprising how easily the subject passed into the armistice document.

After the leaders accepted *reparation des dommages,* they looked at other financial clauses. They approved terms requiring the return of all documents, securities, and specie that Germany had taken from occupied territories. Then the French finance minister quoted a clause from the armistice of 1871, which Prussia had imposed on France, that forbade the export of any public securities that the nation could use to pay reparations. With a touch of irony, the Allied leaders and House added that clause, too.

Foch's terms showed one other obvious gap: they lacked provisions dealing with Russia and the Eastern Front. German forces occupied a vast stretch of Russia running from Estonia south to Ukraine, and a German puppet government sat in Poland. Foch suggested that he prepare separate articles on the Eastern Front, and the Supreme War Council speedily approved the idea.[40] When Foch asked for guidance, however, the answers were slow in coming. Foch noted that the German "evacuation of Russia, Poland, and Roumania was a clear issue, but were we to undertake responsibility for those countries?"

Foch was asking an awkward question. The Allied and Associated Powers had no clear Russian policy. Ostensibly, they had intervened in Russia to thwart German influence there. If they forced Germany to withdraw from Russian territory, their rationale for intervention would disappear. Yet for Bolsheviks to control Russia—and Bolsheviks, the leaders believed, would inevitably fill the vacuum created if both the Germans and the Allies left Russia to its own devices—seemed no more palatable to the Allied leaders than German control.

Neither the Americans nor the British nor the French had any interest in a permanent presence in Russia. The British and French had signed a spheres-of-influence agreement, the Convention of December 23, 1917, which, for the time being, gave each nation dominance in separate parts of Russia, but dominance did not include ownership. The United States, too, had forces in Russia, but clearly they would occupy the territory only temporarily. The Japanese, however, had visions of exploiting Siberia, and many of the eastern European nations hoped to annex tracts of the former Russian Empire.

Another factor that drove discussions over Russia, although the Allied nations did not made it explicit, was that they had accepted a degree of responsibility toward the groups they had encouraged to oppose Bolshevism. The prospect of deserting those people to the mercy of revolutionaries made some of the statesmen uncomfortable. Several Allied plans circulated, among them a British proposal to set up a belt of new nations to prevent Bolshevism's moving west (or Germany's moving east).[41] The nations in that belt would include Finland, the Baltic nations, Poland, Galicia, and Rumania. Now, however, the question was not whether the Allies would withdraw their forces, but what would happen if the Germans withdrew theirs, especially from the Baltic area.

House was the first to respond to Foch's question about whether the Allies should take responsibility for the areas of eastern Europe that the Germans would evacuate. "It was a very difficult problem," he said, "for the withdrawal of the [German] troops would be followed by Bolshevism." Clemenceau minimized the difficulties. Both he and the Italian foreign minister suggested that the Bolshevik threat was a ploy of German propaganda, not a reality.

A consensus did emerge for forcing the Germans to evacuate the east, but Allied and American problems did not end with that decision. The armistice obviously had to require abrogation of the treaties the Germans had imposed on Russia and Rumania, the Treaties of Brest-Litovsk and Bucharest, which gave the Germans important rights in the east. That was easy enough to require. Another question, one that was far more complicated, was how to deal with Russian prisoners of war. If the Allies forced the Germans to return Russian prisoners of war, like the prisoners of war of the other Allied and Associated Powers, it might, Foch said, give the Bolsheviks an army. As a result of Foch's observation, the Allied leaders decided not to order the Germans to return Russian prisoners of war.

Foch, with this guidance, however sparse, prepared articles covering the Eastern Front for the November 2 session of the Supreme War Council. When Foch's terms for the east came under discussion at that meeting, Balfour remarked that as soon as the Germans left Russia, the Bolsheviks would take over the areas evacuated.[42] The inhabitants of an evacuated territory would then face an even worse fate than German occupation. Balfour added that he was trying to entice the Scandinavian nations into intervening in Russia. If they refused, Balfour proposed telling the Germans to leave one-third of their armaments with the anti-Bolshevik populations. He was blind to the probability that, given the current conditions in Russia, his plan would only mean leaving arms for the Bolsheviks.

Balfour also observed that the Allies needed access to Poland. Requiring the Germans to withdraw to their 1914 boundaries would block Allied communications with that new nation. He proposed a clause giving the Allies access to Poland through Danzig or up the Vistula River to supply the population in the interior "or for any other purpose." That suggestion met no objection.

After Balfour's comments, Foch presented his clauses concerning Russia and the Eastern Front. He gave Germany three weeks to evacuate all of Rumania, including Bessarabia, and the Allied leaders and House accepted that proposal without debate. He gave the Germans five weeks to evacuate Danzig and Poland, with Poland defined as the area the nation had ruled before the First Partition of 1772. That boundary included many non-Polish areas, and Foch was treading on a problem that would plague the peacemakers of 1919: the leaders did not agree on a definition of proper boundaries for Poland.

French Foreign Minister Pichon, already trying to build strong states in eastern Europe to create a counterweight against Germany, supported the 1772 boundaries of Poland. It was what the Allies had promised to restore, he said. Balfour contradicted him sharply. The Allies had never agreed to restore the Poland of 1772, only the much less extensive ethnic Poland. Balfour suggested that the Allies simply require that the Germans retire to their 1914 boundaries. That proposal had problems, too, although the Allied leaders accepted it. The German boundaries of 1914 included large ethnically Polish areas, notably in West Prussia, and their remaining under German domination would cause conflict later.

Foch's draft terms for the Eastern Front required that the evacuation of Russia begin at once, a provision that was accepted easily. He required the Germans to free all Russian prisoners of war and maintain them until the Allies told the Germans where to repatriate them. How the Germans were to maintain order among several million bored and underfed former prisoners Foch did not spell out, and the provision disappeared from the final document. The final terms referred to Russian prisoners only in the general directions about prisoners of war, which said that the Germans must return all prisoners according to conditions that the Allied and Associated Powers would fix later. The Allied leaders and House did agree to Foch's last two requirements. The first, after some amendment, forbade the Germans from seizing or requisitioning anything outside their 1914 boundaries, and the other required the Germans to renounce the Treaties of Brest-Litovsk and Bucharest.

In this way, the Supreme War Council backed into terms for the eastern marches. Questions remained, and the Supreme War Council would have to solve them on the afternoon of November 4, their last meeting. For the moment, though, the leaders had at least a draft of terms for the east.

The Allied leaders now had dealt with two gaps Foch had left—financial matters and the Eastern Front. One other question was still pending: naval terms for Germany. The confrontation between the politicians and the naval leaders had waxed increasingly tense, with the British admirals, dismayed at the treatment their draft terms was getting, leading the fight through their dominance over the Allied Naval Council. The only dissent from the unanimity of the Allied Naval Council came from American Admiral Benson, and his position rested less on his personal judgment than on instructions from President Wilson. Wilson ordered him to oppose the surrender of German warships.[43]

Harry Rudin, when he discusses these events, explains Benson's stance as the result of memoranda that the American Naval Planning Section in London prepared.[44] Relative influence is always difficult to assess. The American Naval Planning Section in London prepared a memorandum dated October 30, but it was only a sketchy statement, not fully explained until another memorandum on November 4, too late to affect Benson's position.

Rudin could have measured the influence of the American Naval Planning Section more easily if he had gained access to the original documents, the ones Benson actually received.[45] The navy heavily censored and changed the conclusions of the versions that were printed, the ones Rudin saw. The originals are remarkable for their general xenophobia and particular Anglophobia. For example, the November 4 memorandum stated that the only war likely in the future was one between Great Britain and the United States, and if the British proposed distributing German ships, they did so solely to prepare for that future war. Still, no matter how compelling either memorandum was, the wishes of Benson's commander-in-chief directed him more than any position papers, and the president wanted only internment of the submarines, with the surface fleet being withdrawn to German harbors.[46]

On the afternoon of November 1, the members of the Allied Naval Council discussed the orders the prime ministers and House had given that morning to change the naval terms.[47] The prime ministers and House had instructed the Allied Naval Council to require the Germans to surrender their battle cruisers, some light cruisers, and all submarines. As for the German battleships, the Germans must intern them under guard in a neutral port, not surrender them.

With no change ordered in the clauses dealing with battle cruisers and submarines, discussion in the Allied Naval Council focused on the battleships that their original draft had required Germany to surrender. The Italian admiral observed—shrewdly and correctly—that if the Germans felt beaten badly enough to hand over their submarines and battle cruisers, they would hardly refuse to sign an armistice over the difference between surrendering or interning their battleships. The British admirals remained consistent: armistice and peace terms were synonymous. Wemyss wrote privately that he might agree with Lloyd George in believing the naval terms were too hard and needed easing "*if* terms of armistice could be different to terms of peace, but this is not so."[48]

Wemyss proposed that the Allied Naval Council tell the Supreme War Council that although it might be possible to reduce the number of ships the armistice required Germany to surrender, it was impossible to reduce the number of ships that the peace treaty must order Germany to turn over to the Allied and Associated Powers. Here, Wemyss and the Allied Naval Council were venturing into territory that was none of their business, but they appeared unconscious of any impropriety. Wemyss's fear was that unless the Germans clearly and finally surrendered the ships, they would try to use them as bargaining chips at the coming peace conference, and he warned the members of the Allied Naval Council to assume that the peace conference would eventually return to Germany any ships not surrendered.

The members of the Allied Naval Council, except for the special case of Benson, thus had no intention whatever of following the Supreme War Council's orders. They were planning a counterattack. Reaffirming their earlier recommendations, they agreed to send a letter to the Supreme War Council explaining their "apprehensions" about interning any German vessels in neutral ports instead of requiring surrender of the ships. With that decision to defy the Supreme War Council made, the naval leaders adjourned.[49]

The British naval leaders knew their politics. After supper on November 1, Geddes and Wemyss went to see Foreign Secretary Balfour. They persuaded the Unionist (Conservative) leader to write a letter to Lloyd George "upholding our views & pointing out to P.M. the difficulties he might be incurring if he paid no attention to the A.N.C.'s views."[50] Because Lloyd George was still negotiating with his Unionist allies in his coalition government about a platform for the election, Foreign Secretary Balfour, himself a former Unionist prime minister, could exert great pressure. "I am most anxious on the subject," he wrote Lloyd George,

> and I venture most earnestly to suggest that no final decision *adverse to the views held by* the First Lord of the Admiralty and all his advisors, to the expert views of the Allied Naval Council, and to the *unexpert* views of Bonar [Law, the current head of the Unionist party] and myself should be taken without a little more discussion among the representatives of Great Britain.[51]

It would take a brave prime minister to ignore such a request.[52]

Increasing the pressure, Balfour wrote to Bonar Law that same evening to say he was "anxious" about naval terms.[53] Although internment of the German fleet might give security during the armistice, Britain in the long run needed to destroy the German navy: "If our European Allies are then going to depend on us to police the seas for them, they ought in fairness to make the task as easy as possible."

The Supreme War Council discussed naval terms briefly on November 2.[54] Rear Admiral George Hope, British deputy first sea lord, expounded on the importance of naval operations and the blockade during the war. He contended that although Germany had entered the war with only thirteen Dreadnoughts, now, including ships under construction, Germany had twenty-five; Germany had entered the war with four battle cruisers, and if they completed ships under construction, they would end the war with nine.[55] Unless the Allies and the United States reduced the German navy to the numbers the Allied Naval Council recommended, the Germans would end the war stronger than they were at its start, and the German navy "would remain a permanent menace to the peace of the world."

In answer, Lloyd George said he did not wish to make any final decision on naval terms until it was clear whether the Austro-Hungarians accepted the Allied terms (their response was still pending when this meeting took place): "We should have to decide whether we wished to conclude peace immediately, or whether we wished to continue the war for another year. Before receiving the Austrian reply, he did not wish to take that decision." House tried to push Lloyd George into making an immediate decision, but when Clemenceau supported postponement, House gave in.

On November 3, the day on which House and Lloyd George reached their agreement concerning freedom of the seas, naval terms came up again.[56] The United States' minutes are more colorful than the British.[57] According to the United States' secretary, Lloyd George announced, "Regarding the terms of a naval armistice with Germany, our admirals have their tails up and will not move." He suggested that, instead of "confiscating" some of the German vessels, the Allies intern all of them. House agreed eagerly to the suggestion of interning the German ships, leaving any decision on their fate to the peace conference. Clemenceau added avuncularly, "The more we talk these ships over, the more nearly we come to an agreement."

The Allied leaders and House made no final decision on naval terms that day, but the drift of debate gave a strong hint of what was going to happen. Internment was likely. The leaders adjourned, to meet again the next morning.

At that November 4 meeting, certainly by prearrangement, Lloyd George had American admiral Benson present a statement on naval terms.[58] Benson, following President Wilson's instructions, said that if the Allies and the United States, instead of requiring the surrender of the German battleships, ordered their internment in a neutral port, it would increase the likelihood of the Germans' accepting the terms.

Foch asked why the naval terms were still so exacting. Why should the Allies and the United States continue the war to gain even the internment of those ships in a neutral port? Foch returned to his basic point, that the German fleet had never left port and submarines now conducted naval warfare. The Allied and Associated Powers should not prolong the war to deal with only a potential threat. If Germany accepted the military conditions, Foch said, the war was over. Military conditions alone were sufficient.

Despite Foch's opposition, Lloyd George's naval proposals were not in trouble as long as Clemenceau and House supported some sort of naval clauses. Lloyd George now proposed formally what he had suggested the day before: that the Supreme War Council send the terms back to the Allied Naval Council one more time with instructions to redraft the terms to require the surrender of Germany's submarines only. The Allies would disarm and intern in a neutral port under their supervision all of the designated surface ships—the light cruisers and battle cruisers as well as battleships and destroyers. Lloyd George received approval for his proposal, ending the matter for the moment. Before the Supreme War Council met that afternoon, the members of the Allied Naval Council—very reluctantly—redrafted their terms.[59]

By that afternoon session on November 4, the last meeting of the Supreme War Council, almost everything seemed settled. All of Germany's allies had surrendered, and the Allied leaders had made their plans for an offensive against southeastern Germany. The Allied leaders and House had reached agreement on the Fourteen Points, including a reservation concerning reparations and the effective nullification of freedom of the seas. With slight amendments, they had agreed to Foch's military clauses for the Western Front, and they had written financial terms. The Allied leaders and House had changed the British admirals' demands to require internment of the surface warships, rather than surrender, but interned ships did not threaten the Allies in a major way. Only terms for the Eastern Front still remained on the agenda, and the only open question on that subject came from Balfour's proposal that the Germans arm the civilian population as they withdrew their soldiers. In fact, matters seemed so well in hand that Lloyd George left for London before the afternoon's meeting started.

As the afternoon wore on, problems did come up, but the members of the Supreme War Council dealt with them one way or another.[60] For the last time, the Supreme War Council looked at the military terms for the armistice. The clauses now were renumbered but otherwise unchanged. The first two clauses, which required the cessation of hostilities within six hours after signature and the evacuation of German-invaded territories in the west, as well as Alsace-Lorraine and Luxembourg, within fourteen days, passed without comment. Clause three, requiring repatriation of all inhabitants of those areas, and clause four, requiring the Germans to surrender five thousand guns, thirty thousand machine guns, three thousand trench mortars, and two thousand airplanes, also passed without change.

The great French victory came when clause five, ordering the evacuation of the left bank, Allied occupation of the left bank, bridgeheads at Mainz, Köln, and Koblenz, and a demilitarized zone on the right bank—all to be cleared of German soldiers within twenty-five days—passed without comment. Clause six, ordering the Germans to turn over all the military stores they could not evacuate as their soldiers withdrew, passed.

There was some discussion over clause seven, which required the Germans to surrender 5,000 locomotives, 150,000 railroad cars, and 10,000 motor trucks. Balfour questioned whether the Germans could evacuate territory, repatriate civilians, and return prisoners of war if they had to turn over that great quantity of railroad equipment. Foch claimed they could, noting that the Allies would take care of transporting prisoners.

His chief of staff said that the Germans could retreat on foot, and the generals had calculated the time allowed for German withdrawal on the assumption that German soldiers could march fifteen kilometers per day.

Fifteen kilometers per day would set a rapid pace, considering that the men must move through bottlenecks at the Rhine, where few bridges existed. Moreover, the Germans would have trouble provisioning those troops as they retreated, not only because of the disorganization that would necessarily exist, but also because those same few bridges could not carry supplies forward if masses of retreating soldiers jammed them twenty-four hours a day. Regardless, the clause passed without change.

A requirement that caused great difficulties later was that Germany must pay for the upkeep of occupation forces in the Rhineland. Miscellaneous provisions ordered the Germans to tell the Allies about delayed-action mines, to repatriate prisoners, and to care for sick and wounded prisoners. They all passed with a few slight, technical changes.

The Supreme War Council gave final approval to the financial clauses and dealt with several minor subjects. The draft set no limits on the length of time the armistice would remain in effect. Foch suggested thirty days and, eventually, the Supreme War Council agreed. The armistice would last for thirty days, "with option to extend." It allowed for denunciation by either party on two days' notice. On another matter, the leaders approved a demand for the unconditional surrender of all German forces in East Africa. Then attention focused on the complicated subject of the Eastern Front.

Foch's clauses requiring the Germans to evacuate Rumania, Poland, and Russia were now combined into one new clause, which read: "All German troops to the East shall retire behind the 1914 frontiers of Germany." The Italian foreign minister observed that Foch's wording, "to the East," was vague. That phrase left it uncertain whether the entire Eastern Front was meant. Rumania was at peace with Germany through the Treaty of Bucharest, and the Germans could claim their troops were in friendly country. The British war secretary proposed an entirely new text, which the Supreme War Council adopted: "All German troops at present in any territory, which before the war belonged to Russia, Rumania, or Turkey, shall withdraw within the frontiers of Germany, as they existed on the 1st August 1914."[61] The members of the Supreme War Council also accepted clauses requiring the Germans to begin evacuating the east immediately, to allow Allied access to Poland through Danzig or up the Vistula, and to renounce the Treaties of Bucharest and Brest-Litovsk.

Balfour's clause stimulated the most discussion. It required the Germans to leave a portion of their equipment "in the hands of such local authorities as may be designated by the Allies, for the purpose of enabling the populations concerned to protect themselves against disorder and aggression." Balfour's plan met stiff opposition. French Foreign Minister Pichon opposed it, prophesying that any arms the Germans left behind would fall into Bolshevik hands. Orlando agreed, noting that a half-dozen factions were fighting for supremacy in Russia and that the Allied and Associated Powers ought to avoid involvement in Russian politics. Clemenceau also opposed Balfour's plan, which only Vesnić of Serbia supported.

Pichon added the argument that the adoption of Balfour's plan would let the Bolsheviks say that the Allies were organizing a civil war in Russia. Because that was precisely what the Allies and the United States had done for the last six months, his objection seems pointless. The Bolsheviks would certainly make that charge, but they could make it already because of the Allied and American interventions taking place in Russia's north, south, and east. Balfour's proposal would make that situation no worse, but it garnered no support. Even Foch intervened in the debate to oppose it. Getting no support, Balfour withdrew his proposal.

Discussion then turned to naval terms. The admirals still wanted surrender of the German ships.[62] Geddes told the Supreme War Council that the admirals opposed internment, but the members of the Supreme War Council stood firm. After this prelude, the French minister of marine read the terms the Allied Naval Council had reluctantly approved. They required that German warships be disarmed and kept in a neutral port under Allied supervision. The ships included ten battleships, six battle cruisers, eight light cruisers, and fifty destroyers, almost exactly the same ships the British admirals had specified two weeks earlier, but now listed for internment, not surrender. The Germans must withdraw all their other ships to German bases the Allies designated and disarm them. There was no disagreement over surrender of 160 submarines, nor any objection to continuing the blockade while the armistice was in effect.

The Allied Naval Council included a preface with their draft of terms:

The Allied Naval Council are prepared to concur in the revision of the [requirement for surrender] . . . so as to provide for internment of the ships specified . . . in a neutral country instead of absolute surrender, on the understandings [sic] that this is an armistice term only and that these ships will not, under any circumstances, be returned to Germany on the conclusion of the armistice, or at any time.

Clemenceau chided the admirals, noting that the peace conference would decide the fate of the German fleet. Nevertheless, Admiral de Bon stressed his opposition to revising the terms. The Allied Naval Council, he said, had agreed unanimously that the German navy must not remain as strong as it had been when the war broke out. The Allies could achieve that aim in either of two ways: they could seize the German ships, or they could disarm them in German ports under Allied control, not neutral ports. Nor would the Germans see internment in neutral ports as more lenient than surrender; they would assume that, in either event, the Allies intended to keep the ships.

Clemenceau suddenly reversed himself. Saying he worried whether international law would allow neutrals to keep those warships under surveillance, he proposed interning them in Antwerp, Belgium. De Bon countered that Antwerp was too shallow to accommodate the warships, but Clemenceau stuck to his point. Milner replied that a neutral country would surely accept the responsibility if it meant the end of the war, and Admiral Benson added that if the belligerents agreed, no neutral would object. Geddes said he wished to make it clear that the Allied Naval Council disagreed, "but accepted the decision of the Ministers."[63]

What was happening here is murky. Whether Clemenceau was really toying with changing the naval terms once more, he nevertheless ruled finally, as chairman of the Supreme War Council, that the morning's decision must stand. The armistice would require the Germans to surrender their submarines and to intern specified warships in neutral ports. Desultory discussion took place over other naval terms, but nothing significant happened. At the end, the Supreme War Council adopted the remaining naval terms without further amendment.

They now had a full and complete draft of the armistice for Germany, and the members of the Supreme War Council went on to pass resolutions on the procedure to follow now. They agreed to ask President Wilson to tell the Germans to communicate with Foch and a British admiral to receive armistice terms. Foch and the British admiral could amend "minor technical points" in the document, and the Germans would have seventy-two hours from the time they received the terms to accept or reject them.

The Supreme War Council's message to President Wilson read:[64]

The Allied Governments have given careful consideration to the correspondence which has passed between the President of the United States and the German Government. Subject to the qualifications which follow they declare their willingness to make peace with the Government of Germany on the terms of peace laid down in the President's address to Congress of January 1918, and the principles of settlement enunciated in his subsequent addresses. They must point out, however, that clause 2, relating to what is usually described as the freedom of the seas, is open to various interpretations, some of which they could not accept. They must, therefore, reserve to themselves complete freedom on this subject when they enter the peace conference.

Further, . . . the President declared that invaded territories must be restored as well as evacuated and freed, [and] the Allied Governments feel that no doubt ought to be allowed to exist as to what this provision implies. By it they understand that compensation will be made by Germany for all damage done to the civilian population of the Allies and their property by the aggression of Germany by land, by sea, and from the air.

Then the Supreme War Council adjourned.

The French liked the terms.[65] Through them they got the Rhine and promises of reparations, and they could anticipate crushing their dangerous neighbor in the coming peace treaty. Among the major French leaders, only Poincaré muttered complaints, and he did so for two reasons. First, he had wanted a military victory that would smash the Germans before the Allies offered any terms, and second, his nose was out of joint because Clemenceau, not he, was getting most of the public adulation.

The Italians were unhappy over the resistance they had met to their claims against the Yugoslavs.[66] Orlando brooded over the treatment accorded the Austro-Hungarian fleet. Still, the Italian leaders had succeeded in preventing either the Yugoslavians or the Serbians from getting the items they wanted, so upon sober reflection, the Italians would find more than one reason for which to congratulate themselves and praise their own diplomatic skill.

The British had mixed reactions to the draft armistice. A furious Admiral Beatty sent a flaming telegram to Wemyss, telling him that the Allied Naval Council must not let the civilian leaders override the naval terms already proposed.[67] He said that Wemyss had forecast the Supreme War Council's disregarding naval advice, and assumed that if they did, the admirals could do nothing but protest: "I assume the protest would take the form of the resignation of the Board of Admiralty as a whole." Beatty seems a little too certain where other people's duty lay, but he was absolute in his own opinions, even if he did not, himself, resign in protest. "History will never acquit us," he wrote, "if we miss the present opportunity of reducing the menace to our sea power."

Lloyd George defended the naval terms' calling only for internment of the German warships.[68] When he described the Supreme War Council's meetings to the Imperial War Cabinet, he began by saying that Foch had opposed the British proposals for the surrender of German ships. The general feeling, he reported, grew into the belief that "we were only making it unnecessarily difficult for the Germans to agree to the armistice terms." Therefore, the Supreme War Council had settled on internment, with the clear understanding that the ships would never go back to Germany.

Lloyd George had to face other objections from the Dominion prime ministers—most notably from the prime minister of Australia, who, in his own words, "declined to be bound to the chariot wheel of the Fourteen Points"—but Lloyd George defended what he had done. He told the Imperial War Cabinet that in the Fourteen Points and Wilson's subsequent statements "he could not find a single point which we wanted which was not amply covered, with the exceptions of the points regarding the freedom of the seas and indemnities." Lloyd George was beginning to sound Wilsonian. In any event, he had performed an act worthy of a juggler in keeping the various factions, except the navy, mostly content with the armistice document.

House claimed a victory, but what was it?[69] "The facts are," House wrote in his diary, "I came to Europe for the purpose of getting the Entente to subscribe to the President's peace terms. I left a hostile and influential group in the United States saying frankly they did not approve of the President's terms. . . . On this side I find the Entente Governments as distinctly hostile to the Fourteen Points as our opponents at home." His conclusion was: "The diplomatic battle of the past few days has resulted in complete victory. Our Armistice to Germany carries with it the approval of the President's January 8th address. . . . I have had to persuade; I have had to threatened [sic], but the result is worth all my endeavors."

House did win formal agreement from the Allies. That was a victory, although not, perhaps, an overwhelming one, and House overstated two items. First, he exaggerated the antipathy the Entente governments held at the beginning toward the Fourteen Points. With only a few exceptions, like the British feeling toward freedom of the seas, they had no great objection to them. Second, he exaggerated the degree to which the Fourteen Points committed the Allied governments to any action or policy they chose not to support. The Fourteen Points did not constitute a very precise document originally. Amendments during the course of 1918 had further qualified the actions required, the Cobb-Lippmann Memorandum had introduced further qualifications, and finally House, in discussion with the Allied leaders, had introduced more concessions.

A century earlier, La Rochefoucauld wrote that negotiators almost always abandon the interests of their principals to achieve success in their negotiations. That lets them claim credit for having succeeded in their undertaking. Perhaps La Rochefoucauld only found another way of saying that diplomacy, like politics, is the art of compromise.

House's report to Wilson on November 5 shows no second thoughts.[70] "Earnestly advise I consider we have won a great diplomatic victory in getting the Allies to accept the principles laid down in your January eighth speech and in your subsequent addresses," House wrote. "This has been done in the face of a hostile and influential junta in the United States and the thoroughly unsympathetic personnel constituting the Entente Governments." He added that he doubted "whether any of the heads of governments with which we have been dealing quite realize how far they are now committed to the American peace program." That was foolish. The Allied leaders were only as committed as they felt themselves to be.

Almost immediately, however, it appeared that the Allied governments were more sympathetic to Wilson's peace program than the American people were. On November 5, the United States held its off-year congressional elections. Two weeks earlier, Wilson, in an attempt to aid his party's cause with the electorate, had issued a statement asking the voters to show their approval of the Wilsonian program, both domestic and foreign, by electing Democrats.[71]

For any number of reasons, a Democratic victory was unlikely, and for Wilson to turn the election into a plebiscite on his program was foolish. True, Republican leaders had savagely criticized the president during these pre-armistice negotiations. On that basis, Wilson had some justification for his appeal, and McKinley had done the same thing in 1900. But Wilson's having historical precedent behind his appeal made it no wiser politically. The voters gave the Republicans a resounding victory.

Because he had issued a statement that made the election a vote of confidence, Wilson received a vote of no confidence. If he had remained silent, his prestige might have stayed higher. Wilson himself explained the defeat as a reaction to his domestic policy, not his foreign policy, but the election weakened his hand in international negotiations.[72] With the American people having denied him his vote of confidence, he would go to Europe in December, leaving behind him a Senate that was already hostile, and that promised to become more so when newly elected members took their seats on March 4, 1919.

Woodrow Wilson fretted over the failure of the Allies to endorse the freedom of the seas, but he decided to accept the situation "inasmuch as G[reat] B[ritain] agreed to all other 13 points & did not actually dissent from that [fourteenth] in order to have unity."[73] In a cabinet meeting on November 5, "looking well and happy," Wilson announced that the Allies and House had agreed on armistice terms.[74] The Allies had accepted the Fourteen Points, he said, subject to two "interpretations." One was that the freedom of the seas needed exact definition; the other was that the restoration of Belgium must include financial as well as political restoration. Because the Allied note read that Germany was liable for damages to all civilian populations, it is almost inconceivable that Wilson believed only Belgium would receive "reparation for damages"; the error may lie in the pen of the person reporting the meeting.

Did the leaders of the Allied and Associated Powers feel at this moment that Germany would sign the terms they had drafted? Most had serious doubts. Lloyd George commented that Foch had told him the Germans would not sign the document but that "he would be able to overpower the Germans by Christmas."[75] The armistice terms were still a wish list that established a preliminary peace very favorable to the Allies, not a document the Allied leaders and House thought Germany would sign immediately. In the week that followed the meeting of the Supreme War Council, however, events in Germany took an unpredicted turn that erased earlier calculations.

8

The Germans Sign

On November 5, Woodrow Wilson sent the Germans the Allied note accepting the Fourteen Points with reservations on reparations and freedom of the seas.[1] He added that Marshal Foch was authorized to communicate armistice terms to German representatives. Now the over-riding question was whether Germany would agree to the terms, or, more abstractly, what combination of circumstances could induce a sovereign nation to accept terms like the ones the Allied and Associated Powers had prepared.

Just after the Supreme War Council adjourned on November 4, the Allies, far from thinking about easing any of their terms to lure the Germans into signing, had second thoughts about the naval clauses. The British fretted that no neutral would agree to intern the German warships and proposed adding a clause that, if neutrals refused the task, the Allies would intern the ships in one of their own ports. At British urging, Clemenceau, House, and the Italians agreed to insert "or failing them [neutral ports], Allied ones" in the clause requiring internment of most of the German surface fleet.[2]

Whether Lloyd George planned for something like this change, that addition led to dissimulation on a grand scale. The British claimed that the Allies had to keep all the German ships in the same harbor, and only two convenient neutral ports of sufficient size existed. Both of them—Vigo and Arosa Bay—were Spanish.[3] The British ordered their ambassador in Spain to make certain that the problems of controlling the enemy fleet set an insurmountable obstacle to the Spanish government's agreeing to intern the ships—that is, the ambassador was all but directly ordered to fail in his negotiations with the Spanish.[4] Indeed, the first draft of his instructions included that direct order, but someone crossed it out, expecting him to understand what was needed without explicit orders.

The British had already decided what to do with the ships. The day before the British Foreign Office sent the ambassador his veiled instructions to fail, the Allied Naval Council was making plans to intern the German vessels at the main British naval base of Scapa Flow off northern Scotland.[5] Far from supporting their claim that all German warships had to be kept in a single port, the Allied Naval Council had already decided to send "some" of the German warships to various other Allied ports "as a tangible sign of the German defeat."[6]

One other attempt to modify the naval terms failed. Admiral Beatty was still insisting that the armistice require the surrender of Heligoland, but the first lord of the Admiralty rebuffed him.[7] About all that Beatty gained was a promise to press the point at the coming peace conference.[8] The first lord explained to Beatty that "we have to depart from the idea that Armistice Terms must include everything we wish at the Peace."

Heligoland was about the only item on which that sentiment governed Allied claims. The draft terms, navally and militarily and every other way, were overwhelming. Most of the Allied and American leaders believed the Germans would refuse the terms initially but would accept them within a few months if the Allies and the United States kept up the pressure.

Militarily, of course, the Germans had faced unrelieved disaster since August. They had suffered 2.5 million casualties since the beginning of the year, and during those months, they had broken up 243 infantry battalions, the equivalent of 27 divisions.[9] German morale, too, was deteriorating as military defeats multiplied. Facing the Germans on the Western Front, the Allies and the United States now had 205 divisions; 29 of them were the United States' oversized divisions, which had more than twice the rifle strength of their Allied counterparts, so effectively the Allies had 234 divisions. On the Western Front, the Germans had only about 150 divisions and a rifle strength much inferior to that of the Allies and the United States. But even facing a two-to-one disadvantage, the German army was still fighting with determination.[10]

A series of events that began in Kiel and Wilhelmshafen changed all forecasts. On October 26, the rumor began to spread among the German sailors that their admirals were preparing to order the High Sea Fleet to make a suicidal sortie against the British in a last, grand gesture, and on the thirtieth, open mutiny broke out among the sailors.[11] On November 3, loyal forces fired on a mass demonstration, the first substantial bloodshed of the German revolution, and that evening, demonstrators in Kiel formed a Workers' and Sailors' Council.

That council was not particularly revolutionary, for it demanded only limited reforms, not the total overthrow of the state. The sailors and workers and, very soon, soldiers who made up the council were simply sick of the war. Yet however limited the reforms the sailors and workers and soldiers around Kiel sought, the uprising spread, first to Lübeck and Hamburg, and then inland as far as Köln, Dresden, and Leipzig. In many areas, unrest was already simmering, and news of the Kiel revolt accelerated the formation of revolutionary councils. Revolt was a fire that spread across Germany because flammable material was everywhere, and as revolt spread, it became more insistently radical, particularly in Berlin and Munich.

Bavaria, threatened with invasion from the south and east, saw a mass demonstration in Munich on November 7 amid air-raid alarms and rumors of future battles.[12] The demonstration turned into an uprising, and that evening the last of the Wittelsbach kings slipped out of the capital and fled across the border to Austria.[13] It was an almost bloodless revolution, at least at first, and it antedated the fall of the German emperor. Among the elements of this Bavarian revolution was a demand for a separate peace and, significantly, the new chairman of the Workers', Soldiers', and Peasants' Council also laid claim to being Bavaria's foreign minister.

In Berlin, the situation was growing more and more turbulent. By November 8, a Workers' and Soldiers' Council was threatening a general strike to force the abdication of the emperor. The chancellor, Prince Max of Baden, seeing the situation decay beyond any possible salvation, abdicated in the name of the emperor on the morning of the ninth and, a few hours later, resigned his own office in favor of Socialist Friedrich Ebert; the emperor, meanwhile, fled Germany, seeking asylum in the Netherlands.

Allied intelligence, although getting reports of increasing Bolshevism and riots in Germany, lagged far behind events. On November 4, British intelligence reported that insubordination and the display of revolutionary ideas had increased in the German army.[14] By the sixth, the British army experts were assuming that the emperor would abdicate almost immediately; yet as late as the seventh the Admiralty was reporting that German naval commanders still thought they could restore order.[15] Allied intelligence simply did not understand to what extent military defeat had affected German morale, both civilian and military, and did not grasp the intensity of German antiwar sentiment. Not understanding the strength of those factors, they failed to draw the appropriate conclusion: it had become impossible for Germany to continue the war.

The Allies and the United States kept up the military pressure. Buoyed up by the additional three hundred thousand American soldiers arriving monthly and with sufficient supplies and munitions, the Allied position was excellent, although the weather was beginning to turn bad in France and Flanders, an omen of winter.[16] The Germans continued to retreat in an "exceptionally precipitate manner."[17] Allied and American forces, following a renewal of the general offensive on October 31, were advancing all along the Western Front. Wildly enthusiastic, General Mordacq wrote that now nothing but an armistice could stop them.[18]

The Allies also planned a major offensive in Lorraine, the keystone of the German line. Foch designed a great attack that would involve more than thirty divisions and six hundred tanks.[19] A French army group would attack on a thirty-kilometer front from Metz to the Vosges while the Americans attacked along the French flank.[20] Perhaps responding to a spirit of parsimony concerning the lives of soldiers now that an armistice was possible, Foch postponed that attack several times, and it never began.

The other planned attack against Germany, the one through Bavaria, took shape only slowly, and rivalries in the Balkans, particularly Italian-Yugoslav enmity, disturbed planning for that operation. For those same reasons, the leaders had not solved the problems relating to the Austro-Hungarian battle fleet. On November 2, the Allied leaders and House had ordered that fleet, which Emperor Charles had given to the Yugoslav National Council in Zagreb, to sail to Corfu. The Allies were to intern it there, but the Italians blocked contact between the French admiral at Corfu and Pola, where the main body of the fleet lay at anchor. Not until November 6 could any Yugoslavian representatives get to Corfu to arrange for that sailing.[21]

In the meantime, a committee of admirals met at Paris to make plans for carrying out the Austro-Hungarian armistice.[22] Representatives of the other navies ran over the Italians, who wanted the whole matter left to an Italian admiral. The committee of admirals in Paris required the creation of a naval committee in the Adriatic with representation from each of the four powers—Italy, Great Britain, France, and the United States. Their decision did not mention either Yugoslavs or Serbs, and the admirals stressed that Austria-Hungary must give the naval committee the ships listed in the armistice terms, thus effectively ignoring both the Zagreb National Council's possession of the vessels and the Italians' claim for exclusive control.

While this naval committee was meeting, however, the Italians carried off a coup de main. An Italian admiral sailed into Pola on a pre-Dreadnought battleship accompanied by several smaller vessels and landed two thousand men to secure the harbor.[23] The Yugoslavian commander of the former Austro-Hungarian fleet, former frigate captain Metod Ciril Koch, protested the landing and insisted that Austria-Hungary had transferred the ships to Yugoslav ownership before signing the armistice. The Italian admiral ignored Koch's protests, and the next morning he received the reinforcement of three battleships. With four fully manned and armed battleships now in the harbor, the Italians were more than a match for any countermeasures the Yugoslavs might undertake. Koch made further protests, and the Italian admiral continued to refuse them.[24]

Clemenceau was furious at Italian actions and sent a stinging letter to the Italian prime minister:[25]

> An Italian admiral has taken possession of the fleet of which the Yugo-Slavs were masters and which all the Governments of the Entente, including yours, had ordered to go to Corfu. . . . I regard this as an act contrary to the engagements taken. I had promised you personally that the French Government would recognize no Yugo-Slav Committee before the execution of the armistice conditions. In order for me to keep my promises, it is necessary that the Italian military forces should conform to yours.

Clemenceau sent a copy of that message to London for Lloyd George, and he also sent a copy to the Yugoslavs.[26]

Orlando's response to Clemenceau was disdainful.[27] The special arrangements made concerning the Austrian fleet allowed the ships to go to Corfu under a white flag, he wrote. "Vessels which asked for that authorization obtained it, and had all the time necessary to take advantage of it." Vessels that had not taken advantage of the offer and were still in harbor "fall naturally under the conditions of the armistice."

On November 10, Clemenceau wrote to Orlando again, this time more temperately, perhaps because he now understood the futility of trying to rein in the Italians: "I think that you will agree with me in recognizing that we can have only one form of treatment for all the Austrian ships transferred to the Yugoslavs and flying the flag of Yugoslavia."[28] The Austrian fleet had to be put in Allied hands, not just Italian ones, and Clemenceau asked Orlando to tell the Italian admiral to reach an understanding with his French, British, and American counterparts. That is, Clemenceau backed away from condemning the Italian seizure of the Austro-Hungarian (perhaps Yugoslavian) fleet and now was asking only that the other Great Powers have a share in interning the vessels.

Here, and in other matters, the Yugoslavs might have been more effective if they had fused their various factions, committees, and governments-in-exile and spoken with one voice. Just as important in this case was the Yugoslavian failure to keep control over the sailors in Pola.[29] When the British naval attaché to the Rome embassy went to Pola on November 9, the Italian admiral complained to him about the Bolshevik tendencies of the Yugoslavs ashore and afloat.[30] Suspicious of the Italians, the British captain interviewed Koch, "who informed me he had little power over his men who had organized themselves into Soviets for purposes of looting and disorder." The Italian admiral, the British captain finally concluded, "is handling the situation with tact[,] firmness[,] and success." With the other Allies now admitting that they could do little other than support Italian moves, Orlando became more conciliatory. He agreed that it was up to the other Allies to decide where the Italians should send the ships.[31]

In the meantime, the Italians and the Yugoslavs were having trouble on land. Many of those problems did not reach ignition until later in November, but open friction developed even before the Germans received the armistice terms. The Treaty of London reserved for the Slavs the north end of the bay on which Fiume lay, but it gave Italy Istria, which was north of Fiume, the islands off the coast, Dalmatia south of Fiume as far as Cape Placa, and a protectorate over central Albania even farther south. That is, the Treaty of London gave Italy all of the northeastern coast of the Adriatic except Fiume, but while the coastal towns had a substantial ethnic Italian population, almost no Italians lived outside the towns. Rural and inland areas were overwhelmingly Slavic. In a world in which the national state and the ethnic state were increasingly identical, that division between urban Italians and rural Slavs created instability.

If the Italians limited their claims to the Treaty of London line, they would gain reluctant support from the British and the French, and Yugoslavian protests would probably be futile. In some areas, Yugoslavian actions went beyond protests. In the first flush of their nationalism, the Yugoslavs had little interest in acquiescing to any part of the Treaty of London arrangements. In both Tolmino and Gorizia, north and west of Trieste, and far within the zone Italy intended to annex, Yugoslav forces tried to disarm Austrian soldiers and occupy the cities. In Gorizia, three battalions of Yugoslav troops, a significant force, were successful in taking control of the city.[32]

The Italians were ready to resist any attack on their Treaty of London gains. They also wanted even more territory, including all of Albania, not just its central part. They proposed putting a headquarters, or at least an Italian brigade, at Scutari (modern Shkoder) in northern Albania.[33] Franchet d'Esperey, apparently on his own authority, rejected this Italian proposal for Scutari and said that a mixed force would occupy it. As it turned out, the Serbians beat everyone there, much to Italian annoyance.[34]

The Italians also demanded Montenegro, which the Treaty of London specifically reserved for the Slavs, and the Italians landed an infantry battalion "temporarily" in southwestern Montenegro at Antivari (modern Bar). Sonnino defended this action, claiming that any agreement making the occupation interallied took second place to maintaining public order and that the Italian battalion had landed to protect Italian lives.[35] He added that he would welcome the addition of British and French troops to the occupation force, if and when they arrived.

The Americans, involved in Balkan matters only indirectly, expressed concern over these events.[36] To show the flag, the United States had one regiment on the Italian Front, the 332d Infantry. The Italian government asked for three or four more American regiments to assist in occupying the Treaty of London area, "the plea being that the [Slav] inhabitants would not be hostile to American troops."[37] General Pershing strongly opposed granting the request. The Italians, he thought, would use American regiments to camouflage an advance into Yugoslavian areas.[38] In the weeks to come, Pershing's prophecy came true for the 332d, but at least the United States sent no more troops to that theater.

It irritated the Italians that the other Allies were not supporting them against the Yugoslavs. Orlando talked to the French ambassador and defended the Italian occupation of places along the Dalmatian coast as being in complete conformity with the decisions the Supreme War Council had reached.[39] To the British ambassador, he complained at great length about the Allied attitude toward Italy.[40] The Supreme War Council had disappointed him, he said, because "old friends and Allies and their

interests seemed to count for much less than the newly discovered Jugo-
Slavs." He complained that Clemenceau worried there might be "no Germany on which to put the screw" but seemed oblivious to Orlando's analo-
gous concerns about Austria-Hungary. At the Supreme War Council
meetings, Orlando noted, there had been a tendency to think that all the
"component parts of the old Austria had suddenly become Allies."

After the Yugoslavs had taken over the Austro-Hungarian fleet "by a
sort of trick," Orlando said, he had reluctantly agreed to the Corfu proposal, but he could not agree to recognize a Yugoslav nation at present.
The territorial claims of the National Council at Zagreb went west to the
Isonzo River, roughly the 1914 boundary of Italy and far inside the area
that the Treaty of London had allotted to Italy. Italy had always had the
support of Great Britain and France in its struggles to gain a "livable"
frontier, "and now suddenly a state which had hardly been heard from
before the war, some of the components of which had been among the
hardest fighters against the Allies, seemed to have a monopoly of sympa-
thies and suffrages." Italian friendship was a known Allied asset, Orlando
said, and what this new state might be was uncertain.

In the midst of this bickering, preparations for the Bavarian Offensive
continued.[41] Foch, now the commander-in-chief of all Allied armies, not
just those on the Western Front, planned to have three operational centers in the south. The first was Franchet d'Esperey's Army of the East.
Franchet d'Esperey would stay in Serbia or Bulgaria, keeping order and
representing France. He would transfer some of his troops to General
Henri-Mathias Berthelot in Rumania, who would command the second
center, the newly formed Army of the Danube. The third center was the
group of three armies attacking Bavaria, one army moving north from
Innsbruck and the other two attacking west from the Salzburg-Linz line.

Although the plan for the Bavarian Offensive had serious weaknesses,
it was feasible if speed were not demanded, and something could certainly take place by the following spring. The Allies had a great advantage over Germany in soldiers available in the area. On the Italian front,
the Italians had fifty-seven divisions they could assign to the operation.
In the Balkans, the Allies also had twenty-nine divisions, of which they
might use as few as ten or as many as eighteen for the Bavarian Offensive,
and the Rumanians might mobilize a significant force. The Germans still
had twenty-five weak divisions in Russia and another half-dozen on the
Danube frontier.[42] The divisions in Russia had no feasible way home,
and the divisions on the Danube were cut off because the Hungarians

refused to let them cross Hungarian territory, so none of those forces could reach Bavaria to defend it. Thus, the Germans could get men to protect Bavaria only by drawing them from their armies on the Western Front, and the Germans were already numerically at a disadvantage there. The conclusion was inescapable: because the Germans had no men available to repel the Allied attack on Bavaria, it would eventually overwhelm them.

The Allies, however, faced serious logistical problems with moving soldiers from the Army of the East to take part in that attack, even if Italian objections—presumably based on the presence of Serbian soldiers in that force—could be overcome.[43] The railroad between Belgrade and Niš was in bad condition, which made it almost impossible to send troops directly. Three other routes could move soldiers from the Army of the East to this new theater. One route went through Trieste, but Orlando objected to using Trieste as a transshipment point. The second used the railroad network west of Trieste, but lacking the port at Trieste, the Army of the East could employ only about half the railroad capacity of northeast Italy. Moreover, the Allies needed to repair the railroads in the former battle zone between the Isonzo and Piave Rivers, which would be, in the terse words of a British staff appraisal, a "somewhat lengthy process."[44] The third route was a river one, through the Black Sea to Constanza and up the Danube, but whether the necessary shipping existed was unknown.

On November 5, Clemenceau sent orders to Franchet d'Esperey, informing the general that the Bavarian Offensive would require all the British and French divisions he could spare.[45] He ordered him to occupy the Belgrade-Budapest-Vienna railroad line, to control river transportation on the Danube, and to occupy Rumania, Bulgaria, and the Dardanelles. Clemenceau also ordered him to prepare for action in south Russia in conjunction with the British army, then in Palestine. Given the extravagant nature of those instructions, it is small wonder that the activities of the Army of the East became confused. Moreover, the instructions given to Franchet d'Esperey overlapped those given to General Berthelot, whose Army of the Danube was expected to operate in Rumania and Hungary and to control Danubian communications.

By November 10 or 11, the situation had begun to sort itself out. It would certainly require far longer to mount an offensive against Bavaria than the first optimistic plans had suggested, but by November 11, Italian forces had gained control of the Brenner Pass, critical to movement through Innsbruck.[46] Franchet d'Esperey had ordered British admiral Sir

Ernest Troubridge, a capable officer, to coordinate the war flotillas on the Danube.[47] The advance guard of the Anglo-French Army of the Danube had forced a crossing of the Danube into Wallachia.[48] Nevertheless, with winter advancing, it was unlikely that any decisive activity against Germany from the south or east could occur until the spring.

Among the Great Powers, there was some hurried fence-mending following the Supreme War Council's meeting. House, for example, saw the British ambassador to France and stressed the need to continue Anglo-American friendship after the war.[49] Clemenceau had much the same conversation with the British ambassador.[50] A far stranger conversation took place between Clemenceau and House.[51] To House, Clemenceau said, "You have been so wise and helpful that I beg you to believe my friendship is sincere." Clemenceau promised, House wrote, that he "would not take up any matter at the Peace Conference without having fully apprised me of it, and he intimated that if I objected, he would defer to my judgment." Reporting this conversation to President Wilson, House showed no reservations about these statements, even adding that Clemenceau said he wanted the United States' "moral approval."

Some Anglo-French friction occurred over the occupation of the Straits, but nothing that approached the bitterness of their exchanges over the Near East in October. A French regiment went from Thrace to occupy the Dardanelles, and the British sent an infantry division from Salonika.[52] The French planned to make their fleet equal to the English when the two anchored at Constantinople, but quarrels over the Ottoman Empire, for the moment, were muted.[53]

Whatever the long-range consequences of problems over the Ottoman Empire or the Balkans, the main concern after the Supreme War Council adjourned was the Germans and their reaction to the Allied armistice terms. At 12:30 A.M. on November 6, the Germans radioed Foch, listing their plenipotentiaries and asking for a route to travel.[54] They also asked for an immediate, general cease-fire. Foch radioed back forty-five minutes later, ignoring the cease-fire request and telling the Germans to come to the French posts on the road from Formies to La Capelle to Guise.[55]

This series of preliminary messages led indirectly to the famous "False Armistice" report. The United States' naval attaché at Paris telegraphed a report of this exchange to the American admiral at Brest, but apparently he overstated the situation. The American admiral at Brest showed the telegram to a United Press reporter, who sent out the scoop that caused the American press to announce, excitedly but falsely, that the armistice was already signed.[56]

Just after 6:00 A.M. on November 7, French headquarters warned the 166th Infantry Division near La Capelle to expect the German delegates.[57] Not until 5:00 P.M. did a German lieutenant with a trumpeter come to the French outposts to say that the plenipotentiaries were delayed, and they arrived in their cars only at 8:00 P.M. Matthias Erzberger, the Center Party leader and principal architect of the Reichstag Peace Resolution, led the German delegation. Representing the navy was Captain Ernst Vanselow; his rank was not high, but he was Erzberger's personal friend. Minister to Bulgaria Count Alfred von Oberndorff represented the Foreign Office. The only ranking army member in the delegation was Major General Detlev von Winterfeldt, and he did not represent the Supreme Command; he was the liaison officer between the Supreme Command and the emperor.[58]

The French met the Germans, and they set out from La Capelle.[59] A light mist cleared away, and wan moonlight lit the road. Around midnight, the Germans and their escort reached Hombliers, where the Germans ate a cheerless supper. Setting out again, they reached the broken and abandoned village of Tergnier and boarded a train at 3:00 A.M. At 7:00 A.M. on November 8, the Germans' train pulled onto an empty railroad siding near Rethondes in the Forest of Compiègne, parallel to Foch's railway car. The day before, Foch had arrived with his chief of staff, General Weygand, and British Admiral Wemyss.[60] "It is a curious scene in the middle of the Forest," Wemyss commented, "raining & leaves falling & yet there is nothing sad—at any rate for us."[61]

Two hours after the Germans arrived, the first meeting began.[62] It started on an odd note. After the formal presentation of credentials and the seating of the Germans, Erzberger told Foch that the German delegation had come to hear the Allied proposals. Foch immediately responded: "I have no proposals to make." That nonplused the Germans. Erzberger and the other Germans tried several alternative wordings without hitting upon the precise formula Foch wanted to hear. At last, in frustration, Erzberger read the text of Wilson's Fourth Note, which told the Germans that Foch would give them armistice conditions. Foch finally gave the Germans guidance. He told them he was authorized to inform them of armistice conditions if they requested an armistice. The Germans formally requested one, whereupon Foch told Weygand to read the principal paragraphs of the conditions aloud.

As Weygand read the terms, the Germans paled. When he finished, the Germans requested a cease-fire while discussions over the terms took place. Foch refused the German plea, calling Clemenceau to confirm his decision.[63] The Supreme War Council had given Germany only seventy-two hours to accept or refuse the terms, and the Germans wanted an extension of that time limit to compensate for the difficulties of communications in the unsettled condition of Germany. That request, too, Foch refused.

The German delegates thereupon accepted the armistice in principle, sending a courier off to Berlin with its text to obtain the approval of the German government. Erzberger told his courier he thought the Allies would refuse to consider any counterproposals, but he would try to get modifications to preserve order and prevent famine. Above all, he said, he would try to get a longer period in which to carry out the evacuations and a reduction in the quantity of military material the Allies were requiring Germany to surrender.[64]

It astonished Foch that the German delegates accepted the terms so easily, particularly the clauses on the bridgeheads, the fleet, and the occupation, but became "pale and literally collapsed" when they heard the terms requiring the surrender of their machine guns, cannon, and locomotives. One of the Germans, possibly Erzberger, cried out, "But then we are lost. How are we going to be able to defend ourselves against Bolshevism?"[65] Nevertheless, the Allies' general perception during and after this first session was that the German government would ratify the decision of their delegates and accept the terms. "My impression," Admiral Wemyss commented, "is that they must & will sign."[66]

That afternoon in a private meeting, General von Winterfeldt spoke with Weygand.[67] He accused the Allies of having drawn up excessively severe terms with the aim of having the Germans refuse them, to which Weygand replied that the Allies were merely informing Germany of the conditions under which they would grant an armistice. German arguments that the armistice need not be so severe fell into several groups.[68] First, the Germans swore their army would be incapable of combat again once the armistice was signed, and therefore severe terms were pointless. Second, Bolshevism was making Germany's internal situation precarious, and because it was to Allied advantage to excise that Bolshevik infection, it was in the interest of both the Allies and the Germans to let the army retire in an orderly fashion. To require rapid movement would destroy the army, which was already paralyzed. Finally, von Winterfeldt protested that famine threatened Germany, and it was inhumane to require the surrender of railway equipment and to maintain the blockade. "Germany must be left with an army in good order so that it may suppress revolts, and the country must be provided with food," he said. Weygand showed him no sympathy.

The next day, November 9, the Germans gave Weygand written observations on the armistice terms.[69] In his report, Weygand noted laconically that the Germans simply repeated the arguments of the day before "without saying anything new worth the trouble of noting." After consulting Clemenceau, Foch refused most of the German proposals.[70]

On November 9, Foch met with Clemenceau at Senlis. Clemenceau asked Foch if he had any objection to granting an armistice.[71] "I see only advantages," Foch replied. "To continue the struggle longer would be to play for high stakes. We would kill 50,000 or 100,000 Frenchmen for results that are problematical. . . . Enough blood has been spilled." Foch, however, did not relax the tempo of Allied attacks, although he postponed the scheduled attack in Lorraine again.[72] He was optimistic, telling the liaison officer to the French government that "the Germans are completely broken, even more completely than I had believed. They are accepting everything."[73] In a separate conversation, Foch told Wemyss that if the Germans did not sign, he could beat them on the ground in three weeks.[74]

Toward the evening of November 9, the first news about events in Berlin began to filter in. The information was vague; all the Allies knew at first was that the chancellor had resigned.[75] Wemyss, for one, worried that the fall of the chancellor stripped the German plenipotentiaries of their powers.[76] Clemenceau discounted the effect of the chancellor's fall, if the news was true.[77] Recounting the negotiations in a note to Lloyd George, he noted sardonically that the Germans were protesting they were losing so many machine guns that they would not have enough to fire on their fellow citizens. Clemenceau said Foch had told the Germans they still had their rifles. Shortly after this note, though, Clemenceau became disturbed by the news from Berlin and began to wonder whether the Germans at Rethondes really represented the new government and whether, if those negotiators signed the armistice, the new government would accept it.[78] He cabled Lloyd George, asking him to come to Paris in case swift decisions were necessary.[79]

Lloyd George remarked to the cabinet that the events taking place in Germany resembled what had happened in Russia the previous year.[80] It was important that he consult with Allied and American leaders as soon as possible, "especially as it would seem probable that Marshal Foch was disposed to go on with hostilities with a view of destroying the German

Army and capturing material." He may have misread Foch's intentions at that moment, but no one challenged Lloyd George's claim.

Sir Henry Wilson forecast that the German army would break up but not go socialist. As a precaution, however, he recommended that Allied forces not cross the Rhine, so they could avoid involvement in coming Bolshevik outbreaks.[81] Lloyd George agreed with Sir Henry, saying that "marching men into Germany was marching them into a cholera area." He reminded the cabinet that the Germans had marched into Russia and caught the germs of Bolshevism there. None of these pessimistic comments left the cabinet meeting. The British foreign minister merely cabled Clemenceau to say that unless the matter was truly critical, Lloyd George could not come to Paris until November 13. He suggested that, in the meantime, if there were urgent matters to deal with, Clemenceau could meet with War Cabinet member Lord Curzon, who had stayed on in Paris.[82]

Clemenceau did order Foch to require that the German delegates at Rethondes make two written declarations.[83] First, they had to declare that they represented the new government; second, they had to give assurances that the new government would carry out the armistice provisions. To require promises like those seems an exercise in foolishness. No one in Germany was able to guarantee anything. The new German government authorized Erzberger to sign; the rest would have to be taken on faith.[84]

With Erzberger having his government's authorization to sign the terms in hand, he and Foch began a last, gruelling session of negotiations at 2:15 in the morning of November 11.[85] Erzberger tried to reduce the severity of practically every clause. Fruitlessly, he tried to secure concessions on the Allied intention of maintaining the blockade and tried, also without success, to have Foch allow the return of German prisoners of war.

Foch, despite instructions giving him little discretion, did change a number of articles. He rewrote the terms to require the Germans to surrender only twenty-five thousand machine guns, down from thirty thousand, and seventeen hundred airplanes, down from two thousand. The new figure for airplanes probably represented the actual number of planes the Germans had in service. He also reduced the number of motor trucks demanded from ten thousand to five thousand. He redrew the required neutral zone on the right bank of the Rhine, reducing it to a depth of ten kilometers, and more important, he allowed the Germans to take thirty-one days, not just twenty-five, to carry out the agreed-upon evacuations.

One minor change was an agreement that would allow the German troops in East Africa to keep their arms after they surrendered and allow them to be evacuated instead of requiring their unconditional surrender. That point was one more of symbol than of substance and was ignored when the German forces in East Africa surrendered two weeks later, although the victors treated them courteously.

Foch and Erzberger made an important change in the clauses for the Eastern Front. The Germans protested that the immediate withdrawal of German troops from Russia would expose the population there to Bolshevism, the same argument that had come up in the Supreme War Council. Erzberger convinced Foch, who rewrote the clause to provide for the evacuation of Russia "as soon as the Allies, taking into account the internal situation of those territories, shall decide that the time for this has come." In the meantime, the Germans would maintain their forces in Russia. Balfour would thus indirectly get his proposal that the Germans leave some of their arms, the only difference being that in this new arrangement the Germans would still be carrying them. That clause caused problems some months later, especially in the Baltic nations, where the Germans would claim that they were fighting the Allies' battles in the struggle against Bolshevism.

The naval terms saw modification, too. The Germans protested that they did not have the 160 submarines they were required to surrender, so the Allies amended the terms to require the surrender of all submarines, which was what the British admirals had wanted from the beginning. Although Foch was unrelenting on the maintenance of the blockade, he agreed that the Allies would consider supplying provisions to Germany, but he set no date for beginning either the study or the relief.

Foch lengthened the duration of the armistice from thirty to thirty-six days, at which time it would be either denounced or renegotiated and renewed. At the request of the Germans, he also added a clause establishing a permanent armistice commission to provide communication between the opposing forces during the period of the armistice.

At 5:10 A.M., the Germans, Foch, and Wemyss signed the terms of the Compiègne Armistice. The Germans also read a letter of protest.[86] The German government, the letter said, would try to carry out the terms of the armistice, but the short time allowed for the evacuations, coupled with the surrender of transport, threatened to bring about "anarchy and famine." Nevertheless, the Germans would persevere: "A nation of seventy millions suffers but does not die." Still, a British admiral, who was with Wemyss at Rethondes, described the German delegates over the three days as "very quiet, very servile, and at the end cringing."[87]

At 5:40 A.M., the great radio station at the Eiffel Tower transmitted the news that the armistice was signed.[88]

At 11:00 A.M. the guns fell silent.

Clemenceau told Mordacq on the evening of November 11, "We have won the war, and not without pain, but now we must win the peace, and that will be perhaps more difficult."[89] Clemenceau had already had his emotional outpouring. It had happened on November 8, when he had gotten Foch's telegram reporting that the German delegates had accepted the armistice in principle:[90]

> No sooner had M. Clemenceau finished reading the dispatch than I saw him look at me fixedly. His eyes moistened, and then putting his head in his hands, he began to cry silently. Never in the course of the war had I seen him subject to such an emotion. At the end of a short time, he got hold of himself and cried out, "This is foolish. I am not master of my nerves. I saw 1870 again."

Upon the news of the Germans' signing, House cabled to Wilson: "Autocracy is dead. . . . In this great hour my heart goes out to you in pride[,] admiration[,] and love."[91] One of Wilson's political associates was with him on the evening of November 11. "I shall never forget how happy he looked," he wrote.[92] The crowd was surging along Pennsylvania Avenue, and the president, "unable to remain indoors, had come to the White House gates to look on. . . . In his countenance there was an expression not so much of triumph as of vindication."

In the House of Commons, after announcing the signing of the Compiègne Armistice and reading its terms, Lloyd George said, "Those are the conditions of the Armistice. Thus at eleven o'clock this morning came to an end the cruellest and most terrible War that has ever scourged mankind. I hope we may say that thus, this fateful morning, came to an end all wars."[93]

9

Conclusions

The Compiègne Armistice with Germany was a preliminary peace treaty in which the Allies achieved their major war aims. The British wanted the destruction of the German battle fleet, and they wanted the German economy crippled. They achieved both goals, and they removed any threat that Germany might win hegemony on the Continent. The French wanted an end to the German menace, the return of Alsace and Lorraine, and the establishment of the Rhine as a strategic frontier. For the moment, they had all of that. The Italians, through the Villa Giusti Armistice with Austria-Hungary, had begun making territorial gains to their north and east, and they confidently expected to become the dominant power in the Adriatic and western Balkans. All the Allies welcomed Germany's submission to their demand for reparations, which promised them relief from the debts their wartime expenditures had imposed. The peace treaties of 1919–20 would deal further with all those items, but not change them fundamentally.

The armistice arrangements also included both Allied and German agreement to the Fourteen Points—the major Wilsonian war aims—and President Wilson intended his program to guide the peacemaking. Unfortunately for Wilson's plans, the Fourteen Points would bind the Allies only as far as they let themselves be bound. Eight months after the armistice, the British foreign secretary spoke to the assembled British Empire Delegation at the Paris Peace Conference.[1] He declared that during the negotiations over the armistice terms, he and Lloyd George had "suddenly found themselves faced with the Fourteen Points and the time was too short to discuss them." Because their primary need was to prepare an armistice quickly, "they had no option but to take the Fourteen Points." The foreign secretary was an honorable man, but he was saying that the Americans had coerced the British into accepting the Fourteen Points and implying that because the British had not entered into the bargain freely, the Fourteen Points did not bind them. André Tardieu, Clemenceau's most important political associate, simply ignored the Fourteen Points. "The Armistice of November 11, 1918, was an unconditional surrender on the part of Germany," he wrote two years after it was signed.[2] One scholar's recent excellent study of the Great War labels the armistice simply a "capitulation."[3]

British diplomat Harold Nicolson, looking back at the completed texts of the peace treaties of 1919–20 from the vantage point of the 1930s, exclaimed, somewhat sanctimoniously, that of Wilson's twenty-three conditions—to the original Fourteen Points Nicolson added the statements Wilson made in his other 1918 speeches—the final treaties incorporated only four.[4] Nicolson was unduly conservative in his score keeping, but the Fourteen Points neither provided an agenda for the peace deliberations nor shaped the final peace treaties.

Typical of what happened to the Fourteen Points was the fate of Point Four, which asked for the reduction of armaments. After the peace conference delegates prepared clauses severely limiting Germany's army and navy, they prefaced that section of the treaty with the claim that the disarmament of Germany would "render possible the initiation of a general limitation of the armaments of all nations."[5] Although that phrase became the justification for calling various disarmament conferences in the following years, Point Four did not guide the peacemakers at Paris.

Vague to begin with, the Fourteen Points had become out-of-date in several of their particulars, lost precision in the Cobb-Lippmann Memorandum, and were ignored in the final settlement if they conflicted with the self-defined vital interests of any ally. Yet if the Fourteen Points had been clear and definite, the Allied leaders would have rejected them out of hand. In view of these considerations, it is hard to escape the conclusion that Colonel House's efforts to persuade the Allied leaders to accept Wilson's program were largely wasted energy. The only positive feature of House's struggle was that with it he gave notice to the Allied leaders that the Americans expected some sort of moral justification for the actions they were taking.

Critics of the armistice have focused on the connected questions of whether the armistice was signed too soon or too late. Some participants and commentators have argued that an earlier armistice might have saved lives and even let the German monarchy survive, which, in the long run, might have produced a stable Germany. But, barring the saving of a day or two here and there, it is not clear how the process might have operated much more rapidly. What the Germans said in their First Note was by no means what they agreed to, implicitly and explicitly, in their Third. After the German-American exchanges, the Allied leaders had to gather, draw up and approve terms, and present them to the Germans, a sequence that could not have proceeded much more rapidly than it did.

If some people say the armistice came too late, others maintain it came too soon and should have been even harsher. Particularly in the 1920s and 1930s, people tried to guess whether different armistice terms might somehow have led to a happier world.[6] They tried to figure out whether they might have added some element to the armistice to force the German people to recognize that the Allies and the United States had beaten them. But the armistice the Germans signed took away a great part of their army's weapons and most of their battle fleet. It put more than one-tenth of their nation under enemy occupation and included a multitude of humiliating clauses. If all that did not convince the German people they had lost the war, it is hard to imagine what terms might have done so.

General Sir Frederick Maurice, in his study of these events, pointed out that the German negotiators represented the civilian government, not Supreme Headquarters, and he argued that Foch should have refused to treat with anyone other than the army's leaders.[7] If Foch had done that, Maurice concluded, no intriguer could ever claim that civilians had betrayed the army. Critics of the armistice, like Maurice, who say it should have provided the Germans some indisputable sign of defeat, assume that politics is a rational process in which rational humans engage, and it is not—at least, not on the issues radical German politicians exploited during the years of the Weimar Republic. If the emperor and the German military chiefs had been stripped naked and loaded with chains while they personally signed an armistice, someone, sometime, would still claim betrayal, and others would believe him.

General Henri Mordacq, Clemenceau's loyal assistant in the Ministry of War, writing as much to protect Clemenceau and embarrass Foch as for any other reason, claimed the Allies should have signed the armistice on German soil, not in the Forest of Compiègne.[8] Certainly, doing that might have provided some sort of symbolism, but it is customary for the defeated nation to apply to the victor and come to the victor's headquarters to sign such a document. For Allied generals to go to Germany's Supreme Headquarters or to Berlin might just as well have planted the idea in German minds that the Allies, not the Germans, were the supplicants.

Certainly, the Allies could have demanded more of Germany if they had kept up the war for a few more weeks, but to make that a sensible course, they had to want more than they got on November 11. They also needed to know how near Germany was to collapse, and in the first days of November, they did not know the internal condition of Germany. It is possible to fault Allied intelligence services for not penetrating more deeply into the mysteries of Germany, but it seems wrong to rebuke them for failing to know what the German leaders themselves did not know.[9] Too, the Allies had already made their decisions by November 4, before the situations in Munich and Berlin became catastrophic and public.

Mordacq puts the blame for the Allied failure to ask for more in the armistice on the public's desire for peace and on the faintheartedness of the leaders—other than Clemenceau, of course.[10] Mordacq to the contrary, the reasons the political leaders did not ask for more came less from faintheartedness than from concern about spending lives needlessly. On Christmas Day 1918, Lloyd George was playing golf, and the subject of whether the armistice was premature came up. "I should have been glad to see us enter Germany by force of arms," he said, "but the losses entailed on our side would have been too severe."[11] Colonel House, a year or two after the armistice, noted that "we were striving to get all the fruits of victory without sacrificing new lives; it was difficult to balance our duty toward the cause and our duty toward our brave soldiers."[12]

By requiring unconditional surrender, the Allies and the United States might have guaranteed fulfillment not only of all their past war aims, but also of any new ones they conceived. But unconditional surrender—the complete disarmament of Germany and the occupation of all German territory, total victory after total war—would have required the Allies and the United States to take responsibility for all aspects of Germany's internal administration. Insofar as the Allied and American leaders thought about such a plan in 1918, they were willing to occupy strategic points along the Rhine, but they recoiled from any prospect of running Germany as a whole.[13] Unconditional surrender, therefore, was never seriously discussed.

Conventional wisdom has it that the unconditional surrender policy of World War II was a reaction to these events at the end of World War I. There is, however, some confusion about just what the leaders of the Western democracies, a quarter of a century after the end of World War I, were reacting to. When the Allied leaders in the middle of World War II were trying to decide how to deal with the Axis Powers, the terms of the Compiègne Armistice in 1918 were not really the point at issue. No one objected to a document requiring Germany to surrender, for example, five thousand motor trucks. The objection was to the political promises that accompanied the Compiègne Armistice—that is, the Fourteen Points and the various pre-armistice agreements. Even there, the objection was less to the content of the agreements than to the use to which German propagandists put them later.[14] Therefore, discussion on the relationship between the unconditional surrender doctrine of World War II and the conclusion of World War I is often unfocused.

In fact, the unconditional surrender doctrine of World War II did not come directly from revulsion against the World War I settlement, although certainly the echo of World War I was a major element in decision making. United States president Franklin D. Roosevelt first issued the unconditional surrender doctrine publicly to a press conference at Casablanca on January 24, 1943, but to the assembled reporters, he made no reference to World War I or to the Compiègne Armistice.[15] He referred only to General U.S. ("Unconditional Surrender") Grant, who is supposed to have been the first modern soldier to call for unconditional surrender; that was in 1862 at the siege of Fort Donelson. The point is that if Roosevelt had had World War I and the failure then to demand unconditional surrender on his mind, he would have mentioned that war at his press conference, not make references to U.S. Grant. True, biographer Robert E. Sherwood writes colorfully that Roosevelt had decided there would be "no 'escape clauses' provided by another Fourteen Points" and that the "ghost of Woodrow Wilson" stood beside him.[16] But the evidence points to other motives as the primary reasons for Roosevelt's issuing the doctrine of unconditional surrender, motives mostly having to do with Western-Soviet relations.[17]

It is hard to see how unconditional surrender, like the demands of World War II, could have made drawing up peace terms at the end of World War I any easier than it was in 1919. In 1919, the Germans played no role in making the Versailles Treaty until the very end, when their diplomats, housed behind barbed wire, were allowed to make observations upon what the Allies and the United States had done to them. The important point is that the terms presented to Germany in the Compiègne Armistice of November 11, 1918, omitted nothing the Allies and the United States wanted, and it rendered the Germans helpless.

If the Allied and Associated Powers had no major aims that the November armistice failed to secure, there was no reason to demand unconditional surrender or to fight on. Foch reached that conclusion when he analyzed the armistice in his memoirs.[18] Moreover, he noted that the armistice put the Allies in a military position so overwhelming that it prevented the Germans from resisting any intention the Allies might have.

It was essential to realize, Foch argued, that in November 1918, the Allies did not have the power to bring about the immediate destruction of the German army in the field. The Allies and the United States could have continued forcing the German soldiers to retreat, taking prisoners and capturing guns, but they could not have prevented the Germans from crossing the Rhine and fortifying themselves behind it. The Allies and the United States could have spent many lives to get later perhaps no more than they got in November, and what they got in November, Foch believed, was entirely sufficient.

"Because war is a means," Foch said just before his death, "it is not an end."[19] A nation makes war "solely to make the adversary submit to his will, all his will." The Germans, when they signed the armistice, were submitting to all the will of their foes. When the Allies and the United States signed the armistice, Foch said, they had been sweeping the enemy before them for two months, and they could certainly continue to do so. "But continue for what goal, if the enemy accepts all our conditions . . . ?" After the Compiègne Armistice, Germany was "absolutely obliged to bow to all our exactions." That, he declared, made it a good armistice. "What would it gain to ask more?"

The conclusion to the related questions of whether the armistice came too soon or too late is: the armistice was not possible earlier, leaving aside gaining a day or two, because the Allies had not drafted the document, and if they had drafted a document earlier containing the least they would have settled for, the Germans, before the first week of November, would have rejected it. Nor was the armistice premature, because the Allies got everything they wanted. Finally, there is no reason to believe that any additional exactions would have made the armistice with Germany a substantially better document, either at the time or for the future.

In fact, the worst feature of the armistice was not that it lacked anything necessary, but that it was overwhelming. Wilson had already noted the dangers involved. "Too much success or security on the part of the Allies will make a genuine peace settlement difficult if not impossible," he had cabled to House on October 28.[20] In 1936, with the benefit of hindsight, Lloyd George, too, wrote that the armistice had been far too overwhelming: "Beyond question, it was a disaster that we had to lay Germany prostrate before we could reach a peace settlement."[21]

The reduction of Germany to impotence allowed the Versailles Treaty to make monstrous demands on the nation. If the Germans had retained some strength and been a true participant in making peace, the final settlement might well have been a better one.[22] Moreover, if Germany had kept some power, the United States' diplomats might have served as arbiters between the Allies and Germany. That is, a stronger Germany could have increased the diplomatic leverage of the United States. All that must lie in the realm of speculation, however, because, Lloyd George's later reflections to the contrary, the Allies would never have agreed to an armistice that left Germany significant military resources.

So far as the other Central Powers were concerned, the armistices made with them have aroused far less controversy than the armistice with Germany. Bulgaria lost the war, but all the Salonika Armistice with Bulgaria did was to demonstrate that loss, which the provisions of the Treaty of Neuilly, signed with Bulgaria in November 1919, ratified.

The collapse of the Ottoman Empire created a fertile field for international bickering. At the time when the Turkish leaders signed the Mudros Armistice, they expected eventually to lose all but the ethnically Turkish core of their Ottoman Empire, and so they did. The refusal of the Turkish nationalists later to accept the Treaty of Sèvres marked the beginning of a new era for Turkey, but at the San Remo Conference in 1920, the Allies had already distributed the non-Turkish Ottoman territories among themselves as mandates.

Austria-Hungary, of course, disintegrated, but that disintegration did not stem from the Villa Giusti Armistice or the Belgrade Convention. It was the consequence of unrestrained nationalism. The Treaty of Saint-Germain, made with Austria in September 1919, followed the model of the Versailles Treaty, though many of the terms made little sense for a pocket-sized republic of six million people. The Treaty of Trianon, made with Hungary in June 1920, took away almost all the non-ethnic Hungarian territory, as well as significant numbers of Hungarians, and assigned them to Hungary's neighbors: Rumania, Yugoslavia, Czechoslovakia, and even Austria. It made the Hungarians bitterly resentful, and Hungarian *revanchism* became a dominant theme of interwar diplomacy.

The Fourteen Points guided none of those settlements, which were made on the basis of power politics and the self-interest of the victors. Nor did the armistices themselves have any great bearing on the futures of Bulgaria, Turkey, Austria, or Hungary. It was the German armistice that shaped future events, and it is the German armistice that has caused decades of controversy.

The negotiations leading to the Compiègne Armistice were a critical point in the lives of those who participated in them, but no one—neither the politicians, nor the diplomats, nor the military and naval leaders—rose to greatness at the occasion. The type of leader that modern technological war brought forth was a man convinced of his own infallibility, a man undaunted by reverses, a man who could withstand relentless pressure and a killing schedule day after day. This type of man—and Clemenceau, Lloyd George, Foch, and the other Europeans all represented it—was necessary for fighting and winning the war, but other qualities might have served diplomacy and the construction of peace better.

Clemenceau, with ideas on armistice terms for Germany little if any different from Foch's, was determined not to let the military gain primacy in the negotiations. He managed to win at small cost the items he wanted most: Alsace-Lorraine, occupation of the Rhineland, and the promise of reparations. Foch, too, acted capably in getting what he wanted as terms, although he never garnered the power he sought over the negotiations. Nevertheless, it is curious how completely he dominated the construction of military, if not naval, terms. It was his draft that served as the basis for construction of military terms; no other draft of military terms ever received line-by-line discussion after the Conference of Prime Ministers early in October. The draft that the Military Representatives created in cooperation with other military and naval persons dropped into complete obscurity and was never heard of again. Some of Haig's views did make it into discussion through Lloyd George, but those were general ideas, not specific terms. It was Foch who was overwhelming, and in getting what he wanted, he separated himself both from the national commanders-in-chief and from the Military Representatives, playing a lone hand.

One surprising conclusion of this study bears on that point. That conclusion is the small amount of cohesiveness that existed among the military commanders of the various nations. Despite civilian assumptions that military people view similar problems in a similar way, and despite civilian assumptions that military persons unite against civilians, there was as much divergence among the generals as there was among the politicians. Perhaps the explanation lies in the positions these generals held. Generals who rise to high staff command or to the head of a national army must be as much politicians as warriors. Their roles require them to have talents and attributes that move them from the category of "typical" soldiers—and perhaps, too, assumptions about the military mind are wanting.

In contrast with the generals, the naval leaders showed great solidarity in the meetings of the Allied Naval Council, but that solidarity came from the tradition of British primacy permeating naval decisions during the war. The naval leaders broke their solid front at the critical moment, when the politicians demanded that they scale down their naval demands.

Of all the major leaders involved in making the armistice with Germany, Lloyd George is the most difficult to assess. During the weeks discussed here, he made statements supporting and opposing every position, with the notable exception of his opposition to freedom of the seas. From his amazingly mercurial approach, it is possible to conclude that he had no firm position on most subjects and simply let himself drift in the winds of debate. Whatever emerged he could then claim as his own. Another interpretation, however, is probably the correct one: Lloyd George had a consistent policy and took various and changing positions in debate to see what arguments would emerge. He had a peace policy from the beginning that was roughly similar to the Fourteen Points, stripped of the freedom of the seas and with reparations added, and he achieved it. His seeming vacillations were a tactical system whereby he learned what might be said and who would say it. He got what he wanted, but at the price of his colleagues' distrust.

The Italian delegates at the Supreme War Council, Orlando and Sonnino, managed to keep their Treaty of London claims, although no specific mention of that treaty appears in the armistice terms for either Austria-Hungary or Germany. They fared less well in retaining French and British friendship. If the Italians had been less grasping, they might have received greater Allied support, but less in the way of territory. In the long run, the additional land they wanted was probably worth strained relations, if they could keep that region in the final treaty and hold it in the face of ethnic unrest during the years to come.

Woodrow Wilson judged the mood of the Allied leaders, quite correctly from the American point of view, as brutal, greedy, and intransigent. On the other hand, from the time of the First German Note, people had warned him that the German overtures were only a deceitful snare designed to gain time for the German armies. Wilson had to avoid playing into German hands, while not, he hoped, giving the Allies free rein; and in his own country, harsh cries for vengeance rang louder than any public demand for a peace of reconciliation.

During early and mid-October, as Wilson continued his bilateral negotiations with the Germans, military and political events combined to make it more and more likely that this German peace initiative would bear fruit. Every word exchanged began to seem starkly important, then and later, and Wilson managed the negotiations effectively. Good planning, however, received the aid of good fortune when, as a result of the November Revolution, German resistance disappeared and the German emperor fell.

Wilson sincerely believed in his Fourteen Points and seems to have assumed that even if they were blurred in details, the Allied leaders would accept their spirit, to which he thought they would be bound. But Wilson wanted something impossible. He wanted to play the antithetical roles of participant and impartial arbiter, and he never realized, either in the fall of 1918 or in the negotiation of the peace treaties the following year, that he could not be both at once. Nevertheless, Wilson's idealism and his willingness to show a degree of generosity to a defeated opponent did inspire many people, not only in the United States but also in Allied nations, and perhaps he laid the first bricks, if not a complete foundation, for a better world than he was viewing in 1918.

Unlike the Allied prime ministers, Colonel House was not a true plenipotentiary. He was Wilson's agent. Still, he was able to act more independently than he might have otherwise because of the rapid pace of events and the delays inherent in communicating in code over a cable system between different hemispheres. House did not block reparations claims, he failed on freedom of the seas, he allowed the French to take the Rhineland, and he let the Austro-Hungarian armistice avoid a firm link to the Fourteen Points. Even if the value of his trying to get Allied acceptance to the Fourteen Points is debatable, he did win superficial Allied adherence to the Wilsonian program. Whether it was wise or worthwhile to have done so, that was the task with which Wilson had charged him, and no one else was likely to have done much better. Whatever House's shortcomings, he ended with the respect and affection of the European leaders, no mean feat under the circumstances.

Many of the issues that arose in the armistice negotiations continued to dominate proceedings at the Paris Peace Conference the following year. The freedom of the seas died in the spring of 1919, but other issues that surfaced during the armistice negotiations remained very much alive. Italian-Serb-Yugoslav quarrels continued well beyond the time of the peace conference. So did the Russian question.

What to do about Russia was a mystery. The Allied leaders believed that Bolshevism was a temporary aberration and that, once the world returned to peace and normality, Bolshevism would die of its own rabid bite. Meanwhile, the centrifugal force of nationalism in Russia was forming a ring of ethnic states on the periphery of the old imperial core.

In November 1918, some already existed: Finland, Estonia, Latvia, Lithuania, and Poland, and others fleetingly.[23] Discussion in the Supreme War Council over the boundaries of Poland had revealed some of the problems that would confront the peacemakers later. At the time of the armistice, attention was focused on the emergence of these new nations, not on drawing their frontiers. The following spring would see the peacemakers try to deal with the intractable problems of drawing proper ethnic lines of demarcation in Eastern Europe.

The problems of dealing with Russia that surfaced in discussions over the armistices—lack of information, concern for the anti-Bolsheviks, the inability to affect the situation directly—continued to cast shadows on the peace conference the following year. Whether a totally different policy, such as the recognition of Lenin's regime as the legitimate government over the core of old imperial Russia, would have made any real difference is doubtful, but the leaders never seriously considered it. The amendment that Foch agreed to include in the armistice, delaying German withdrawal from Russia until the Allies ordered it, did not help to solve the Russian puzzle. The Germans remained in Russia too long, and the situation became difficult before the Allies forced them to evacuate their soldiers in the fall of 1919.[24]

During the peace conference, the French tried diligently to get Allied agreement to some sort of arrangement for the Rhineland that would separate that territory, its six million people, and its resources from Germany. They failed at the conference table, and they failed when they sponsored a revolution in the Rhineland demanding autonomy. In the Versailles Treaty, they did get the occupation of the left bank for fifteen years and a promise, never carried out, that they might continue the occupation "if at that date the guarantees against unprovoked aggression by Germany are not considered sufficient by the Allied and Associated Governments."[25]

Unlike the provisions concerning land forces in the Bulgarian and Turkish armistices, the Compiègne Armistice did not demand that German land formations demobilize. Although it required the surrender of large quantities of equipment, it did not directly demand that the Germans demobilize their army. That caused uneasiness in the spring of 1919, when the German army remained, on paper at least, a formidable force, while political calls for Allied demobilization grew louder. The Versailles Treaty fixed that omission: not only did it forbid Germany's keeping much in the way of weapons, it also limited the size of the German land army to one hundred thousand men.[26]

Through the surrender of German submarines and the internment of other warships, the Compiègne Armistice effectively dismantled the German navy. The Versailles Treaty reduced it to about the size of Argentina's.[27] The Allies obtained no great advantage from the "or failing them, Allied ports" clause that had snaked its way into the armistice. The Allies interned the German warships in the British naval base of Scapa Flow, and the German caretaker forces left aboard the vessels scuttled them in June 1919, much to Allied consternation.[28] Admiral Beatty finally got his wish concerning Heligoland: the Versailles Treaty required demilitarization of the island.[29]

Leaving the blockade in force at the beginning of the armistice was an appropriate military measure, but its continuance during the months that followed caused great suffering in Germany. A blockade is an unfocused weapon, its effect as great against noncombatants as it is against armaments factories. The Allies, in keeping the blockade in force after January or February 1919—by which time, it had ceased to serve any visible military purpose—were exacting revenge on the civilian population of Germany, not legitimately protecting themselves from a military threat.

During the negotiation of the armistice, no one ever gave exact figures for the reparations the Allies expected to claim, although every indication was that the sum would be very large. That forecast was fulfilled, but not in the Versailles Treaty itself. The Allies had such difficulty in dealing with the problem among themselves that they simply claimed most of Germany's movable assets in the treaty and required the Germans to sign what was, in effect, a promissory note for an unspecified additional amount.[30] This demand for reparations, upon which all the Allies insisted, would constrict the peace conference and would poison international relations through the coming decade. Not until 1921 was a bill presented to the Germans, and then the Allies set Germans reparations at 132 billion gold marks. The sum was never paid.

Another unsettled question was whether Anglo-American cooperation, forged in wartime, would hold together under the stress of postwar naval and commercial competition. The danger, of course, was that the European powers would unite against the United States, diplomatically and commercially. Though that might happen in the short run, no great danger existed in the long run. The European nations needed the United States' economy to reconstruct their own shattered systems. Equally important, France and Italy would try to exclude Great Britain from the Continent, which would give the British nowhere to turn except to the United States. Relations among the other Allies was poor, too. Franco-Italian quarrels went deep, and Italian-Slav confrontations threatened to become open warfare during the period of the peace conference and after.

All that lay in the future. On November 11, 1918, it was still uncertain whether the new German government would—or could—carry out the armistice terms. Wiseman wrote House on the twelfth, saying that the leaders in London were confident that Germany could carry out the terms, but he himself was less sure.[31] With the advantage of hindsight, it is easy to say that the Allies did not have to worry about the German government's trying to satisfy the terms. Unless the new government could magically restore the morale of the soldiers and find armaments and supplies, there was no chance of any organized German military action impeding the Allies and the United States.

The only danger the Allies and the United States faced was that public order in Germany would break down so completely that the new government could not carry out the terms. General Bliss thought the Compiègne Armistice arrangements would cause a radical revolution in Germany. "The political leaders here have been unanimous in their dread of a Bolshevik revolution in Germany," he wrote to the secretary of war, "but it seems to me that they have done and are permitting the [Allied] military to do everything to make such a revolution possible."[32]

If revolution did occur, however, it would pose no military threat to the Allies and the United States. Indeed, it would leave Germany even more helpless to Allied dictates than it was. The only peril was the chance that radicalism might spread to the Allied armies, too. But on November 11, there was little sign of that in the French, British, or American armies, even though no one—no Allied leader, nor American, nor German—could begin to guess what might happen once the warring nations laid down their arms.[33]

All these events in the waning months of 1918 illustrate wonderfully well the problems of waging a coalition war, or, more precisely, ending a coalition war by forging a coalition peace. Mutual mistrust, conflicting national ambitions, indifference to the hopes and fears of one's partners, and intolerance toward the errors of one's partners all contributed in the fall of 1918 to shaping the negotiations over the armistice.

In earlier months, in the darkest days of the war, those problems could be, and were, overwhelmed by the will to survive. But when the leap toward victory began, and particularly when what amounted to the drafting of peace terms became central to events, differences among the victors emerged in all their virulence to steer events. That is the essence of coalition war and coalition peace.

Rudin ends his study of the armistice with the observation that the anniversary of the day the Compiègne Armistice with Germany was signed, November 11, was more celebrated around the world than June 28, the date the Versailles Treaty between Germany and the Allied and Associated Powers was signed in 1919.[34]

That difference, he wrote, was a "monument to the simple truth that men find it easier to end a war than to make a peace." But the Compiègne Armistice was both: it was a cessation of hostilities and it was a preliminary peace. The truth is that at Compiègne the two were joined in a single document.

Abbreviations in Notes

AAE	Archives des Affaires Étrangères, Ministère des Affaires Étrangères, Paris, France
AFGG	France, État-major des Armées, Service historiques, *Les armées françaises dans la Grande Guerre*
AN	Archives Nationales, Paris, France
BDIC	Bibliothèque de Documentation Internationale et Contemporaine, Nanterre, France
BN	Cabinet des Manuscripts, Bibliothèque Nationale, Paris, France
BOU	Manuscripts, Bodleian Library, Oxford University, Oxford, England
BL	Manuscripts, British Library, London, England
CCCU	Manuscripts, Churchill College, Cambridge University, Cambridge, England
HLRO	House of Lords Record Office, London, England
HCY	Edward M. House Collection, Yale University, New Haven, Connecticut
IORL	India Office Records and Library, London, England
IWM	Manuscripts, Imperial War Museum, London, England
LC	Manuscripts Division, Library of Congress, Washington, D.C.

LRO   Liverpool Record Office, Liverpool, England

NA   National Archives, Washington, D.C.

NLS   Manuscripts, National Library of Scotland, Edinburgh, Scotland

NMM   Manuscripts, National Maritime Museum, London (Greenwich), England

PRO   Public Record Office, London (Kew), England

SHAT   Service Historique de l'Armée de Terre, Archives de la Guerre, Vincennes, France

U.S. Army   United States, Department of the Army, Historical Division, *The United States Army in the World War, 1917–1919*

Notes

PREFACE

1. Charles Hardinge, Lord Hardinge, *Old Diplomacy* (London: Murray, 1947), 229. The British War Cabinet had ordered the army and navy leaders to prepare material on armistice terms for Germany, but nothing had come of it yet. War Cabinet 480, 1 October 1918, CAB 23/8, PRO. Edmonds states that the General Staff had studied armistice terms before October 1918, but no fruits of that effort seem to have reached high-level discussion. J. E. Edmonds and R. Maxwell-Hyslop, *Military Operations, France and Belgium, 1918*, Great Britain, Committee of Imperial Defence, Historical Section, 5 vols. (London: H.M. Stationery Office, 1947), 5:183. See also David Stevenson, *French War Aims Against Germany, 1914–1919* (Oxford: Clarendon Press, 1982), 110.

2. Michael Howard, *The Franco-Prussian War* (New York: Macmillan, 1962), 438–43.

3. Heinrich Friedjung, *The Struggle for Supremacy in Germany, 1859–1866*, trans. A. J. P. Taylor and W. L. McElwee (London: Macmillan, 1935), 266–79. The Russo-Japanese War was unusual in that the two warring nations made no armistice until the Peace of Portsmouth was practically ready for signature. Eugene P. Trani, *The Treaty of Portsmouth* (Lexington: University of Kentucky Press, 1969), 78.

4. Almodovar del Rio to William Day, 7 August 1898, U.S. Department of State, *Foreign Relations of the United States, 1898* (Washington, D.C.: Government Printing Office, 1901), 822–33. Basis for Establishment of Peace, 12 August 1898, U.S. Department of State, *Treaties and Other International Agreements of the United States of America, 1776–1945*, comp. Charles I. Bevans, 13 vols. (Washington, D.C.: Government Printing Office, 1968–76), 11:613–14.

5. For example, Great Britain, Foreign Office, *British Documents on the Origins of the War, 1898–1914,* ed. G. P. Gooch and Harold Temperley, 11 vols. in 13 pts. (London: H.M. Stationery Office, 1926–38), vol. 9, pt. 1:438–42, pt. 2:248–49, 1049–51.

6. Stevenson makes the astute comment that war aims are not a fixed item but are "cast in the conditional tense." *French War Aims Against Germany,* v.

7. General Sir Frederick Barton Maurice, *The Armistices of 1918* (New York: Oxford University Press, 1943); Harry R. Rudin, *Armistice, 1918* (New Haven, Conn.: Yale University Press, 1944); Brigadier C. N. Barclay, *Armistice, 1918* (South Brunswick, N.J.: A. S. Barnes, 1968); Pierre Renouvin, *L'Armistice de Rethondes: 11 novembre 1918,* Trente journées qui ont fait la France (Paris: Gallimard, 1968); Gordon Brook-Shepherd, *November 1918: The Last Act of the Great War* (London: Collins, 1981); Stanley Weintraub, *A Stillness Heard Round the World: The End of the Great War: November, 1918* (New York: Truman Talley Books, E. P. Dutton, 1985).

INTRODUCTION: THE SITUATION, SEPTEMBER 1918

1. The bulk of the following account comes from Erzberger. Mathias Erzberger, *Erlebnisse im Weltkrieg* (Stuttgart: Deutsche Verlagsanstalt, 1920), 328–30.

2. Solf to von Hintze, Berlin, 10 November 1918, Germany, Reichskanzlei, *Preliminary History of the Armistice,* trans. Carnegie Endowment for International Peace (New York: Oxford University Press, 1924), 150; Erzberger, *Erlebnisse,* 335.

3. Renouvin, *Armistice,* 47–48.

4. Austro-Hungarian Peace Note, U.S. Department of State, *Papers Relating to the Foreign Relations of the United States, 1918,* supplement 1, *The World War,* 2 vols. (Washington, D.C.: Government Printing Office, 1933), 1:306–9 (hereafter cited as *Foreign Relations, 1918, World War*).

5. Address of President Wilson to a Joint Session of Congress, 11 February 1918, *Foreign Relations, 1918, World War* 1:108–13.

6. In September 1918, the Army of the East had twenty-nine divisions: eight French, six Serbian, ten Greek, four English, and one Italian; facing them were three Bulgarian armies, an Austrian army corps, and the German Eleventh Army. General Henri Mordacq, *Le ministère Clemenceau: journal d'un témoin,* 4 vols. (Paris: Plon, 1930–31), 2:246.

CHAPTER 1. THE CONFERENCE OF
PRIME MINISTERS AND THE FIRST GERMAN NOTE

1. Milne to War Office, 26 September 1918, file no. 163316, and Minute by H. G. N[icolson], 27 September 1918, FO 371/3447, PRO; Franchet d'Esperey to Clemenceau, 27 September 1918, 6 N 71, SHAT; Lt. Col. [G. G.?] Heywood to

GHQ, Salonika, 13 October 1918, Appendix, WO 158/765, PRO.

2. Franchet d'Esperey to Clemenceau, 27 September 1918, and note 60, France, État-major des Armées, Service Historiques, *Les armées françaises dans la Grande Guerre*, tome 8, *Le campagne d'Orient*, 3 vols., with 3 vols. of documents and 1 vol. of maps annexed (Paris: Imprimerie Nationale, 1934), 8, Annexes, 2:913–14 (hereafter cited as *AFGG* 8); Clemenceau to Franchet d'Esperey, 27 September 1918, 6 N 71, SHAT.

3. Paul Cambon, London, to Pichon, 27 September 1918, and Balfour for Lloyd George to Clemenceau, 28 September 1918, both in 6 N 71, SHAT.

4. Franchet d'Esperey to Ministry of War, 30 September 1918, *AFGG* 8, Annexes, 2:980. For a procès-verbal, see Franchet d'Esperey to Clemenceau, 24 October 1918, filed 7 November 1918, 6 N 71, SHAT.

5. Cyril Falls, *Military Operations: Macedonia,* Great Britain, Committee of Imperial Defence, Historical Section, 2 vols. (London: H.M. Stationery Office, 1935), 2:251. See also British Salonika Force, War Diary, 28 September 1918, WO 95/4757, PRO.

6. R. W. Bliss to Lansing, The Hague, 27 September 1918, *Foreign Relations, 1918, World War* 1:322. See also R. W. Bliss to American Embassy, London, 27 September 1918, London Embassy Correspondence, 1918, vol. 58, RG 84, NA.

7. Lansing to R. W. Bliss, 27 September 1918, *Foreign Relations, 1918, World War* 1:324.

8. Lansing to T. N. Page, Rome, et al., 2 October 1918, *Foreign Relations, 1918, World War* 1:334; Barrère, Rome, to Ministry of Foreign Affairs, 1 October 1918, 6 N 71, SHAT. The British responded officially only on 6 November, saying then they agreed with the United States' position. London Embassy Correspondence, 1918, vol. 58, RG 84, NA.

9. Derby to Lloyd George, 30 September 1918, file no. 165014, FO 371/3447, PRO; Clemenceau to Jusserand, 1 October 1918, 6 N 71, SHAT.

10. Derby to Balfour, 11 October 1918, 920 DER(17) 28/2/1, LRO. Clemenceau warned the French ambassador in Washington to avoid conversations on the subject. Clemenceau to Jusserand, 20 October 1918, 6 N 71, SHAT.

11. Clemenceau to Paul Cambon for Lloyd George, 30 September 1918, 6 N 71, SHAT. See also Raymond Poincaré, *Au service de la France,* 11 vols. (Paris: Plon, 1926–33, 1974), 10:369.

12. Hankey diary, 3 October 1918, HNKY 1/16, CCCU; Balfour to Colville Barclay [British chargé in Washington], 10 October 1918, file no. 169743, FO 371/3442, PRO. As late as 7 October, Clemenceau suggested using Bulgarian troops in concert with Allied forces, which would require a peace treaty. Clemenceau to Franchet d'Esperey and Gen. H.-M. Berthelot, 7 October 1918, 6 N 71, SHAT. The Italians were ready to accept Bulgaria as a cobelligerent. Lord Robert Cecil, Report of Conversation with Baron Sonnino, 12 October 1918, file no. 171073, FO 371/3444, PRO.

13. Lord Granville, Athens, to Balfour, 26 October 1918, file no. 148849, FO 371/3160, PRO; Lt. Col. [G. G.?] Heywood to GHQ, Salonika, 13 October 1918, WO 158/765, PRO. See also Henry Dundas Napier, *Experiences of a Military Attaché in the Balkans* (London: Drane's, 1924), 242. It is difficult to avoid speculation about whether the Bulgarian situation would have changed if Germany and Austria-Hungary had fought on for another six months.

14. See note 3 above. Derby to Lloyd George, 30 September 1918, file no. 165014, FO 371/3447, PRO.

15. Derby to Lloyd George, 2 October 1918, and Foreign Office to Sir R. Rodd, 2 October 1918, both in file no. 165842, FO 371/3434, PRO. See also Derby to Arthur [Balfour], Paris, 2 October 1918, Balfour Papers, Add. MSS 49744, BL, and Derby diary, 2 October 1918, 920 DER(17) 28/1/1, LRO.

16. Maurice, Lord Hankey, *The Supreme Command, 1914–1918,* 2 vols. (London: Allen and Unwin, 1961), 2:840, and Hankey diary, 5 October 1918, HNKY 1/6, CCCU.

17. Hankey diary, 5 October 1918, HNKY 1/6, CCCU; Derby diary, 5 October 1918, 920 DER(17) 28/1/1, LRO.

18. I.C.-76, Procès-verbal of a Conference, 5 October 1918, 1700, CAB 28/5, PRO. These records are British. The British secretary to the War Cabinet, M. P. A. Hankey, generally served as secretary to these conferences, and the French and Italians used his minutes. The usual interpreter, Paul Mantoux, was French, and some of his notes are preserved in the Paul Mantoux Papers, BDIC.

19. Hankey diary, 5 October 1918, HNKY 1/6, CCCU. The liaison was Hugh Frazier, first secretary of the United States' embassy in Paris.

20. Foch had already given Clemenceau advice on how to exploit the Bulgarian surrender: cut the German rail lines to Constantinople, occupy strategic points in Bulgaria, and push a bridgehead across the Danube. Foch Memorandum, 4 October 1918, 6 N 71, SHAT.

21. Henry Wilson diary, 5 October 1918, HHW 1/32, IWM. Selections from the Wilson diary have been printed in Major General Sir C. E. Callwell, *Field Marshal Sir Henry Wilson, His Life and Diaries,* 2 vols. (London: Cassel, 1927); it is very dangerous to use Callwell's version without comparing it to the original.

22. Hankey diary, 5 October 1918, HNKY 1/6, CCCU.

23. There is still confusion over the precise course of events in Germany, the General Staff records that might solve the puzzles having been destroyed in 1945. For a narrative focusing on the German Foreign Office, see Klaus Schwabe, *Woodrow Wilson, Revolutionary Germany, and Peacemaking, 1918–1919: Missionary Diplomacy and the Realities of Power,* trans. Rita Kimber and Robert Kimber (Chapel Hill: University of North Carolina Press, 1985), 31–39.

24. Oederlin [Swiss chargé] to Wilson, 6 October 1918, enclosing Max of Baden to Wilson, *Foreign Relations, 1918, World War* 1:337–38, formally presented on 7 October. See also Maurice, *Armistices of 1918,* 27.

25. Their note of 14 September had requested negotiations over peace terms, not an armistice. This note was Ekengren to Lansing, 7 October 1918, enclosing Imperial and Royal Government to Wilson, *Foreign Relations, 1918, World War* 1:341. The Austro-Hungarian story is a complicated one: Hungarian leaders, for example, made overtures to the British, who saw no profit in separate negotiations. See minutes to file no. 166364, FO 371/3437, PRO.

26. I.C.-77, Procès-verbal of a Conference, 6 October 1918, 1500, CAB 28/5, PRO.

27. For the Sixtus Affair, see Z. A. B. Zeman, *The Gentlemen Negotiators: A Diplomatic History of the First World War* (New York: Macmillan, 1971), 131–42. For the 1917 events from a German perspective, see Gerhard Ritter, *Staatskunst und Kriegshandwerk: Das Problem des Militarismus in Deutschland,* vol. 4, *Die Herrschaft des Deutschen Militarismus und die Katastrophe von 1918* (Munich: R. Oldenburg, 1968), chap. 1, pt. 1.

28. Mordacq, *Clemenceau* 2:250.

29. See note 24 above.

30. Hankey, *Supreme Command* 2:853.

31. See preface, note 1. Of course, only six months earlier, the military leaders had been drafting plans for the evacuation of Paris and the defense of the British islands against invasion. See such documents as Organisation of Lines of Communication in Event of Operations in United Kingdom, May 1918, WO 33/878, PRO, and Derby to Foreign Office, 20 June 1918, file no. 111908, FO 371/3214, PRO.

32. The Allies treated Luxembourg, here and later, as a German-occupied neutral country despite the close collaboration of Luxembourg's ruler with Germany.

33. See General Bliss's analysis, Bliss to Adjutant General, 7 October 1918, U.S. Department of the Army, Historical Division, *The United States Army in the World War, 1917–1919* 10:5 (hereafter cited as *U.S. Army*).

34. Henry Newbolt, *Naval Operations,* vol. 5, *From April 1917 to the End of the War,* Great Britain, Committee of Imperial Defence, Historical Section (London: Longmans, Green, 1931), 351–52; Draft, ADM 116/1931, PRO.

35. See note 26 above.

36. I.C.-78, Procès-verbal of a Conference, 7 October 1918, 10:30, CAB 28/5, PRO. This meeting was not, strictly speaking, part of the Conference of Prime Ministers, because only British leaders met with the marshal.

37. I.C.-79, Procès-verbal of a Conference, 7 October 1918, 1500, CAB 28/5, PRO.

38. Franchet d'Esperey to Armies, 4 October 1918, WO 95/4757, PRO, and Instructions for Armies, GHQ, Salonika, 5 October 1918, 5346/3, *AFGG* 8, Annexes, 3:87. See also Paul Azan, *Franchet d'Esperey* (Paris: Flammarion, 1949), 213, and Falls, *Military Operations: Macedonia* 2:260–61.

39. Franchet d'Esperey also ordered four French divisions to march into Albania, which the Treaty of London had awarded to Italy as a protectorate. That

movement does not appear in the Instructions for Armies, 5 October 1918, note 38 above, but is reported in Henrys to Franchet d'Esperey, 3 October 1918, *AFGG* 8, Annexes, 3, 60–63. See also ibid., 73, and Carte 17, "Le dispositif des AAO prévu par le plan d'action du 5 octobre 1918 et modifié le 10 octobre 1918," *AFGG* 8, Map volume.

40. See note 38 above.

41. He also agreed to stop the French troop movement toward Albania. His orders on both subjects went as Clemenceau to Franchet d'Esperey, 7 October 1918, *AFGG* 8, Annexes, 3:126, and the attached note concerning Albania. Cf. Franchet d'Esperey to Princep, 8 October 1918, *AFGG* 8, Annexes, 3:141, and Instructions, Salonika, 10 October 1918, *AFGG* 8, Annexes, 3:168–70. See also Azan, *Franchet d'Esperey,* 212–16, and Troopers (London) to Milne, 8 October 1918, WO 95/4757, PRO.

42. At this same time, the Italians ordered General Lord Cavan, commander of the British corps in Italy, to take command of the reserve. WO 106/835, PRO. That removed Cavan from the front lines of the coming Austro-Hungarian occupation. Cavan's unpublished memoirs show no concern over the matter. "Recollections, Hazy But Happy," chap. 12, CAVN 1/3, CCCU.

43. Guy Pedroncini, *Les mutineries de 1917* (Paris: Presses Universitaires de France, 1967).

44. Continuing French military concern over the morale of the soldiers is seen in Fayolle to Mangin, 3 October 1918, Mangin Papers, 149 AP 20, AN.

45. The Military Representatives and the Supreme War Council both came from the Rapallo Agreement of November 1917. Minutes of a Conference, Rapallo, 7 November 1917, Annex 1, *U.S. Army* 2:72.

46. Bliss to N. D. Baker, 9 October 1918, Bliss Papers, box 74 (9a/1–28), LC.

47. Bliss was unnecessarily suspicious. The prime ministers were already giving their views, or at least Lloyd George was, to Hugh Frazier, the United States' diplomatic liaison officer with the Supreme War Council. See, for example, Frazier's 141 of 7 October 1918, *Foreign Relations, 1918, World War* 1:344–45.

48. See Bliss to Adjutant General for Baker and March, 8 October 1918, *U.S. Army* 10:6–7.

49. Ludendorff speaking at the office of the imperial chancellor, 9 October 1918. Germany, Reichskanzlei, *Preliminary History of the Armistice,* 56.

50. Henry Wilson diary, 8 October 1918, HHW 1/32, IWM.

51. The committee justified this addition by referring to the speech President Wilson had made on 27 September 1918. See chapter 2.

52. Appendix 1 to I.C.-80, Conference of Prime Ministers, 8 October 1918, 1500, CAB 28/5, PRO. See also Ferdinand Foch, *Mémoires pour servir à l'histoire de la guerre de 1914–1918,* 2 vols. (Paris: Plon, 1931), 2:270–72.

53. Maxime Weygand, *Idéal vécu,* vol. 1 of *Mémoires* (Paris: Flammarion, 1953), 623; iaem, *Foch* (Paris: Flammarion, 1947), 260.

54. Points Seven and Eight of the Fourteen Points proposed "restoration" of Belgium and the invaded territory of France, but Wilson in his 11 February 1918 speech to Congress said that there should be no "punitive damages." *Foreign Relations, 1918, World War* 1:110.

55. Renouvin discusses Aristide Briand's 1917 efforts to gain the Rhine through the use of diplomacy. *Armistice*, 211–12.

56. Foch claimed later that those southern bridgeheads would let him turn the German defenses, but he was stretching. Foch, *Mémoires* 2:272.

57. I.C.-80, Conference of Prime Ministers, 8 October 1918, 1500, CAB 28/5, PRO. See also Report of Conversation between Lord Robert Cecil and Baron Sonnino, [8 October 1918], file no. 171073, FO 371/3444, PRO.

58. Such is Lord Robert Cecil's summary, Derby to Foreign Office, 8 October 1918, file no. 169092, FO 371/3442, PRO.

59. Hankey diary, 8 October 1918, HNKY 1/6, CCCU.

60. Frazier to Lansing, 144, 8 October 1918, *Foreign Relations, 1918, World War* 1:346.

61. Henry Wilson diary, 9 October 1918, HHW 1/32, IWM.

62. See chapter 2 for citation to, and extended discussion of, the First Wilson Note.

63. I.C.-81, Conference of Prime Ministers, 9 October 1918, CAB 28/5, PRO. See also Hankey diary, 9 October 1918, HNKY 1/6, CCCU.

64. Apparently, Hankey had written the actual document. Henry Wilson diary, 9 October 1918, HHW 1/32, IWM, and Hankey, *Supreme Command* 2:854–55. This telegram and one adopted immediately afterward were sent through the diplomatic liaison officer as Frazier to Lansing, 147 and 148, both of 9 October 1918, *Foreign Relations, 1918, World War* 1:353–54. Quotes below are translated from the French text in the procès-verbal of the meeting.

65. Foch, who did not like Clemenceau, stresses that Lloyd George forced the idea on a reluctant French prime minister. Foch, *Mémoires* 2:273.

66. Frazier to Lansing, 145, 9 October 1918, *Foreign Relations, 1918, World War* 1:351–52.

67. Henri Mordacq, *Pouvait-on signer l'armistice à Berlin?* (Paris: Grasset, [1930]), 3–4, 14.

CHAPTER 2. WOODROW WILSON, THE FOURTEEN POINTS, AND THE GERMAN NOTES

1. Renouvin, *Armistice*, 396.

2. John Maynard Keynes, *The Economic Consequences of the Peace* (New York: Harcourt, Brace and Howe, 1920), 56–57, 60. Many other commentators use the word "contract." See, for example, Bernadotte Schmitt, "Peace Treaties of 1919–1920," *Proceedings of the American Philosophical Society* 104 (1960):102.

3. David Lloyd George, *Memoirs of the Peace Conference,* 2 vols. (New Haven, Conn.: Yale University Press, 1939), 1:145.

4. The text used is *Foreign Relations, 1918, World War* 1:15–16. See also Charles Seymour, ed., *The Intimate Papers of Colonel House,* 4 vols. (Boston: Houghton Mifflin, 1926–28), 3:317–38, and Inquiry Memorandum no. 887, 22 December 1917, U.S. Department of State, *Papers Relating to the Foreign Relations of the United States, 1919, The Paris Peace Conference,* 13 vols. (Washington, D.C.: Government Printing Office, 1942–47), 1:41–53 (hereafter cited as *Foreign Relations, 1919, Paris Peace Conference*). For general discussions, see L. E. Gelfand, *The Inquiry* (New Haven, Conn.: Yale University Press, 1963), 135–53, Arno J. Mayer, *Political Origins of the New Diplomacy* (New Haven, Conn.: Yale University Press, 1959), 329–67, and Charles Seymour, *American Diplomacy in the World War* (Baltimore: Johns Hopkins University Press, 1934), 282–90.

5. Wilson to Lansing, 12 March 1918, *Congressional Record* (12 June 1918), 65th Cong., 2d sess., 1918, pt. 56:7653.

6. For legal and historical background, see Pitman B. Potter, *The Freedom of the Seas in History, Law, and Politics* (New York: Longmans, Green, 1924).

7. Wilson to House, private code series 6, 31 October 1918, Wilson Papers, Series 2, LC.

8. The British had read the European and Near Eastern treaties to him, and Russian revolutionaries had published them. He also knew of the Far Eastern arrangements. Foreign Office, Statement on Japanese Claims to Pacific Islands North of the Equator, 15 October 1918, Cabinet Paper G.T.-6078, CAB 24/67, PRO. See also Balfour to Barclay, 10 October 1918, file no. 169743, FO 371/3442, PRO.

9. Address by Lloyd George at Caxton Hall, London, 5 January 1918, *New York Times,* 6 January 1918.

10. Wilson speaking to Sir William Wiseman, Memorandum by Wiseman, 16 October 1918, John Snell, ed., "Wilson on Germany and the Fourteen Points," *Journal of Modern History* 26 (1954): 364–69.

11. 11 February 1918, *Foreign Relations, 1918, World War* 1:108–13; 4 July 1918, ibid., 268–71; 27 September 1918, ibid., 316–21.

12. Seymour, *Intimate Papers of Colonel House* 3:37; Wilson to House, 21 July 1917, Ray Stannard Baker, *Woodrow Wilson, Life and Letters,* 8 vols. (New York: Doubleday Page, Doubleday Doran, 1927–28), 7:180–81.

13. Lloyd George, *Memoirs of the Peace Conference* 1:38.

14. Ibid., 158.

15. Wythe Williams, *The Tiger of France: Conversations with Clemenceau* (New York: Duell, Sloan and Pearce, [1949]), 186, and Mordacq, *Clemenceau* 2:295 n.1.

16. Barclay to [Balfour], Washington, 7 October 1918, Balfour Papers, Add. MSS 49748, BL.

17. House's is the only full account of these discussions, and he credits himself for whatever success appeared. House diary, 9 October 1918, HCY. See also Lan-

sing desk diary, 7 and 8 October 1918, Lansing Papers, box 3, LC. A lenient draft in the Wilson Papers, Series 2, LC, offers no evidence on who was responsible for strengthening it.

18. Schwabe, *Woodrow Wilson, Revolutionary Germany, and Peacemaking,* 41–42, gives a summary of the advice Wilson was getting.

19. Private memorandum, 7 October 1918, Lansing Papers, box 1, LC. There is no evidence that Lansing actually presented this memorandum to Wilson, but his position was a defensible one, and he probably voiced it.

20. Private memorandum, 12 October 1918, Lansing Papers, box 1, LC.

21. Lansing desk diary, 8 October 1918, Lansing Papers, box 3, LC. The text is Lansing to Oederlin for Prince Max, 8 October 1918, *Foreign Relations, 1918, World War* 1:343.

22. Daniels diary, 8 October 1918, Daniels Papers, box 3, LC.

23. Bliss to Adjutant General for Baker and March, 8 October 1918, *U.S. Army* 10:5. See also Tasker Bliss, "The Armistices," *American Journal of International Law* 16 (1922):513, 515, and Barclay to Foreign Office, enclosing Wiseman to Reading and Drummond, 9 October 1918, file no. 169743, FO 371/3442, PRO.

24. Lansing desk diary, 9 October 1918, Lansing Papers, box 3, LC. On Wiseman's status, see W. B. Fowler, *British-American Relations, 1917–1918: The Role of Sir William Wiseman* (Princeton, N.J.: Princeton University Press, 1969).

25. Barclay to Foreign Office, 9 October 1918, enclosing Wiseman to Reading and Drummond, 9 October 1918, file no. 169742, FO 371/3442, PRO. For Reading's response, see Reading to Wiseman, 10 October 1918, Balfour Papers, FO 800/255, PRO.

26. Balfour to Barclay and handwritten addition, 10 October 1918, file no. 169743, FO 371/3442, PRO, and Balfour to Barclay, 14 October 1918, file no. 171764, FO 371/3444, PRO.

27. Polk diary, 9 and 10 October 1918, HCY.

28. Barclay to Foreign Office, very urgent, very secret, 10 October 1918, file no. 170667, FO 371/3444, PRO.

29. Wiseman to Reading and Drummond, 13 October 1918, Balfour Papers, Add. MSS 49741, BL. See also Balfour to Barclay, draft, [13 October 1918], file no. 171764, FO 371/3444, PRO, and Barclay to Foreign Office, 14 October 1918, file no. 172297, FO 371/3444, PRO.

30. Schwabe, *Woodrow Wilson, Revolutionary Germany, and Peacemaking,* 47–50.

31. Oederlin to Lansing, 14 October 1918, enclosing Solf to Wilson, *Foreign Relations, 1918, World War* 1:357–58. See also Ludendorff to von Haeften, Berlin, 11 October 1918, Germany, Reichskanzlei, *Preliminary History of the Armistice,* 62, and Conference of 12 October 1918, ibid., 63.

32. House diary, 15 October 1918, HCY. Seymour, when he edited the following passage, changed the pronouns, from "we" to "he," and dropped the "I" from before "offered." *Intimate Papers of Colonel House* 4:83.

33. Sir Eric Geddes to Lloyd George, personal and confidential, 13 October 1918, Wiseman Papers, drawer 90, folder 53, HCY.

34. Lansing desk diary, 14 October 1918, Lansing Papers, box 3, LC; Note on Cabinet Meetings, 23 October 1918, A. W. Lane and L. H. Wall, eds., *The Letters of Franklin K. Lane, Personal and Political* (Boston: Houghton Mifflin, 1922), 293; Daniels diary, 14 October 1918, Daniels Papers, box 3, LC; House diary, 14 and 15 October 1918, HCY.

35. Barclay to Balfour, 14 October 1918, Milner Papers, box 127, BOU. See Lansing to Wilson, 14 October 1918, enclosing Balfour to Barclay, 6182, 6183, and 6184 of 13 October 1918, Wilson Papers, Series 2, LC. For further discussion of those telegrams, see chapter 3.

36. War Cabinet 485, 14 October 1918, 1200, CAB 23/8, PRO.

37. Wilson Papers, Series 2, LC. See also Daniels diary, 14 October 1918, Daniels Papers, box 3, LC. Schwabe argues that domestic politics was also a factor in Wilson's becoming harsher. *Woodrow Wilson, Revolutionary Germany, and Peacemaking,* 51, 54.

38. Sent as Lansing to Oederlin, 14 October 1918, for the German Government, *Foreign Relations, 1918, World War* 1:358–59.

39. Brook-Shepherd argues that, on the contrary, this passage demonstrates Wilson intended the overthrow of monarchy in both Germany and Austria-Hungary. *November 1918,* 241–42. That seems to make too much of what the president was actually saying.

40. Barclay to Foreign Office, 16 October 1918, file no. 174313, FO 371/3442, PRO.

41. Lansing to Laughlin, 14 October 1918, *Foreign Relations, 1918, World War* 1:361, and similar to U.S. embassies in France and Italy. See also Barclay to Foreign Office, 14 October 1918, file no. 172225, FO 371/3442, PRO. Cf. file no. 172297, FO 371/3444, PRO.

42. Poincaré, *Au service* 10:388. See Émile E. Herbillon, *Du général en chef au gouvernement: souvenirs d'une officier de liaison pendant la Grande Guerre,* 2 vols. (Paris: Tallandier, 1930), 2:328–29, and Réné M. M. L'Hôpital, *Foch, l'armistice et la paix* (Paris: Plon, 1938), 26. See also War Cabinet 486, 15 October 1918, 1130, CAB 23/8, PRO, and Reading to Wiseman, 15 October 1918, House-Wiseman Correspondence, HCY. See also minutes on file no. 172216, FO 371/3444, PRO, and Derby to Balfour, 17 October 1918, 920 (DER)17 28/2/1, LRO.

43. Schwabe, *Woodrow Wilson, Revolutionary Germany, and Peacemaking,* 55.

44. Full Session of 17 October 1918, Germany, Reichskanzlei, *Preliminary History of the Armistice,* 78–99.

45. Oederlin to Lansing, 22 October 1918, enclosing Solf to Wilson, 20 October 1918, *Foreign Relations, 1918, World War* 1:379–81.

46. Barrie Pitt writes about the "bravado" of the Third German Note. *1918: The Last Act* (New York: Norton, 1962), 263.

47. Renouvin, *Armistice,* 133.

48. Derby to Foreign Office, 23 October 1918, file no. 177183, FO 371/3445, PRO.

49. Holograph draft, Balfour to Barclay, 21 October 1918, repeated to Paris and Rome, file no. 175883, FO 371/3444, PRO.

50. Lansing desk diary, 21 October 1918, Lansing Papers, box 3, LC.

51. The United States kept no official records of cabinet meetings. Only three accounts of this cabinet meeting exist, and they disagree with each other: Daniels diary, 22 October 1918, Daniels Papers, box 3, LC; Lane and Wall, *Letters of Franklin K. Lane,* 293–96; David F. Houston, *Eight Years with Wilson's Cabinet, 1913–1920,* 2 vols. (Garden City, N.Y.: Doubleday, Page, 1926), 1:308–17.

52. Thomas J. Knock believes that Wilson expected his acceptance of basic Allied military terms to force the Allies to accept his program. *To End All Wars: Woodrow Wilson and the Quest for a New World Order* (New York: Oxford University Press, 1992), 175.

53. Wilson read his text to Lansing, Daniels, and Gen. Peyton C. March. Lansing desk diary, 23 October 1918, Lansing Papers, box 3, LC. Note sent as Lansing to Oederlin for German Government, 23 October 1918, *Foreign Relations, 1918, World War* 1:381–82.

54. Sir Eric Geddes to Lloyd George, private and personal, 13 October 1918, Wiseman Papers, drawer 90, folder 53, HCY.

55. Wiseman to Reading and Drummond, 16 October 1918, Wiseman Papers, drawer 91, folder 108, HCY, published in Snell, "Wilson on Germany and the Fourteen Points," 364–69.

56. Barclay to Foreign Office, 19 October 1918, Milner Papers, box 131, BOU.

57. For list of telegrams, see *Foreign Relations, 1918, World War* 1:383.

58. Inga Flota makes much of Wilson's sending this correspondence to the Allies without recommendation. Inga Flota, *Colonel House in Paris: A Study of American Policy at the Paris Peace Conference, 1919* (Princeton, N.J.: Princeton University Press, 1980), 40. That does not describe the situation. The act of sending it to the Allies was a recommendation.

59. Oederlin to Lansing, 28 October 1918, transmitting Solf to Wilson, 27 October 1918, *Foreign Relations, 1918, World War* 1:395–96. It was the dismissal of Ludendorff on 26 October that freed Prince Max to send this note. Rudin, *Armistice, 1918,* 211–12.

CHAPTER 3. GREAT BRITAIN AND THE ARMISTICE

1. Lloyd George *"was a prime minister without a party."* Lord Beaverbrook, *The Decline and Fall of Lloyd George* (New York: Duell, Sloan and Pearce, 1963), 9.

2. R[obert] C[ecil] to his cousin, Arthur [Balfour], Paris, 7 October 1918, Balfour Papers, FO 800/201, PRO.

3. David Lloyd George, *War Memoirs,* 6 vols. (London: Ivor Nicholson and Watson, 1933–36), 6:3255.

4. Lloyd George, *Memoirs of the Peace Conference* 2:518–20.

5. Balfour to Sir Rennell Rodd, 14 October 1918, Milner Papers, box 131, BOU. The British also argued that the Rome Congress Agreement (1918) superseded the Treaty of London (1915), but got nowhere. Policy Commission of the British War Mission, 9 October 1918, Balfour Papers, FO 800/212, PRO.

6. Lord Robert Cecil, Memorandum, 8 October 1918, Cabinet Paper G.T.-5955, approved by cabinet and printed as appendix to War Cabinet 485, 14 October 1918, CAB 23/8, PRO. Cf. War Cabinet 482A, 3 October 1918, CAB 23/14, PRO, and Cecil to Pichon, 8 October 1918, Curzon Papers, Eur F.112/276, IORL. See also Lloyd George Papers, F/52/2/37, HLRO. The French demanded that the British keep the wartime agreements. French Embassy Memorandum, 22 October 1918, Curzon Papers, Eur F.112/276, IORL.

7. War Cabinet 482A, 3 October 1918, CAB 23/14. See other opinions favoring cooperation with the United States, such as Derby to Sir Eric Drummond, Paris, 7 October 1918, Balfour Papers, Add. MSS 49378, BL.

8. The Army Council forecast a shortage of 171,000 men by mid-1919. Army Council Memorandum, 24 October 1918, Cabinet Paper G.T.-6099, CAB 24/67, PRO. On Ireland, see the series of Cabinet Papers presented between 7 and 9 October, G.T.-5918, -5919, and -5929, CAB 24/66, PRO.

9. J. M. Bourne, *Britain and the Great War, 1914–1918* (London: Edward Arnold, 1989), 187.

10. Fortnightly Report on Pacifism and Revolutionary Organisations in the United Kingdom [Number 23], 7 October 1918, Cabinet Paper G.T.-5986, CAB 24/66, PRO.

11. War Cabinet 480, 1 October 1918, CAB 23/8, PRO. See also Bolshevik Propaganda, 12 October 1918, Cabinet Paper G.T.-5986, CAB 24/66, PRO.

12. The procès-verbal is Draft Notes of a Conference Held at Danny, 13 October 1918, Cabinet Paper G.T.-5967, CAB 24/66, PRO. See also Hankey diary, 13 October 1918, HNKY 1/5, CCCU. Those present were Andrew Bonar Law (chancellor of the Exchequer and Conservative, properly Unionist, leader), A. J. Balfour (secretary of state for Foreign Affairs), Winston Churchill (minister of Munitions), Lord Milner (secretary of state for War), Lord Reading (ambassador to the United States), Rosslyn Wemyss (first sea lord), Henry Wilson (chief of the Imperial General Staff), Philip Kerr (Lloyd George's secretary), and M. P. A. Hankey (secretary of the War Cabinet).

13. War Cabinet 484 (Imperial War Cabinet 35), 11 October 1918, CAB 23/8, PRO.

14. Balfour got more bloodthirsty as the war entered its final phase; he had just proposed systematic terror-bombing of German cities. A. J. B[alfour], Reparation for Acts of Devastation, Reprisals, 8 October 1918, Cabinet Paper G.T.-

5931, CAB 24/66, PRO.

15. Henry Wilson diary, 13 October 1918, HHW 1/32, IWM.

16. Thus reported by Balfour to War Cabinet 485, 14 October 1918, CAB 23/8, PRO. See also Policy Committee of the British War Mission, Memorandum, 9 October 1918, enclosed in Northcliffe to War Cabinet, 10 October 1918, Balfour Papers, FO 800/212, PRO. Lloyd George quotes part of that memorandum in his *War Memoirs* 6:3284–85.

17. See chapter 2.

18. War Cabinet 485, 14 October 1918, CAB 23/8, PRO. See also Hankey to Lloyd George, 18 October 1918, Lloyd George Papers, F/23/3/17, HLRO.

19. Bonar Law to Balfour, 5 October 1918, Robert Blake, *Unrepentant Tory: The Life and Times of Andrew Bonar Law, 1858–1923* (New York: St. Martin's, 1956), 384–85.

20. War Cabinet 486, 15 October 1918, CAB 23/8, PRO. From 14 to 19 October, the leaders sent a number of memoranda to each other. See also Harold I. Nelson, *Land and Power: British and Allied Policy on Germany's Frontiers, 1916–1919* (Toronto: University of Toronto Press, 1963), 61–68.

21. Lloyd George, *War Memoirs* 6:3404. Sir Henry's greatest admirers were French soldiers, surely unusual for Britain's highest staff officer. See, for example, Weygand, *Mirages et réalité*, vol. 2 of *Mémoires* (Paris: Flammarion, 1957), 25–26. Clemenceau despised him. Derby diary, 2 October 1918, 920 DER(17) 28/1/1, LRO.

22. On Bolshevism, see Henry Wilson diary, 15 and 17 October 1918, HHW 1/32, IWM. On President Wilson, see entry of 15 October 1918. On the Irish situation, see entries of 11, 13, and 16 October 1918.

23. Haig diary, 21 October 1918, H 132, NLS.

24. Henry Wilson diary, 16 October 1918, HHW 1/32, IWM; War Cabinet 487, 16 October 1918, CAB 23/8, PRO.

25. *War Memoirs* 6:3378.

26. 30 November 1918, H 132, NLS.

27. Haig diary, 10 October 1918, H 132, NLS. See also Raymond Recouly, *Le mémorial de Foch: Mes entretiens avec le maréchal* (Paris: Éditions de France, 1929), 47–48.

28. Haig diary, 13 October 1918, H 132, NLS.

29. Haig to Henry Wilson, 13 October 1918, Henry Wilson to Haig (personal), 13 October 1918, and Henry Wilson to Haig, 14 October 1918, all in H 132, NLS.

30. Henry Wilson diary, 19 October 1918, HHW 1/32, IWM, and Haig diary, 19 October 1918, H 132, NLS.

31. The minutes are in the most secret series, War Cabinet X-29, 19 October 1918, CAB 23/17, PRO. The diaries of Haig and Sir Henry agree with each other and the minutes. See also Lloyd George, *War Memoirs* 6:3299–3304. Admiral Wemyss attended, but no representative of the newly independent air force was present. The chief of the Air Staff gave his recommendations only on 22 October

in Main Requirements of the Royal Air Force, Cabinet Paper G.T.-6076, CAB 24/67, PRO.

32. Hankey to Curzon, 21 October 1918, Curzon Papers, Eur F.112/121b, IORL.

33. Milner diary, 19 October 1918, Milner Papers, box 281, BOU.

34. Lloyd George, *War Memoirs* 6:3300.

35. Perhaps Lloyd George was being an Easterner to the last.

36. Wemyss to Beatty, 16 October 1918, BTY/13/40/6, NMM.

37. Beatty to Wemyss, 17 October 1918, BTY/13/40/7, NMM.

38. Rear Admiral W. S. Chalmers, *The Life and Letters of David, Earl Beatty* (London: Hodder and Stoughton, 1951), 328.

39. Wemyss to Beatty, 18 October 1918, BTY/13/40/9, NMM.

40. There is a serious contradiction between the minutes and Wemyss, Admiralty Memorandum for War Cabinet, 19 October 1918, Cabinet Paper G.T.-6042, CAB 24/67, PRO, which printed what Wemyss supposedly presented. The memorandum asked for the surrender of the German warships, but the minutes of War Cabinet X-29, CAB 23/17, PRO, have him only requiring the withdrawal of German ships to specified bases. Lloyd George's immediate reaction, however, suggests that, at the meeting, Wemyss demanded the surrender of warships.

41. Regular cabinet meetings were numbered consecutively. The most secret meetings were the X series. Between those two was a secret series in which the number given is that of the previous ordinary meeting followed by the suffix *A* (and, if necessary, *B*). This meeting was War Cabinet 489A, 21 October 1918, CAB 23/14, PRO. The minutes of this meeting were rearranged later. See also the diaries of Haig, Henry Wilson, and Milner.

42. See ADM 116/1649, PRO. See also Newbolt, *Naval Operations* 5:352–53.

43. Milint (Mudros) to Director of Military Intelligence, 10 October 1918, Milner Papers, box 127, BOU. See also Admiralty Memorandum for War Cabinet, 12 October 1918, ADM 1/8451/276, PRO.

44. Lloyd George to Clemenceau, 15 October 1918, 6 N 54, SHAT, and Clemenceau to Lloyd George, 21 October 1918, Lloyd George Papers, F/52/2/43, HLRO.

45. Lloyd George used the same argument to the War Cabinet the next day. War Cabinet 489B, 22 October 1918, CAB 23/14, PRO.

46. Milner did advise withholding information from the French. Milner to Balfour, 21 October 1918, Balfour Papers, FO 800/206, PRO. See also Balfour to Barclay, 22 October 1918, *Foreign Relations, 1918, World War* 1:384.

47. War Cabinet X-31, 23 October 1918, CAB 23/17, PRO.

48. War Cabinet 490A, 24 October 1918, CAB 23/14, PRO.

49. Milner diary, 23 October 1918, Milner Papers, box 281, BOU, and Henry Wilson diary, 22 October 1918, HHW 1/32, IWM.

50. Derby to [Balfour], 24 October 1918, ADM 116/1651, PRO.

51. War Cabinet 491A, 25 October 1918, CAB 23/14, PRO.

52. War Cabinet 491B, 26 October 1918, CAB 23/14, PRO, and Paul Cambon to Balfour, 27 October 1918, Balfour Papers, Add. MSS 49745, BL.

53. Henry Wilson diary, 21 October 1918, HHW 1/32, IWM.

54. Sir Henry's plan, printed as Cabinet Paper G.T.-6069, CAB 24/67, was presented to the cabinet on 22 October but not discussed. War Cabinet 489B, CAB 23/14, PRO.

55. War Cabinet 489A, 21 October 1918, CAB 23/14, PRO.

56. Beatty supplemented his remarks with notes sent as Beatty to Hankey, 23 October 1918, printed as Cabinet Paper G.T.-6107, CAB 24/68, PRO. Cf. The Views of the Commander in Chief Grand Fleet on the Naval Terms of the Armistice, 21 October 1918, BTY/7/11/2, NMM. See Wemyss to Beatty, 19 October 1918, BTY/13/40/11, NMM.

57. Sir Eric Geddes to Balfour, 24 October 1918 and Derby to [Balfour], 24 October 1918, both in ADM 116/1651, PRO. The War Cabinet agreed later that the Admiralty would have representation at the coming meeting. War Cabinet 491B, 26 October 1918, CAB 23/14, PRO.

58. War Cabinet 491B, 26 October 1918, CAB 23/14, PRO.

59. Beatty on 27 October complained to the chief of the Naval Staff that he had not been consulted on "minimum terms." BTY/13/40/12, NMM.

60. War Cabinet 491B, 26 October 1918, CAB 23/14, PRO.

61. War Cabinet 489A, 21 October 1918, CAB 23/14, PRO. See chapter 2.

62. 21 October 1918, H 132, NLS.

63. 21 October 1918, HHW 1/32, IWM.

64. Ibid. Sir Henry redrafted his own proposals several days later. He would let the Germans keep their small arms, but would seize all other weapons. The Germans must evacuate the Rhineland and Russia's 1914 frontiers, but the Allies would not occupy that territory. Memorandum, 24 October 1918, WO 158/25, PRO.

65. War Cabinet 489A, 21 October 1918, CAB 23/14, PRO.

66. War Cabinet 490, 24 October 1918, CAB 23/8, PRO.

67. War Cabinet 491A, 25 October 1918, CAB 23/14, PRO.

68. War Cabinet 491B, 26 October 1918, CAB 23/14, PRO.

69. Hankey diary, 25 October 1918, HNKY 1/6, CCCU. War Cabinet 491A, 25 October 1918, CAB 23/14, PRO.

70. War Cabinet 491B, 26 October 1918, CAB 23/14, PRO.

71. A Note on the Early Conclusion of Peace, 24 October 1918, Cabinet Paper G.T.-6019, CAB 24/67, PRO, most of which Smuts seems to have presented on 26 October.

72. War Cabinet 491, 24 October 1918, CAB 23/8, PRO.

73. War Cabinet 491B, 26 October 1918, CAB 23/14, PRO.

CHAPTER 4. FRANCE, CLEMENCEAU, AND FOCH

1. P. Miquel, *Poincaré* (Paris: Arthème Fayard, 1961), 370–72.

2. Two different and partisan accounts exist of the events described hereafter. That given by the head of Clemenceau's military cabinet, Mordacq, *Clemenceau* 2:262–64, contradicts Poincaré, *Au service* 10:377–85. Mermeix [Gabriel Terrail] has a garbled account of the incident. *Les négociations secrètes et les quatre armistices* (Paris: Ollendorff, [1922]), 221–22. Philippe Erlanger accepts the version that Clemenceau's partisans present. *Clemenceau* (Paris: Grasset/Paris-Match, 1968), 535–36. Cf. Georges Wormser, *Le septennat de Poincaré* (Paris: Presses Universitaires de France, 1977), 146–48. Jean-Baptiste Duroselle has the latest word here in *Clemenceau* (Paris: Fayard, 1988), 709–10.

3. Herbillon, *Du général en chef au gouvernement* 2:325.

4. Duroselle quotes the critical passage in *Clemenceau,* 710.

5. Poincaré, *Au service* 10:373, 380–84. Cf. Georges Clemenceau, *Grandeurs et misères d'un victoire* (Paris: Plon, 1930), 92. See also Miquel, *Poincaré,* 375–76, and Duroselle, *Clemenceau,* 710.

6. In the months that followed these events, Clemenceau and Foch, after a bitter quarrel, broke with each other, and admirers of either of the two principals are entirely untrustworthy in their descriptions of the other's behavior.

7. Weygand, *Idéal vécu,* 617; Haig diary, 5 October 1918, H 132, NLS.

8. Mordacq, *Clemenceau* 2:244, 249; Derby to Balfour, 2 October 1918, Balfour Papers, Add. MSS 49744, BL, reported the French point of view, that it was an "appalling situation." The British assessment was less harsh than the French. Serial No. 12, Notes on the American Army, M.O.–1, 3 October 1918, Cabinet Paper G.T.-5874, CAB 24/65, PRO.

9. Pershing diary, 3 October 1918, Pershing Papers, box 4–5 (two boxes were consolidated, giving a hyphenated reference), LC. See also Haig diary, 5 October 1918, H 132, NLS, and Herbillon, *Du général en chef au gouvernement* 2:323. Somehow, within the next few days, Foch smoothed the matter over and Pershing was mollified. Pershing diary, 8 October 1918, Pershing Papers, box 4–5, LC.

10. Weygand, *Idéal vécu,* 618; Haig diary, 6 October 1918, H 132, NLS.

11. Mordacq, *Pouvait-on signer,* 6–7; idem, *Clemenceau* 2:258–59.

12. Poincaré, *Au service* 10:377.

13. Clemenceau, *Grandeurs et misères,* 61, 64, 69. Foch's quote below is from Mordacq, *Clemenceau* 2:270, 274–75. See also Bacon to Henry Wilson, 15 October 1918, WO 158/84, PRO, and Mordacq, *Pouvait-on signer,* 8–9.

14. Weygand, *Idéal vécu,* 628, and Mordacq, *Clemenceau* 2:277–78; Foch to Pétain, 16 October 1918, France, Ministère de la guerre, État-major de l'armée, Service historique, *Les armées françaises dans la Grande Guerre,* tome 7, *Le campagne offensive de 1918 et la marche au Rhin (18 juillet 1918–28 juin 1919),* 2 vols. with 1 vol. of documents and 2 vols. of maps annexed (Paris: Imprimerie Nationale,

1938), 7, Annex, 422; this set hereafter cited as *AFGG* 7. See also Pershing diary, 13 October 1918, Pershing Papers, box 4–5, LC, and Foch, *Mémoires* 2:245–46.

15. War Cabinet 489, 21 October 1918, CAB 23/8, PRO. Haig diary, 21 October 1918, H 132, NLS.

16. For Milner's assignment, see chapter 3. For Milner's instructions, see Henry Wilson diary, 23 October 1918, HHW 1/32, IWM. On 25 October, British anxieties diminished when Haig got command of two American divisions. Mordacq, *Clemenceau* 2:267–68. See also Bacon to Henry Wilson, 15 October 1918, WO 158/84, PRO.

17. Another danger lay in what Pershing would do when he learned of all this, which he inevitably did. For example, Gen. James G. Harbord to Pershing, 4 November 1918, Harbord Papers, Pershing-Harbord Letters, 1917–1922, LC.

18. Clemenceau, *Grandeurs et misères,* 63. Col. Mott claims that Clemenceau was just carrying on a grudge against Pershing. T. Bentley Mott, *Twenty Years as Military Attaché* (New York: Oxford University Press, 1937), 259.

19. L'Hôpital, *Foch,* 27–30. See Foch, *Mémoires* 2:276–78, and Herbillon, *Général en chef au gouvernement* 2:326. Cf. Stevenson, *French War Aims,* 122.

20. *"Conseil du gouvernement"* in the original. Foch's using "government" in the singular is significant, because it suggests that he thought of himself as an adviser to France alone, not to the Allied governments collectively.

21. L'Hôpital, *Foch,* 31–33. See also Recouly, *Mémorial de Foch,* 48–49.

22. Mordacq, *Clemenceau* 2:284.

23. L'Hôpital, *Foch,* 33–34. See also Foch, *Mémoires* 2:279.

24. L'Hôpital, *Foch,* 37–39. See also Recouly, *Mémorial de Foch,* 45.

25. Recouly, *Mémorial de Foch,* 45.

26. Foch did complain that from this time on, Clemenceau was extremely jealous of his authority. Ibid., 44. Relations between the two worsened during the peace conference the next year, and they made a final break in April 1919.

27. Weygand, *Idéal vécu,* 634–35. Foch (*Mémoires* 2:280) mentions the meeting only in passing.

28. Weygand, *Idéal vécu,* 635.

29. Weygand states that when Clemenceau summoned Foch, the Allied governments had already accepted an armistice. Ibid. Cf. Weygand, *Foch,* 259.

30. Stevenson, *French War Aims,* 124.

31. Foch's chief of staff had used almost those exact words to a British liaison officer a week before, and it is impossible to tell whether Clemenceau was deliberately quoting the marshal or whether these phrases were simply being passed back and forth. Du Cane to Henry Wilson, 17 October 1918, WO 158/84, PRO.

32. They did add a clause requiring the continuance of the blockade, but they added no other naval clauses. As a result of technical studies Mordacq had carried out, they made minor changes in other articles. Mordacq, *Clemenceau* 2:292.

33. Pétain proposed these new bridgeheads on 15 October. Renouvin, *Armistice*, 197.

34. Foch, *Mémoires* 2:273. C. J. C. Grant said later that when General Mangin saw Foch on 3 November, Foch showed him Moltke's 1864 book, which claimed the Mainz crossing was essential, and for that reason, Foch included it. Memorandum, 1 March 1919, WO 158/106, PRO.

35. Henri Mordacq, *L'Armistice du 11 novembre: Récit d'un témoin* (Paris: Plon, 1937), 156; André Tardieu, *The Truth about the Treaty* (Indianapolis: Bobbs-Merrill, 1921), 60.

36. John J. Pershing, *My Experiences in the World War*, 2 vols. (New York: Frederick A. Stokes, 1931), 2:359. The first entry in his diary concerning the armistice came only on 13 October, Pershing Papers, box 4–5, LC.

37. Pershing diary, 23 October 1918, Pershing Papers, box 4–5, LC.

38. Unsent letter, Haig to Foch, 23 October 1918, H 132, NLS. With the query omitted, Haig sent the letter almost verbatim to Foch on 25 October. Ibid.

39. Haig diary, 24 October 1918, H 132, NLS. Haig thought Pershing backed him. Haig diary, 23 October 1918, H 132, NLS.

40. A sanitized version of this episode is in Edmonds and Maxwell-Hyslop, *Military Operations, France and Belgium* 5:439–40. Cf. Du Cane to Henry Wilson, 25 October 1918, WO 158/92, PRO.

41. Haig diary, 27 October 1918, H 132, NLS. See also Foch to Haig, 26 October 1918, WO 158/106, PRO, and Derby diary, 26 October 1918, 920 DER(17) 28/1/1, LRO.

42. The Belgian chief of staff, the Belgian analogue of commander-in-chief, was invited but unable to get to the meeting. Mordacq, *Clemenceau* 2:292. Vice Admiral F. F. J. de Bon of the French navy was present but did not speak. The chiefs of staff to Foch, Haig, and, for the last half of the meeting, Pershing, were also present. Memorandum, 25 October 1918, box 1573, RG 120, NA.

43. Proceedings of a Military Conference at Senlis (Contemporary Translation), Notes on Conference Held at Senlis, 25 October 1918, *U.S. Army* 10:19–22. The document is a French procès-verbal with annotations by Colonel Boyd, one of Pershing's aides. See also Pershing, *My Experiences* 2:359–63, and Foch, *Mémoires* 2:280–82. Haig's and Pershing's diaries give little additional information.

44. Haig's exact words here caused a minor crisis. He said the U.S. Army "had suffered a great deal on account of its ignorance of modern warfare." After the meeting Pershing protested, and Haig hastened to correct the transcript, explaining that his remarks, made in French, had been "misinterpreted." Haig to Pershing, 27 October 1918, H 132, NLS. Pershing replied that Haig's explanation was satisfactory. Pershing to Haig [30 October 1918], H 132, NLS.

45. He proposed forcing the Germans to surrender 126,000 railroad cars and 2,500 locomotives or 100,000 cars and 5,000 locomotives.

46. Pershing, *My Experiences* 2:362–63, and the procès-verbal differ slightly.

Quotations here are from the procès-verbal.

47. Pershing diary, 25 October 1918, Pershing Papers, box 4–5, LC.

48. As sent, Pershing to Adjutant General, Paris, 25 October 1918, drawer 15, folder 45, HCY. As received, 26 October 1918, 1712, Wilson Papers, Series 2, LC.

49. Haig diary, 25 October 1918, H 132, NLS.

50. Foch to Clemenceau, [26 October 1918], L'Hôpital, *Foch*, 60–65. For the official English-language translation, see Bliss Papers, General Correspondence, vol. 230, LC. Clemenceau had written Orlando to get the views of General Diaz. Derby to Foreign Office, 24 October 1918, file no. 177715, FO 371/3445, PRO.

51. Foch gave no explanation of those numbers; Pétain did not mention machine guns or trench mortars at Senlis.

52. In a footnote, Foch explained that the new numbers represented the quantity taken from France and Belgium, which was 2,500 locomotives and 135,000 cars; the difference between that number and the total Foch demanded represented the equipment necessary to service the left bank when the Allies occupied it.

53. Possibly Foch appended naval clauses because of Pershing's proposals concerning submarines. Foch demanded the surrender of 150 submarines; the German surface fleet must withdraw to Cuxhaven, Heligoland, and Baltic ports; the Allies would occupy Cuxhaven and Heligoland; and the Germans must reveal the positions of their mine fields.

54. Weygand, *Idéal vécu*, 636.

55. Eyre Crowe, Conversation with de Fleuriau, 16 October 1918, file no. 173395, FO 371/3444, PRO. Cf. Memorandum, 22 October 1918, Paul Cambon Papers, series 1, dossier 22, AAE.

56. The last minutes on Crowe's memorandum came on 5 November, after the prime ministers and House had reached agreement on armistice terms and agreement of a sort on the Fourteen Points.

57. Memorandum by Cecil, 28 October 1918, file no. 181024, FO 371/3445. Summary sent to Derby, Paris, 30 October 1918, ibid.

58. Derby to Foreign Office, 24 October 1918, file no. 177715, FO 371/3445, PRO.

59. Lloyd George to Clemenceau, 25 October 1918, file no. 179593, FO 371/3445, PRO; War Cabinet 491A, 25 October 1918, CAB 23/14, PRO. See also Balfour to Derby, 25 October 1918, drawer 12, folder 32, HCY.

60. Rennell Rodd, Rome, to Foreign Office, 26 October 1918, file no. 179365, FO 371/3445, PRO.

61. Draft, Lloyd George to Rodd, 27 October 1918, file no. 179365, FO 371/3445, PRO.

62. Rodd to Foreign Office, enclosing Orlando to Lloyd George, 27 October 1918, file no. 179470, FO 371/3445, PRO.

63. Milner to Lloyd George, 27 October 1918, file no. 179303, FO 371/3445, PRO.

64. Milner diary, 28 October 1918, Milner Papers, box 281, BOU; Rodd to Foreign Office, 28 October 1918, file no. 179584, FO 371/3445, PRO.

CHAPTER 5. THE FOURTEEN POINTS, HOUSE, AND THE ALLIED PRIME MINISTERS

1. House diary, 22 October 1918, HCY.

2. Seymour, *Intimate Papers of Colonel House* 4:88.

3. D. H. Miller (the law partner of House's son-in-law) to House, 8 October 1918, Wilson Papers, Series 2, LC; House diary, 13 October 1918, HCY.

4. Wilson may already have stated his intention to attend the conference. Lansing desk diary, 14 October 1918, Lansing Papers, box 3, LC.

5. House diary, 26 October 1918, HCY; Haig diary, 26 October 1918, H 132, NLS.

6. House to Wilson, USS *Northern Pacific,* 22 October 1918, *Foreign Relations, 1919, Paris Peace Conference* 1:155.

7. House diary, 26 October 1918, HCY.

8. Ibid. In the published version of House's diary, the editor excised this mention of Bliss and many others. Seymour, *Intimate Papers of Colonel House* 4:93. See also House to Wilson, private code series 1, [26?] October 1918, Wilson Papers, Series 2, LC. House sent him a summary of Foch's terms. House to Wilson, private code series 2, 27 October 1918, Wilson Papers, Series 2, LC.

9. Bliss to N. D. Baker, 27 October 1918, and addendum, 1500, Bliss Papers, box 74 (9a/1–32), LC; House diary, 27 October 1918, HCY.

10. David F. Trask, *General Tasker Howard Bliss and the "Sessions of the World," 1919,* Transactions of the American Philosophical Society, n.s., 56, pt. 8 (Philadelphia: American Philosophical Society, 1966), 7. See Balfour Memorandum, 15 April 1919, Balfour Papers, Add. MSS 49750, BL, and Col. R. H. Beadon, *Some Memories of the Peace Conference* (London: Williams, 1933), 16.

11. Bliss's relations with Pershing remained correct and formal, although some of the officers of the AEF were not among Bliss's admirers. See, for example, Harbord to Pershing, 5 April 1919, Pershing-Harbord Letters, Harbord Papers, LC.

12. Bliss to House, 28 October 1918, Bliss Papers, box 69 (2/4a–2), LC. See also the explanatory letter, Bliss to C. S. Seymour, 14 June 1928, Seymour, *Intimate Papers of Colonel House* 4:114–15.

13. Mordacq, *Clemenceau* 2:296; Mordacq, *Armistice du 11 novembre,* 204. Mordacq judged Bliss's terms as harsher than Foch's. Ibid., 244. L'Hôpital quotes part of the memorandum, so Foch probably knew about Bliss's terms, too. L'Hôpital, *Foch,* 67–68.

14. Henry Wilson diary, 29 October 1918, HHW 1/32, IWM.

15. Bliss reported this Milner interview in a penciled note on scratch paper; he gave no date, only "3:40 P.M." Drawer 3, file 13, HCY. Seymour quotes it as if it were a formal letter and dates it 28 October 1918. Seymour, *Intimate Papers of Colonel House* 4:116. Bliss also described the Milner interview in a letter to Seymour,

14 June 1928, ibid., 116 n.1–117 n.1, and dated the interview 27 October, but Bliss's draft did not exist until the morning of the twenty-eighth. Bliss also referred to a typed version of the report. Cf. Bliss to N. D. Baker, 10 November 1918, Bliss Papers, box 74 (9a/1–33), LC, from which comes Bliss's quote following.

16. Wilson to House, private code series 1, 28 October 1918, Wilson Papers, Series 2, LC.

17. Schwabe focuses upon a garbled sentence in the first decoding of the telegram. Instead of reading, properly, "The position of Haig and Milner and Pétain as reported by our commander-in-chief is therefore safer than Foch's," it read, "The position of Haig and Milner and Pétain as reported and Pershing is therefore subordinate to Foch." *Woodrow Wilson, Revolutionary Germany, and Peacemaking,* 88. Schwabe adds that ultimately it made little difference to House's position. Ibid., 89. I agree.

18. Seymour, *Intimate Papers of Colonel House,* 4:152 n.1, and House diary, 29 October 1918, HCY. Not everyone liked Lippmann's ideas; a French critic described him as a "pacifist, ignorant of European things, [and] of a simplistic and theoretical mind." E. de Martoune, "Alsace-Lorraine," n.d., Klotz Papers, BDIC. Cobb was a staunch Wilsonian liberal.

19. The memorandum is printed in *Foreign Relations, 1918, World War* 1:405–13. I was allowed to read Lippmann's working papers and drafts on the subject in the Lippmann Papers, Yale University, but under the conditions of access, I was not permitted to quote directly from them.

20. Lippmann expanded on this idea in Supplementary Interpretation Prepared for Colonel House by WL, 2 November 1918, Lippmann Papers, Yale. In that memorandum, he stressed the role of the league.

21. House to Lansing for Wilson, 5, 29 October 1918, 1500, *Foreign Relations, 1918, World War* 1:405–13.

22. Wilson to House, private code series 4, [30 October 1918], Wilson Papers, Series 2, LC.

23. The Germans had broken the codes used, and they read this document as official. Schwabe, *Woodrow Wilson, Revolutionary Germany, and Peacemaking,* 82.

24. Derby to Arthur [Balfour], 23 October 1918, Lloyd George Papers, F/52/2/44, HLRO.

25. House diary, 28 October 1918, HCY.

26. Pratt to William S. Benson, 25 October 1918, Benson Papers, box 10, LC.

27. House to Lansing for Wilson, 8, 30 October 1918, *Foreign Relations, 1918, World War* 1:421, and House to Lansing for Wilson, 10, 30 October 1918, 1700, ibid., 424.

28. W. Stull Holt, "What Wilson Sent and What House Received: or Scholars Need to Check Carefully," *American Historical Review* 65 (1960): 569–71.

29. 9 November 1918, HHW 1/32, IWM.

30. For example, House's private code series 6, 5 November 1918, was decoded

correctly except for one incomplete phrase in the second-to-last sentence. Lloyd George Papers, F/60/1/8, HLRO.

31. Crosby to MacAdoo, 7 December 1918, London Embassy Correspondence, 1918, RG 84, NA.

32. House to Lansing for Wilson, 10, 30 October 1918, *Foreign Relations, 1918, World War* 1:424.

33. The British minutes (taken by Hankey) are I.C.-83, Notes of a Conversation in M. Pichon's Rooms at the Quai d'Orsay, Paris, Tuesday, October 29, 1918, at 3 P.M., CAB 28/5, PRO. The United States kept separate minutes, a full set of which is in HCY. The United States' minutes for this meeting are entitled Meeting at the F.O., October 29, 1918, at 3 o'c. P.M. In Paul Mantoux's Papers in the BDIC are his translator's notes, partly published in Jacques de Launau, *Secrets diplomatiques* (Brussels: Brepols, 1963). Unless otherwise stated, all quotations henceforth come from the British minutes.

34. The smaller nations did not accept their exclusion from the negotiations with good grace. For example, the Portuguese minister to Great Britain protested his nation's being barred from the inner circle of the Paris talks. Foreign Office to Derby for Balfour, 2 November 1918, file no. 183201, FO 371/3445, PRO.

35. House to Lansing for Wilson, 8, 30 October 1918, *Foreign Relations, 1918, World War* 1:422.

36. Hankey, *Supreme Command* 2:859, and Lloyd George, *Memoirs of the Peace Conference* 1:44–45.

37. House seemed both hurt and outraged at what he saw as Lloyd George's betrayal of what he had seen as an agreement at lunchtime. House to Lansing for Wilson, 9, 30 October 1918, Wilson Papers, Series 2, LC. House's son-in-law, international lawyer Gordon Auchincloss, drafted the text of this telegram.

38. 29 October 1918, HNKY 1/6, CCCU.

39. House to Lansing for Wilson, 8, 30 October 1918, *Foreign Relations, 1918, World War* 1:422.

40. Sources saying it did have an effect depend on House for their information. See for example, Stephen Bonsal, *Unfinished Business* (Garden City, N.Y.: Doubleday, Doran, 1944), 2. Paul Cambon, who was reading the minutes, but who was not present, thought the whole exchange was prearranged. P. Cambon to de Fleuriau, 1 November 1918, Paul Cambon, *Correspondance, 1870–1940*, ed. Henri Cambon, 3 vols. (Paris: Grasset, 1940–46), 3:279.

41. See chapter 3.

42. 26 October 1918, Victoria, Lady Wester Wemyss, *The Life and Letters of Lord Wester Wemyss* (London: Eyre and Spottiswoode, 1935), 386.

43. Wemyss, Notes, 27 October–3 November 1918, WMYS 7/11/4, CCCU.

44. Ibid.

45. Conference of Naval Representatives, Paris, 28 October 1918, afternoon, Allied Naval Council, Report of the Sixth Meetings Held . . . October 28th to

November 4th, 1918, BTY/7/11/9, NMM. Technically, this first meeting was not a formal session because no Japanese delegate was present.

46. Wemyss described the Americans as "tiresome—sententious and stupid." Notes, 27 October–3 November 1918, WMYS 7/11/4, CCCU.

47. Ibid.

48. First Session, 29 October 1918, afternoon, Allied Naval Council, Report of the Sixth Meetings, BTY/7/11/9, NMM.

49. The final draft includes a formal American reservation to that clause. Benson wrote for instructions, recommending acceptance. Benson to Secnav, n.d. [29 or 30 October 1918], Benson Papers, misc. no. 3 file, box 36, LC; Wilson to House, unnumbered, 28 October 1918, transmitted as Opnav to Sims, 3998, n.d., Wilson Papers, Series 2, LC. See also David F. Trask, *Captains and Cabinets: Anglo-American Naval Relations, 1917–1918* (Columbia: University of Missouri Press, 1972), 332.

50. At the same time, Foch wrote Clemenceau to warn him of British efforts to demand too much in the naval armistice terms. Foch to Clemenceau, 29 October 1918, Foch, *Mémoires* 2:284.

51. The draft of naval terms that Lloyd George read was probably the preliminary draft the Allied Naval Council had put together on 28 October, but the final touches the naval leaders gave the document changed it very little.

52. House to Lansing for Wilson, 8, 30 October 1918, *Foreign Relations, 1918, World War* 1:422–23.

53. Mordacq, *Clemenceau* 2:355.

54. House to Lansing for Wilson, 8, 30 October 1918, *Foreign Relations, 1918, World War* 1:422. Hankey claimed the meeting was also set to exclude Balfour. Hankey diary, 30 October 1918, HNKY 1/6, CCCU.

55. The evidence is insufficient but suggestive. There is no doubt such a meeting took place; the question is precisely when. General Mordacq, a witness, claims it took place before the meeting with Lloyd George. Mordacq, *Clemenceau* 2:297. Mordacq is sometimes careless in dating events, but in his support, other matters he mentions in the same passage are confirmed in House to Lansing for Wilson, 12, 30 October 1918, Wilson Papers, Series 2, LC.

56. Flota raises the possibility of such an arrangement but comes to no conclusion. *Colonel House in Paris*, 53.

57. House to Lansing for Wilson, 12, 30 October 1918, Wilson Papers, Series 2, LC. House diary, 29 [30] October 1918, HCY. House's diary for this period was evidently written in bursts as he found time and then backdated.

58. House to Lansing for Wilson, 12, 30 October 1918, Wilson Papers, Series 2, LC. See also House diary, 30 October 1918, HCY. House told Wilson of his plan to make that threat in a telegram sent later that day at 1600, House to Lansing for Wilson, 9, 30 October 1918, Wilson Papers, Series 2, LC.

59. House to Lansing for Wilson, 12, 30 October 1918, Wilson Papers, Series 2,

LC. Cf. Poincaré, *Au service* 10:396, and Hankey diary, 30 October 1918, HNKY 1/6, CCCU.

60. House to Lansing for Wilson, 12, 30 October 1918, Wilson Papers, Series 2, LC. See also Mordacq, *Clemenceau* 2:297.

61. The evening before, Lloyd George was reported as believing that Henry Wilson's and Foch's terms were too harsh and Haig's too mild and that stiff naval terms were necessary. Henry Wilson diary, 29 October 1918, HHW 1/32, IWM.

62. Lloyd George apparently still wanted milder naval terms than the Allied Naval Council was proposing. Derby diary, 30 October 1918, 920 DER(17) 28/1/1, LRO.

63. House, in fact, planned to urge that the conference meet in Lausanne.

64. Milne to Franchet d'Esperey, 19 October 1918, *AFGG* 8:3, Annexes, 2:301.

65. See chapter 3, and Newbolt, *Naval Operations* 5:351–57. See also Lloyd George, *War Memoirs* 6:3313, and Hankey, *Supreme Command* 2:844–45.

66. Vice Admiral Sir Somerset Calthorpe to Admiralty, 28/29 October 1918, ADM 1/8541/276, PRO, and Calthorpe to Amet, 30 October 1918, ADM 116/1931, PRO.

67. Paul Cambon to Ministère des Affairs Étrangères, 24 October 1918, Paul Cambon Papers, series 1, carton X, dossier 24, AAE. See also Henry Wilson diary, 26 October 1918, HHW 1/32, IWM, Lloyd George, *War Memoirs* 6:3311, and Poincaré, *Au service* 10:394–95.

68. I.C.-84, Notes of a Conversation, 30 October 1918, 1500, CAB 28/5, PRO.

69. Paul Cambon to de Fleuriau, Paris, 1 November 1918, Paul Cambon, *Correspondance* 3:279, and House diary, 30 October 1918, HCY. Hankey thought the whole debate was artificial and was the result of French political pressures. Hankey, *Supreme Command* 2:843.

70. Calthorpe to Admiralty, 31 October 1918, ADM 1/8541/276, PRO.

71. Maurice, *Armistices of 1918*, 26. For successive drafts of the armistice and the document as signed, see Newbolt, *Naval Operations*, appendix D, pt. 3, 5:418–23.

72. See chapter 4. Pershing to Adjutant General, Paris, 25 October 1918, Wilson Papers, Series 2, LC. There is also a copy in the House Papers, drawer 15, folder 45, HCY.

73. Harris (March) for Baker to Pershing, unnumbered, 27 October 1918, rec'd 29 October 1918. Slightly different versions of this telegram exist. Cf. Wilson Papers, Series 2, LC, and drawer 15, folder 45, HCY.

74. Separately, Wilson sent naval terms to House that were no more rigorous. Wilson to House, unnumbered, 28 October 1918, sent as Opnav to Sims for House and Benson, Wilson Papers, Series 2, LC. The draft Wilson worked from was Sims to Opnav, 25 October 1918, Wilson Papers, Series 2, LC. See also Pratt to Benson, [28 October 1918], Benson Papers, Box 10, LC.

75. The following events are described briefly by Frank E. Vandiver, *Black Jack:*

The Life and Times of John J. Pershing, 2 vols. (College Station: Texas A&M University Press, 1977), 2:982–83, and in greater depth by Donald Smythe, S.J., *Pershing: General of the Armies* (Bloomington: Indiana University Press, 1986), 220–22. Cf. my "Pershing and the Armistice," *Journal of American History* 55 (1968):281–91.

76. Pershing to Allied Supreme War Council, 30 October 1918, *U.S. Army* 10:28–30; House to Lansing for Wilson, 14, 31 October 1918, Wilson Papers, Series 2, LC. When Renouvin analyzes these events, he recognizes the possibility that Pershing was maneuvering tactically, but he gives at least equal weight to the general's wanting a personal victory in battle before peace came. *Armistice,* 260–61.

77. House diary, 30 October 1918, HCY; House to Lansing for Wilson, 14, 31 October 1918, Wilson Papers, Series 2, LC. No discussion of the subject is recorded in the procès-verbal. Hankey quotes Lloyd George as saying the letter was written for political purposes and adding, "Perhaps being a Republican." Diary, 30 October 1918, HNKY 1/6, CCCU.

78. [House] to Pershing, 30 October 1918, drawer 15, folder 45, HCY.

79. Pershing diary, 30 October 1918, Pershing Papers, box 4–5, LC, and House to Lansing for Wilson, 14, Series 2, LC.

80. Pershing to Adjutant General, Paris, rec'd 31 October 1918, 1710, sent to Wilson as an enclosure in Baker to Wilson, 1 November 1918, and filed in Wilson Papers, Series 2, LC. Foch, of course, had not presented terms at Senlis; Pétain had.

81. Pershing to House, 30 October 1918, drawer 15, folder 45, HCY.

82. House diary, 30 October 1918, HCY.

83. Pershing to House, 30 October 1918, drawer 15, folder 45, HCY. It is possible that this letter was drafted in more or less complete form on the thirtieth and not sent until the following day.

84. Pershing diary, 1 November 1918, Pershing Papers, box 4–5, LC.

85. 2 November 1918, HCY. Pershing commented in his diary that he had had a "long and very satisfactory talk" with House but gave no details. 2 November 1918, Pershing Papers, box 4–5, LC.

86. House to Lansing for Wilson, 36, 2 November 1918, Wilson Papers, Series 2, LC.

87. N. D. Baker to Wilson, 31 October 1918, Wilson Papers, Series 2, LC. Other copies were arriving by diplomatic channels.

88. Wilson to House, private code series 6, 31 October 1918, Wilson Papers, Series 2, LC.

89. Draft letter, Baker to Pershing, 5 November 1918, enclosed in Baker to Wilson and the whole enclosed in Wilson to Baker, 7 November 1918, Baker Papers, box 8, LC. Baker consulted Lansing on the matter. Lansing desk diary, 5 November 1918, Lansing Papers, box 3, LC.

90. There is no evidence it was sent.

91. Foch telegraphed his views to Pershing the next day. Mott to Boyd for

Pershing, 31 October 1918, *U.S. Army* 10:31. See Mott, *Twenty Years as Military Attaché*, 267, and his chapter 17, "Why Pershing's Plea for Unconditional Surrender Was Rejected," ibid., 274–80. See also Pershing diary, 31 October 1918, Pershing Papers, box 4–5, LC.

92. I.C.-84, Notes of a Conversation, 30 October 1918, 1500, CAB 28/5, PRO.

93. Cf. the United States' minutes, Meeting at the F.O., 30 October 1918, 3 P.M. HCY.

CHAPTER 6. THE AUSTRO-HUNGARIAN ARMISTICE

1. Ekengren to Lansing, transmitting Imperial and Royal Government to Wilson, 7 October 1918, *Foreign Relations, 1918, World War* 1:341.

2. Lansing to Ekengren for Imperial and Royal Government, Washington, 19 October 1918, *Foreign Relations, 1918, World War* 1:368. See Wilson to Senator J. S. Williams, 17 October 1918, Wilson Papers, Series 2, LC. See also Barclay to Foreign Office, 16 October 1918, file no. 174313, FO 371/3442, PRO.

3. Betty Miller Unterberger, *The United States, Revolutionary Russia, and the Rise of Czechoslovakia* (Chapel Hill: University of North Carolina Press, 1989), 316. The United States had recognized the Czecho-Slovak National Council on 3 September 1918. Ibid., 285–86.

4. Ekengren to Lansing, 29 October 1918, *Foreign Relations, 1918, World War* 1:404–5. See also Poincaré, *Au service* 10:395–96, and Henry Wilson diary, 28 October 1918, HHW 1/32, IWM.

5. Ivo J. Lederer, *Yugoslavia at the Paris Peace Conference: A Study in Frontiermaking* (New Haven, Conn.: Yale University Press, 1963), 40.

6. Ibid., 31.

7. T. N. Page to Lansing, Rome, 22 October 1918, *Foreign Relations, 1918, World War* 1:379, and T. N. Page to Lansing, Rome, 30 October 1918, ibid., 1:432. See also Mordacq, *Clemenceau* 2:326, and Giraud to Foch, 17 October 1918, *AFGG* 7, Annexes, 442–43.

8. Poincaré, *Au service* 10:399.

9. See chapter 5, and I.C.-84, Notes of a Conversation, 30 October 1918, 1500, CAB 28/5, PRO.

10. House to Lansing for Wilson, 13, 30 October 1918, *Foreign Relations, 1918, World War* 1:427.

11. Henry Wilson diary, 30 October 1918, HHW 1/32, IWM. See also Poincaré, *Au service* 10:396.

12. Members of the ad hoc military committee were Sir Henry Wilson (chairman), the four Military Representatives, General Pershing, and Philip Kerr, Lloyd George's secretary.

13. Conference of Naval Representatives, 28 October 1918, and Appendices B and D, and First Session, 29 October 1918, both in Allied Naval Council, Report of

the Sixth Meetings, BTY/7/11/9, NMM.

14. Austria-Hungary had three Dreadnought-class battleships, the fourth, *Szent Istvan*, having been sunk in June 1918. The number was reduced to two on 1 November 1918, when the *Viribus Unitis* was sunk. They had three battleships of almost Dreadnought type (the *Radetzky* class) and nine pre-Dreadnought battleships.

15. The following is from the United States' minutes, Meeting at the F.O., October 30, 1918, at 3 P.M., HCY.

16. Committee of the Allied Naval Council on . . . Naval Conditions [for] . . . Austria-Hungary, Second Session, 31 October 1918, morning, and Third Session, 31 October 1918, afternoon, both in Allied Naval Council, Report of the Sixth Meetings, BTY/7/11/9, NMM.

17. In these discussions of the Austro-Hungarian naval terms, the Italian representative seldom spoke; it was not necessary for him to do so because first the British and then Admiral de Bon fought Italy's battles for him.

18. I.C. 85 (SWC), Procès-verbal of the First Meeting of the Eighth Session of the Supreme War Council, 31 October 1918, 1500, CAB 28/5, PRO. The minutes list thirty-eight persons present. The procès-verbaux of this and other formal Supreme War Council sessions are printed in parallel French and English columns.

19. Henry Wilson diary, 31 October 1918, HHW 1/32, IWM. For petulant comments on the failure of the secretariat, see Hankey, *Supreme Command* 2:846. See also House to Lansing for Wilson, 23, 31 October 1918, Wilson Papers, Series 2, LC.

20. See Map 2. On duplicating the Treaty of London line in the armistice, see minute by C. H. Smith to file no. 181812, 2 November 1918, FO 371/3445, PRO.

21. Barrère to Ministère des Affaires Étrangères, 12 November 1918, 6 N 73, SHAT.

22. By old laws, the merchant fleet was actually two fleets, one Austrian, registered in Trieste, and the other Hungarian, registered in Rikh (Fiume). Various provinces also had ownership rights over particular vessels.

23. House to Lansing for Wilson, 23, 31 October 1918, Wilson Papers, Series 2, LC.

24. Meeting of British, French, and Italian M.F.A.'s, morning November 1st, [1918], Prepared by E[ric] D[rummond], HCY. The conclusions of that meeting, but not a procès-verbal, appear as I.C.-86, 1 November 1918, CAB 28/5, PRO.

25. At some point, Clemenceau made an arrangement with the Italians in which he promised not to recognize Yugoslavia for the time being. Clemenceau to Orlando, n.d., enclosed in de Fleuriau to Davies, 6 November 1918, Lloyd George Papers, F/50/3/44, HLRO.

26. Earlier in the month, it had issued manifestos, but had not taken the decisive step of constituting itself as a government. See Dragovan Šepić, "The Question of Yugoslav Union in 1918," *Journal of Contemporary History* 3 (1968):37.

27. Lederer, *Yugoslavia*, 43.

28. I.C.-87, Notes of a Conversation, 1 November 1918, 1100, CAB 28/5, PRO, amd I.C.-88 (SWC), Procès-verbal of the Second Meeting of the Eighth Session of the Supreme War Council, 1 November 1918, 1500, CAB 28/5, PRO.

29. National Council at Zagreb to Wilson, 1 November 1918, 6 N 71, SHAT.

30. Sharp to Lansing, 1 November 1918, *Foreign Relations, 1918, World War* 1:860–61. See also H. W. V. Temperley, ed., *A History of the Peace Conference of Paris,* [Royal] Institute of International Affairs, 6 vols. (London: Henry Frowde, Hodder and Stoughton, 1924; reprint, London: Oxford University Press, 1969), 4:199–200.

31. Wilson to House, private code series 7, [1 November 1918], Wilson Papers, Series 2, LC.

32. I.C.-90, Notes of a Conversation, 2 November 1918, 1130, CAB 28/5, PRO. See also Poincaré, *Au service* 10:407–8.

33. I.C.-92, Notes of a Conversation, 3 November 1918, 1500, CAB 28/5, PRO. The National Council at Zagreb protested Italian attacks that sank a battleship and a torpedo boat on 1 November. Tresi to Allied Powers, 2 November 1918, 6 N 71, SHAT.

34. The Italians prevented the French admiral at Corfu from communicating with the fleet, and the situation gradually unraveled to Italian advantage. Gauchet to Marceau, 3 November 1918, 6 N 53, SHAT. See chapter 8.

35. I.C.-89, Notes of a Conversation, 2 November 1918, 1000, CAB 28/5, PRO. Present were all the Military Representatives and army commanders, with the exception of Pétain and Diaz.

36. Derby to Foreign Office, 3 November 1918, file no. 182497, FO 371/3445, PRO.

37. Sir J. E. Edmonds and H. R. Davies, *Military Operations, Italy, 1915–1919,* Great Britain, Committee of Imperial Defence, Historical Section, 4 vols. in 1 (London: H.M. Stationery Office, 1949), 367–78.

38. Mordacq, *Pouvait-on signer,* 159; Pershing diary, 2 November 1918, Pershing Papers, box 4–5, LC.

39. Procès-verbal of a Meeting of Foch, Bliss, Henry Wilson, and di Robillant, 3 November 1918, 1600, *AFGG* 7, Annexes, 757–58. See Bliss to House, 4 November 1918, Bliss Papers, box 69 (2/4a–3), LC, and [Report of] Foch, Bliss, H. Wilson, and di Robillant, 3 November 1918, Appendix I to War Cabinet, Paris Conference, November 1918, 4 November 1918, CAB 28/5, PRO. See also I.C.-92, Notes of a Conversation, 3 November 1918, 1500, CAB 28/5, PRO.

40. The American 332d Infantry Regiment, fighting on the Italian Front to show the American flag, would not join that attack.

41. Simultaneously, one or two Czech divisions then fighting in Italy would somehow go from Italy to Bohemia.

42. Gen. Delmay Radcliffe to Sir Henry Wilson, 8 November 1918, WO 106/835, PRO. See also Cavan to Henry Wilson, 4 November 1918, WO 79/68, PRO. The major critique of the plan is Major General Sir P. A. M. Nash, Inter-Allied Trans-

portation Council, to Sackville-West, 4 November 1918, enclosing memorandum, Concentration on Bavarian Front, CAB 25/97, PRO. See also [British] Army Council, 6 November 1918, WO 106/842, PRO.

43. I.C.-93, Procès-verbal of Conference of Heads of Governments, 4 November 1918, 1100, CAB 28/5, PRO.

44. On 4 November, five Serbian divisions were on a line from Montenegro to the outskirts of Belgrade, so the Italians already faced problems. Situation, 4 November 1918, WO 153/1021, PRO.

45. Temperley, *History of the Peace Conference* 4:112–17.

46. Unterberger, *United States, Revolutionary Russia, and the Rise of Czechoslovakia,* 317–18.

47. Šepić argues that it existed on paper from the Geneva Conference of 6–9 November 1918. "The Question of Yugoslav Union in 1918," 37–38, 42–43. Even if that interpretation is correct, the union occurred too late to influence events here.

48. On Hungary, see Michael Karolyi, *Memoirs of Michael Karolyi: Faith Without Illusion,* trans. Catherine Karolyi (New York: E. P. Dutton, 1957), 114–27.

49. Temperley, *History of the Peace Conference* 4:118–19.

50. For a narrative, see Bogdan Krizman, "The Belgrad Armistice of 13 November 1918," *Slavonic and East European Review* 48 (1970):67–87.

51. Gen. Jean Bernachot, *Les armées françaises en orient après l'armistice de 1918,* France, Ministère des armées, État-major de l'armée de terre, Service historique, 2 vols. (Paris: Imprimerie Nationale, 1970), 1:20. See Karolyi, *Memoirs,* 130–37. See also Clemenceau to Franchet d'Esperey, 6 November 1918, 4 N 10, SHAT.

52. Azan, *Franchet d'Esperey,* 225–32.

53. Military Convention Regulating the Conditions Under Which the Armistice, Signed Between the Allies and Austria-Hungary, Is To Be Applied in Hungary, 13 November 1918, U.S. Department of State, *Foreign Relations, 1919, Paris Peace Conference* 2:183–84. Cf. Franchet d'Esperey to Corvisant, 20 November 1918, enclosed in Spiers to War Office, WO 106/405, PRO.

CHAPTER 7. THE ALLIES, HOUSE, AND THE TERMS FOR GERMANY

1. I.C.-87, Notes of a Conversation, 1 November 1918, 1100, and Appendix [Foch's terms of 26 October 1918], CAB 28/5, PRO.

2. No secretary was present at that 31 October meeting. Weygand, *Idéal vécu,* 635, and Foch, *Mémoires* 2:285, have substantially the same text. Some sources suggest that Foch made the following statement first on 1 November; it makes no difference. See also the variation in Paul Mantoux to House, 6 July 1920, Seymour, *Intimate Papers of Colonel House* 4:91.

3. I.C.-85 (SWC), Procès-verbal of the First Meeting of the Eighth Session of the Supreme War Council, 31 October 1918, 1500, CAB 28/5, PRO.

4. I.C.-87, Notes of a Conversation, 1 November 1918, 1100, and Appendix [Foch's terms of 26 October 1918], CAB 28/5, PRO. See also chapter 4.

5. This change of depth at Gersheim amended the Senlis draft. No reason was given for the change, but because of the terrain along the Upper Rhine, it was sensible. In negotiations between Foch and the Germans, the depth would be reduced still more. The draft presented to the Supreme War Council still included the bridgehead at Strasbourg, but at Foch's suggestion, it was dropped.

6. See also Foch, *Mémoires* 2:286.

7. Hankey diary, 30 October 1918, HNKY 1/6, CCCU.

8. Geddes had discussed naval terms at breakfast with Lloyd George, Law, and Milner. Milner diary, 1 November 1918, Milner Papers, box 281, BOU.

9. Wemyss to Sir Oswyn Murray, 2 November 1918, ADM 116/1651, PRO. A copy was enclosed in Wemyss to Beatty, 2 November 1918, BTY/13/40/14.

10. House to Lansing for Wilson, 30, 1 November 1918, 1600, *Foreign Relations, 1918, World War* 1:438.

11. Private code series 3, [29] October 1918, Wilson Papers, Series 2, LC.

12. It was at least 30 October when House received this cable, so it had no bearing on his actions earlier.

13. House to Lansing for Wilson, 29, 1 November 1918, Wilson Papers, Series 2, LC.

14. Wilson to House, private code series 5, [30 October 1918], Wilson Papers, Series 2, LC.

15. House diary, 31 October 1918, HCY.

16. House to Wilson, private code series 5, [31 October 1918], Wilson Papers, Series 2, LC.

17. House to Lansing for Wilson, 12, 30 October 1918, Wilson Papers, Series 2, LC.

18. Private code series 6, 31 October 1918, Wilson Papers, Series 2, LC.

19. House was exceedingly grateful for those few words. House diary, 3 November 1918, HCY.

20. See chapter 5. Wilson's cables rejecting the House-Lloyd George agreement, his private code series numbers 5 and 6, were sent five days before House's private code series number 6, the first of the private code series cables for which there is indisputable evidence of the private code's having been broken.

21. I.C.-88 (SWC), Procès-verbal of the Second Meeting of the Eighth Session of the Supreme War Council, 1 November 1818, 1500, CAB 28/5, PRO.

22. Charles à Court Repington, *After the War* (Boston: Houghton Mifflin, 1922), 406.

23. House diary, 1 November 1918, HCY.

24. House diary, 1 [2] November 1918, HCY.

25. Tom Clarke, *My Northcliffe Diary* (London: Victor Gollancz, 1931), 116.

26. Reginald Pound and Geoffrey Harmsworth, *Northcliffe* (London: Cassell, 1959), 668–69.

27. Milner diary, 1 November 1918, Milner Papers, box 281, BOU. For the letter, see Blake, *Unrepentant Tory,* 383–86, and *Liberal Magazine* 26 (December 1918): 585–87.

28. House to Lansing for Wilson, 38, 3 November 1918, 1100, rec'd idem, 1533, *Foreign Relations, 1918, World War* 1:448.

29. I.C.-92, Notes of a Conversation, 3 November 1918, 1500, CAB 28/5, PRO.

30. Notes of a Conversation at Colonel House's Residence, 3 November 1918, HCY.

31. Appendix to British Minutes.

32. House to Lansing for Wilson, 41, 3 November 1918, 2100, rec'd idem, 2057, *Foreign Relations, 1918, World War* 1:455–57.

33. Wilson to House, private code series 9, 4 November 1918, [Mrs. Whalen's transcription], Wilson Papers, Series 2, LC.

34. House diary, [3 November 1918], HCY.

35. Lloyd George, *Memoirs of the Peace Conference* 1:44–46.

36. He did. House to Lansing for Wilson, 41, 3 November 1918, *Foreign Relations, 1918, World War* 1:455–57. Wilson did nothing about it.

37. I.C.-88 (SWC), Procès-verbal of the Second Meeting of the Eighth Session of the Supreme War Council, 1 November 1918, 1500, CAB 28/5, PRO. Not including the secretariat or the interpreter, the minutes list thirty-six persons in attendance. The military leaders present included Foch and Weygand, but not Pétain; Haig and Henry Wilson, but not Wemyss or Beatty; and Bliss and Benson, but not Pershing.

38. *Dommages* was translated contemporaneously as "damage done," a cumbersome choice. "Losses" is better, both for translation and for what Clemenceau meant. It is a word that suggests no limits.

39. I.C.-91 (SWC), Procès-verbal of the Third Meeting of the Eighth Session of the Supreme War Council, 2 November 1918, 1500, CAB 28/5, PRO.

40. I.C.-88 (SWC), Procès-verbal of the Second Meeting of the Eighth Session of the Supreme War Council, 1 November 1918, 1500, CAB 28/5, PRO.

41. Memorandum by Lt. Col. J. H. Kisch, 21 October 1918, WO 32/5670, PRO.

42. I.C.-91 (SWC), Procès-verbal of the Third Meeting of the Eighth Session of the Supreme War Council, 2 November 1918, 1500, CAB 28/5, PRO.

43. Opnav to Amnavpar, [c. 1 November 1918], Benson Papers, box 36, LC.

44. *Armistice,* 302–3.

45. The printed versions Rudin used were Memorandum 64, Principles Governing Disposition of German Vessels That Are Surrendered, 30 October 1918, United States, Office of Naval Records and Library, *American Naval Planning Section, London* (Washington, D.C.: Government Printing Office, 1923), 456, and Memorandum 65, United States Naval Interests in the Armistice, 4 November

1918, ibid., 457–60. The uncensored versions of those memoranda were not distributed until later. Bliss received uncensored copies only on 17 December 1918, Bliss Papers, box 76 (17-1), LC.

46. Navy Department to Benson, copies to Bliss and House, 3 November 1918. A copy is in the Bliss Papers, Correspondence, vol. 230, LC. See House diary, 29 October 1918, HCY. See also Benson to House, 2 November 1918, Seymour, *Intimate Papers of Colonel House* 4:131.

47. Fifth Session, 1 November 1918, afternoon, Allied Naval Council, Report of the Sixth Meetings, BTY/7/11/9, NMM.

48. Wemyss, Notes, 28 October–3 November 1918, WMYS 7/11/4, CCCU.

49. That evening they met again and approved documents embodying their proposals. Sixth Session, 1 November 1918, evening, Allied Naval Council, Report of the Sixth Meetings, BTY/7/11/9, NMM.

50. Wemyss, Notes, 28 October–3 November 1918, WMYS 7/11/4, CCCU.

51. Balfour to Lloyd George, 1 November 1918, Balfour Papers, FO 800/199, PRO.

52. But he was furious with Geddes. Hankey diary, 4 November 1918, HNKY 1/6, CCCU.

53. Balfour to Law, 1 November 1918, Balfour Papers, FO 800/201, PRO.

54. I.C.-91 (SWC), Procès-verbal of the Third Meeting of the Eighth Session of the Supreme War Council, 2 November 1918, 1500, CAB 28/5, PRO.

55. Geddes to Lloyd George, with copies to Hankey, Balfour, Bonar Law, and Wemyss, 2 November 1918, confirmed those extravagant figures. ADM 116/1651, PRO.

56. I.C.-92, Notes of a Conversation, 3 November 1918, 1500, CAB 28/5, PRO.

57. Notes of a Conversation, 3 November 1918, 1500, HCY.

58. I.C.-93, Procès-verbal of a Conference of Heads of Governments, 4 November 1918, 1100, CAB 28/5, PRO.

59. Seventh Session, 4 November 1918, afternoon [before 1500], Allied Naval Council, Report of the Sixth Meetings, BTY/7/11/9, NMM.

60. I.C.-95 (SWC), Procès-verbal of the Fourth Meeting of the Eighth Session of the Supreme War Council, 4 November 1918, 1500, CAB 28/5, PRO. Mermeix prints the French procès-verbal. *Négociations secrètes,* 253–66. Forty-two persons, including four Japanese (the ambassador to France and his military and naval advisers) and representatives from Belgium, Greece, Portugal, Serbia, and Czechoslovakia, are listed in the minutes as attending, exclusive of the secretariat and interpreters.

61. To avoid any ambiguity, the final text listed Austria-Hungary as well as those other nations.

62. Seventh Session, 4 November 1918, Allied Naval Council, Report of the Sixth Meetings, BTY/7/11/9, NMM.

63. Lloyd George had told Balfour, who opposed internment in a neutral coun-

try, that Geddes supported the idea. Balfour privately asked Geddes if that were so, and Geddes claimed that Lloyd George was lying. Derby diary, 3 November 1918, 920 DER(17) 28/1/1, LRO.

64. *Foreign Relations, 1918, World War* 1:468–69.

65. Herbillon, *Du général en chef au gouvernement* 2:343. See also Poincaré, *Au service* 10:406.

66. Rodd to Balfour, 11 November 1918, Balfour Papers, FO 800/203, PRO.

67. Beatty to Wemyss, 5 November 1918, BTY/13/40/16, NMM.

68. War Cabinet 497, Imperial War Cabinet 36, 5 November 1918, CAB 23/8, PRO.

69. House diary, 4 November 1918, HCY.

70. House to Wilson, private code series 6, 5 November 1918, Wilson Papers, Series 2, LC. The quotation is from the first decoding.

71. Joseph Tumulty, *Woodrow Wilson as I Know Him* (Garden City, N.Y.: Doubleday, Page for the *Literary Digest,* 1921), chap. 35, "Appeal for a Democratic Congress," 322–34. See also Renouvin, *Armistice,* 169–72.

72. Address to Democratic National Committee, 28 February 1919, Tumulty, *Woodrow Wilson,* 332–33.

73. These were the conclusions reached at a conference of Wilson, Lansing, Baker, and Daniels. Daniels diary, 4 November 1918, Daniels Papers, box 3, LC.

74. Houston, *Eight Years with Wilson's Cabinet* 1:320–21.

75. War Cabinet 497, Imperial War Cabinet 36, 5 November 1918, CAB 23/8, PRO. See also Derby diary, 5 November 1918, 920 DER(17) 28/1/1, LRO.

CHAPTER 8. THE GERMANS SIGN

1. Wilson's Fourth Note, Lansing to Sulzer for German Government, *Foreign Relations, 1918, World War* 1:468–69.

2. Text filed under date of 5 November 1918 in 6 N 42, SHAT. See Balfour to Derby, 6 November 1918, file no. 184668, FO 371/3445, PRO, and Derby to Foreign Office, 7 November 1918, file no. 185027, FO 371/3445, PRO. The British admirals were not informed of the change immediately. Wemyss to Beatty, 5 November 1918, BTY/13/40/18, NMM, and Paper 453, 7 November 1918, ADM 167/55, PRO. Wilson got the amendment only in House to Lansing for Wilson, 60, 8 November 1918, Wilson Papers, Series 2, LC.

3. Wemyss to Balfour, 12 November 1918, Balfour Papers, FO 800/201, PRO.

4. Foreign Office to Sir A. Hardinge, 14 November 1918, file no. 188838, FO 371/3446, PRO.

5. Emergency Meeting, Allied Naval Council, 13 November 1918, ADM 116/1651, PRO.

6. Procès verbal de la union tenue . . . 11 November 1918, ADM 137/1794, PRO.

7. Beatty to Admiralty for Wemyss, 8 November 1918, and Geddes to Nicolson,

9 November 1918, enclosing Beatty to Geddes with attachments, 8 November 1918, ADM 116/1651, PRO.

8. Geddes to Beatty, 9 November 1918, enclosed in Geddes to Nicolson, 9 November 1918, ADM 116/1651, PRO. As it turned out, Beatty did get a mention of Heligoland in an additional protocol, which allowed the Allies to occupy Heligoland as a penalty if the German ships failed to sail for their internment at the time set. Derby to Foreign Office, 11 November 1918, file no. 186910, FO 371/3446, PRO. See also Cmdr. W. T. Bagot's report, 8 December 1918, ADM 1/8546/319, PRO. The power was not used.

9. Military Situation in Various Theatres, no. 127, 1 November 1918, and no. 128, 7 November 1918, WO 106/319. See also Daily Summary of Intelligence Received, 3–4 November 1918, WO 157/37, PRO.

10. Daily Summary of Intelligence Received, 6–7 November 1918, WO 157/37, PRO.

11. Newbolt, *Naval Operations* 5:369–70. On this and the following events in Germany, see the excellent summary in Rudin, *Armistice, 1918,* 244–65.

12. On Bavaria, see Allan Mitchell, *Revolution in Bavaria, 1918–1919* (Princeton, N.J.: Princeton University Press, 1965), 30–33, 86–109, and Richard Grunberger, *Red Rising in Bavaria* (New York: St. Martin's, 1973), 31–35.

13. Ludwig III did not formally abdicate, although he released the Bavarian army officers and civil servants from their oath of allegiance to him.

14. Daily Summary of Intelligence Received, 3–4 November 1918, WO 157/37, PRO.

15. Daily Summary of Intelligence Received, 7–8 November 1918, WO 157/37, PRO. See also War Cabinet 499, 7 November 1918, and War Cabinet 500, 8 November 1918, both in CAB 23/8, PRO.

16. Mordacq, *Pouvait-on signer,* 84–85. See Foch to Commander-in-Chief of French Armies of North and Northeast, 5 November 1918, WO 158/106, PRO. See also War Cabinet 497, Imperial War Cabinet 36, 5 November 1918, CAB 23/8, PRO.

17. Daily Summary of Intelligence Received, 9–10 November 1918, WO 157/37, PRO.

18. Mordacq, *Armistice du 11 novembre,* 62. See also Daily Summary of Intelligence Received, 8–9 November 1918, WO 157/37.

19. Foch, *Mémoires* 2:263–64.

20. De Castlenau to Foch, 23 October 1918, *AFGG* 7, Annexes, 553ff., and Foch to de Castlenau, 3 November 1918, ibid., 739. See also Foch to Pershing, 27 October 1918, ibid., 637, and Foch to Pershing, 3 November 1918, ibid., 741.

21. Sir C. DesGraz, Corfu, to Foreign Office, 6 November 1918, file no. 184981, FO 371/3160, PRO. See also Gauchet to Kelly, 8 November 1918, ADM 137/716, PRO.

22. Memorandum, Steps to Be Taken, 4 November 1918, Benson Papers, box 31, LC; Procès-verbal, 5 November 1918, ADM 116/1651, PRO.

23. Naval Attaché's Office, Rome, to Admiralty, 5 November 1918, enclosing Capt. Dennis A. H. Larking to Wemyss, ADM 116/1651, PRO. Larking was the British naval attaché at Rome.

24. Wireless intercept, Koch to President Wilson, 6 November 1918, Daily Summary of Intelligence Received, 9–10 November 1918, WO 157/37, PRO; Larking to Admiralty, 8 November 1918, ADM 116/1651, PRO.

25. Clemenceau to Orlando, n.d., enclosed in de Fleuriau to Davies, 6 November 1918, Lloyd George Papers, F/50/3/44, HLRO.

26. Ibid. Lloyd George gave Clemenceau his full support, [? Davies] to de Fleuriau, 6 November 1918, Lloyd George Papers, F/50/3/45, HLRO. Poincaré, *Au service* 10:406–8.

27. Orlando to Clemenceau, 9 November 1918, enclosed in Derby transmitting Clemenceau to Lloyd George, 10 November 1918, file no. 186282, FO 371/3446, PRO.

28. Clemenceau to Barrère for Orlando, 10 November 1918, 6 N 71, SHAT.

29. Not only was there radicalism, there was uncontrolled desertion, and one battleship was down to a crew of 48. Radcliffe to Henry Wilson, 10 November 1918, WO 106/835, PRO.

30. Larking to Admiralty, 10 November 1918, ADM 116/1651, PRO.

31. Barrère to Pichon, 12 November 1918, 6 N 53, SHAT. See also Marine, Paris, to Admiralty, 9 November 1918, ADM 116/1651, PRO.

32. Radcliffe, Rome, to Henry Wilson, 8 November 1918, WO 106/835, PRO, and Radcliffe to War Office, 9 November 1918, Daily Summary of Intelligence Received, 10–11 November 1918, WO 157/37, PRO.

33. Daily Summary of Intelligence Received, 4–5 November 1918, WO 157/37, PRO.

34. Daily Summary of Intelligence Received, 7–8 November 1918 and 12–13 November 1918, WO 157/37, PRO.

35. Italian Embassy to British Foreign Office, 7 November 1918, file no. 285703, FO 371/3160, PRO.

36. Lansing to Sharp, 9 November 1918, *Foreign Relations, 1918, World War* 1:869.

37. Pershing diary, 9 November 1918, Pershing Papers, box 4–5, LC.

38. Pershing diary, 9 November 1918, Pershing Papers, box 4–5, LC, and Pershing to House, 10 November 1918, drawer 15, folder 45, HCY.

39. Barrère to Pichon, 12 November 1918, 6 N 53, SHAT.

40. Rodd to Balfour (private), 11 November 1918, Balfour Papers, FO 800/203, PRO. A copy of this "private" letter is in the Lloyd George Papers, F/56/2/11, HLRO.

41. Poincaré, *Au service* 10:408–9; Mordacq, *Pouvait-on signer,* 76. See also Daily Summary of Intelligence Received, 14–15 November 1918, WO 157/37, PRO.

42. Military Situation in Various Theatres, no. 128, 7 November 1918, WO 106/319, PRO.

43. See chapter 6. War Cabinet 497, Imperial War Cabinet 36, 5 November 1918, CAB 23/8, PRO.

44. Military Situation in Various Theatres, no. 128, 7 November 1918, WO 106/319, PRO.

45. Mordacq, *Clemenceau* 2:332–34.

46. Daily Summary of Intelligence Received, 12–13 November 1918, WO 157/37, PRO.

47. Flynt for Admiralty to Balfour, 11 November 1918, file no. 186950, FO 371/3160, PRO.

48. Communiqué of the Army of the East, 12 November 1918, Mordacq, *Clemenceau* 2:358.

49. D[erby] to Arthur [Balfour], 7 November 1918, Balfour Papers, Add. MSS 49744, BL.

50. Derby diary, 8 November 1918, 920 DER(17) 28/1/1, LRO.

51. House diary, 9 November 1918, HCY, and House to Wilson, private code series 8, [9 November 1918], Wilson Papers, Series 2, LC.

52. War Cabinet 498, 4 November 1918, CAB 23/8, PRO.

53. Poincaré, *Au service* 10:409.

54. For the German internal debate over accepting armistice terms, see Schwabe, *Woodrow Wilson, Revolutionary Germany, and Peacemaking,* 95ff.

55. Both quoted in House to Lansing for Wilson, 58, 7 November 1918, *Foreign Relations, 1918, World War* 1:481.

56. Lansing to House, 7 November 1918, 1100, House to Lansing, 7 November 1918, 1800, and House to Lansing enclosing Auchincloss to Polk, 8 November 1918, *Foreign Relation, 1918, World War* 1:480, 483. Weintraub discusses the incident at length, *Stillness,* 17–40.

57. Maxime Weygand, *Le onze novembre* (Paris: Flammarion, 1947), 18–21.

58. The British military thought very little of von Winterfeldt. "He is said to be a soldier of no note, an intriguer who would sink to any deceits in order to carry out his objects." Daily Summary of Intelligence Received, 6–7 November 1918, WO 157/38. See also Derby to Foreign Office, 7 November 1918, FO371/3446, PRO.

59. Weygand, *Onze novembre,* 21–26.

60. Brig. Gen. Charles Grant to Director of Military Operations, 7 November 1918, WO 106/1456, PRO. French officials claimed Foch was "assisted by," not "associated with," Admiral Wemyss. Mordacq, *Armistice du 11 novembre,* 2. It is Foch's phrase, too, *Mémoires* 2:288.

61. Wemyss, Dictated Memorandum, 7–11 November 1918, WMYS 5/7, CCCU.

62. Foch quotes his official report at length. *Mémoires* 2:291–320. See also Weygand, *Idéal vécu,* 639, and Erzberger, *Erlebnisse,* 330–31. Additional material is in the report of the British interpreter, Cmdr. W. T. Bagot, 8 December 1918, ADM 1/8546/319, PRO.

63. Mordacq, *Clemenceau* 2:341.

64. Erzberger, *Erlebnisse,* 332.

65. Mordacq, *Clemenceau* 2:344.

66. Wemyss, Dictated Memorandum, 7–11 November 1918, WMYS 5/7, CCCU; Mordacq, *Clemenceau* 2:343. See also Pershing diary, 8 November 1918, Pershing Papers, box 4–5, LC.

67. Foch, *Mémoires* 2:298–301 (Weygand's report).

68. Weygand, *Onze novembre,* 46–47. See also Pershing diary, 12 November 1918, Pershing Papers, box 4–5, LC.

69. The German observations were substantially those printed in Germany, Waffenstillstandkommission, 1918–19, *Der Waffenstillstand, 1918–1919,* 3 vols. (Berlin: Deutsche Verlagsgesellschaft für Politik und Geschichte, 1928), 1:22–57. Three columns give terms presented, German observations, and terms signed.

70. Mordacq, *Clemenceau* 2:346.

71. Mordacq, *Clemenceau* 2:352. Mordacq dates this conversation on 10 November, but it took place the day before. He dates the exchange correctly, but gives slightly different wording in *Armistice du 11 novembre,* 192.

72. Foch, *Mémoires* 2:291. See also Mordacq, *Armistice du 11 novembre,* 13.

73. Herbillon, *Du général en chef au gouvernement* 2:346.

74. Wemyss, Dictated Memorandum, 7–11 November 1918, WMYS 5/7, CCCU.

75. Mordacq, *Clemenceau* 2:347. That news was not confirmed until 0300, 10 November. Mordacq, *Armistice du 11 novembre,* 16. Bliss on 10 November was still noting rumors about the emperor's abdication. Bliss to N. D. Baker, 10 November 1918, Bliss Papers, box 74 (9a/1–33), LC.

76. Wemyss, Dictated Memorandum, 7–11 November 1918, WMYS 5/7, CCCU.

77. Derby to Foreign Office, [9] November 1918, file no. 186248, FO 371/3446, PRO, and Clemenceau to Lloyd George, 9 November 1918, Lloyd George Papers, F/50/3/46, HLRO.

78. Mordacq, *Armistice du 11 novembre,* 15–16, and Commodore, Paris, to Geddes and Beatty, 9 November 1918, ADM 1/8542, PRO.

79. Clemenceau to Lloyd George, [9 November 1918?], Lloyd George Papers, F/50/3/47, HLRO.

80. War Cabinet 500A, 10 November 1918, CAB 23/14, PRO.

81. "Our real danger now," Sir Henry wrote in his diary that evening, "is not the Boches but Bolshevism," HHW 1/32, IWM.

82. Balfour to Derby, 10 November 1918, file no. 185314, FO 371/3445, PRO. See also Balfour to Lord Stamfordham, 10 November 1918, Balfour Papers, FO 800/201, PRO, and Milner diary, 10 November 1918, Milner Papers, box 281, BOU.

83. Mordacq, *Clemenceau* 2:347.

84. Ebert, Imperial Chancellor, to Erzberger, 10 November 1918, Germany, Reichskanzlei, *Preliminary History of the Armistice,* 149–50.

85. For a procès-verbal, see *Der Waffenstillstand* 1:66ff. See also L'Hôpital, *Foch,* 88–89, and Foch, *Mémoires* 2:304. Cf. Erzberger, *Erlebnisse,* 335. Foch had called

Paris saying he expected the Germans to sign that morning. Mordacq, *Clemenceau* 2:348.

86. Derby to Foreign Office, 11 November 1918, file no. 186908, FO 371/3446, PRO.

87. Rear Admiral Hope, quoted in Derby to Arthur [Balfour], 14 November 1918, enclosing Derby diary, 12 November 1918, Balfour Papers, Add. MSS 49744, BL. The French were uniformly courteous to the Germans, but sometimes French courtesy had an edge; from reports, the mess waiters served the German delegation 1870 champagne. Charles Grant to War Office, 17 November 1918, WO 158/84, PRO.

88. From Foch, *AFGG* 7, Annexes, 877.

89. Mordacq, *Clemenceau* 3:5. The original is italicized.

90. Ibid. 2:343–44.

91. House to Wilson, private code series, 13, [11 November 1918], Wilson Papers, Series 2, LC.

92. Tumulty, *Woodrow Wilson*, 321.

93. Great Britain, *Parliamentary Debates* (Commons), 5th ser., 110:2452–63 (11 November 1918).

CHAPTER 9. CONCLUSIONS

1. British Empire Delegation, 1 June 1919, CAB 29/28/1, PRO.

2. Tardieu, *Truth about the Treaty,* 43.

3. Trevor Wilson, *The Myriad Faces of War: Britain and the Great War, 1914–1918* (Cambridge: Polity Press, 1986), 606.

4. Harold Nicolson, *Peacemaking, 1919* (London: Constable, 1934), 44.

5. Versailles Treaty, Article 159.

6. Rudin, *Armistice, 1918,* 392–99. The quest has continued; Renouvin, entitled a chapter, "L'Armistice a-t-il été prématuré?" *Armistice,* 255–67.

7. Maurice, *Armistices of 1918,* 55. Gerhard L. Weinberg states that the failure to make the military leaders sign led the Allied political leaders of World War II to demand that the military leaders of the Axis Powers be the people who signed the surrender instruments. *A World at Arms: A Global History of World War II* (New York: Cambridge University Press, 1994), 827.

8. Mordacq, *Armistice du 11 novembre,* 202, 209–11.

9. Mordacq, *Clemenceau* 2:340–42, and *Pouvait-on signer,* 89–93.

10. Ibid., 126, 152–56, and Mordacq, *Clemenceau* 2:315–23. Cf. Weygand, *Idéal vécu,* 626, and Herbillon, *Du général en chef au gouvernement* 2:347.

11. Lord Riddell, *Lord Riddell's Intimate Diary of the Peace Conference and After, 1918–1923* (New York: Reynal and Hitchcock, 1934), 6–7.

12. House to Mantoux, 3 July 1920, quoted in Mordacq, *Armistice du 11 november,* 191.

13. Lloyd George, for example, objected to occupying even the few German cities inside the proposed bridgeheads on the right bank. See chapter 7.

14. Chester Wilmot in his classic study of World War II is clearer than many writers. He comments that the idea was to offer Germany no chance to claim bad faith over something like the Fourteen Points: "They would offer Germany no points at all." *The Struggle for Europe* (New York: Harper Colophon, 1963), 123.

15. Transcript of [FDR] Press Conference, Casablanca, 24 January 1943, U.S. Department of State, *Foreign Relations of the United States: The Conferences at Washington, 1941–42, and Casablanca, 1943* (Washington, D.C.: Government Printing Office, 1968), 727. Roosevelt had apparently gotten Churchill's approval the day before. Editorial Note to Roosevelt-Churchill Luncheon Meeting, 23 January 1943, ibid., 704.

16. Robert E. Sherwood, *Roosevelt and Hopkins: An Intimate History* (New York: Harper, 1948), 697.

17. The idea was to assure the Soviet leaders that in spite of the failure of the Western democracies to open a Second Front, they were determined not to accept a separate peace. Leon Sigal claims that the doctrine was more propaganda than a true war aim. Leon V. Sigal, *Fighting to a Finish: The Politics of War Termination in the United States and Japan, 1945* (Ithaca, N.Y.: Cornell University Press, 1988), 90. Weinberg argues that the timing of issuing the doctrine was a response to criticism over Allied accommodations with Darlan, although he does claim that its origin lies in the failures at the end of World War I. *World at Arms,* 433.

18. Foch, *Mémoires* 2:269, 322, and Weygand, *Idéal vécu,* 633.

19. Recouly, *Mémorial de Foch,* 30 (original in italics).

20. Private code series 1, Wilson Papers, Series 2, LC. See also *Congressional Record* (11 November 1918), 65th Cong., 2d. sess., 1918, pt. 56:11543.

21. *War Memoirs* 6:3308–9.

22. Schwabe, following a different line of reasoning, reaches the same conclusion. *Woodrow Wilson, Revolutionary Germany, and Peacemaking,* 93–94.

23. See, for example, Stanley W. Page, *The Formation of the Baltic States* (Cambridge: Harvard University Press, 1959), esp. 62–109. See also Hans Erich Volkmann, *Die deutsche Baltikumpolitik zwischen Brest-Litvosk und Compiègne: Ein Beitrag zur Kriegszeildiskussion* (Köln: Bohlau, 1970).

24. A. Niessel, *L'Évacuation des pays baltiques par les allemandes* (Paris: Charles LaVauzelle, 1933).

25. Versailles Treaty, Article 429, section 3.

26. Versailles Treaty, Articles 159–72.

27. Versailles Treaty, Articles 181–97; Article 181 limited the German navy to six pre-Dreadnought battleships, six light cruisers, twelve destroyers, and twelve torpedo boats. They were forbidden to have submarines.

28. See Friedrich Ruge, *Scapa Flow, 1919: The End of the German Fleet,* trans. Derek Masters, ed. A. J. Watts (Annapolis: U.S. Naval Institute, 1973).

29. Versailles Treaty, Article 115.

30. Versailles Treaty, Articles 232 and 233.

31. Wiseman to House, London, 12 November 1918, House-Wiseman Correspondence, HCY.

32. Bliss to Baker, 10 November 1918, Bliss Papers, box 74 (9a/1–33), LC.

33. Even French army morale, suspect since the mutinies of 1917, was high, the leaders thought. EMA, 2d Bureau, Bulletin confidentielle résumant la situation morale à l'intérieure, 15 November 1918, 6 N 147, SHAT. The Allied leaders were less sure of Italian stability, and the Allies watched them carefully, with the commander of the British forces in Italy even plotting an escape route for his men to use if the Italians went Bolshevik. Cavan to Sir Henry Wilson, 14 November 1918, WO 79/68, PRO.

34. *Armistice*, 399.

Selected Bibligraphy

UNPUBLISHED MATERIAL

France

Governmental

Archives de la Guerre. Vincennes.
Archives des Affaires Étrangères. Ministère des Affaires Étrangères, Paris.

Personal Papers

Cambon, Paul. Archives des Affaires Étrangères, Ministère des Affaires Étrangères, Paris.
Clemenceau, Georges. Fonds Clemenceau, Archives de la Guerre, Vincennes.
Klotz, L.-L. Bibliothèque de Documentation Internationale et Contemporaine, Nanterre.
Mangin, Charles. Archives Nationales, Paris.
Mantoux, Paul. Bibliothèque de Documentation Internationale et Contemporaine, Nanterre.
Pichon, Stephen. Archives de l'Institut de France, Paris.
Poincaré, Raymond. Cabinet des Manuscrits, Bibliothèque Nationale.

Great Britain

Governmental

Admiralty. Public Record Office, London.
Cabinet Office. Public Record Office, London.

Foreign Office. Public Record Office, London.
War Office. Public Record Office, London.

Personal Papers

Beatty, David Beatty, Admiral of the Fleet Earl. National Maritime Museum, London (Greenwich).

Balfour, Arthur James Balfour, Earl of. Manuscripts, British Library, London; and Foreign Office Special Collections, Public Record Office, London.

Cavan, Frederick Lambert, Field Marshal Earl. Churchill College, Cambridge University.

Cecil of Chelwood, Robert Cecil, Viscount. Manuscripts, British Library, London.

Curzon of Keddleston, George Nathaniel Curzon, Marquess. India Office Records and Library, London.

Derby, E. G. V. Stanley, Earl. Liverpool Record Office, Liverpool.

Haig of Bemersyde, Douglas Haig, Field Marshal the Earl. National Library of Scotland, Edinburgh.

Hankey of the Chart, Maurice Hankey, Lord. Churchill College, Cambridge University.

Lloyd George of Dwyvor, David Lloyd George, Earl. House of Lords Record Office, London.

Milner, Arthur Milner, Viscount. New College, in the custody of Manuscripts, Bodleian Library, Oxford University.

Wester Wemyss, Rosslyn E. Wemyss, Admiral of the Fleet Lord. Churchill College, Cambridge University.

Wilson, Field Marshal Sir Henry Hughes. Manuscripts, Imperial War Museum, London.

Wiseman, Sir William. House Collection, Yale University, New Haven, Connecticut.

United States

Governmental

General Records of the Department of State. National Archives, Washington, D.C.

Records of the American Expeditionary Forces, 1917–1923. National Archives, Washington, D.C.

Records of the Foreign Service Posts of the Department of State. National Archives, Washington, D.C.

Personal Papers

Baker, Newton D. Manuscripts Division, Library of Congress, Washington, D.C.

Benson, William S. Manuscripts Division, Library of Congress, Washington, D.C.

Bliss, Tasker Howard. Manuscripts Division, Library of Congress, Washington, D.C.

Cobb, Frank. Additional Accession to Woodrow Wilson Papers, Manuscripts Division, Library of Congress, Washington, D.C.

Daniels, Josephus. Manuscripts Division, Library of Congress, Washington, D.C.

Harbord, James G. Manuscripts Division, Library of Congress, Washington, D.C.

House, Edward M. House Collection, Yale University, New Haven, Connecticut.

Lansing, Robert. Manuscripts Division, Library of Congress, Washington, D.C.

Lippmann, Walter. Yale University, New Haven, Connecticut.

Pershing, John J. Manuscripts Division, Library of Congress, Washington, D.C.

Polk, Frank. House Collection, Yale University, New Haven, Connecticut.

Wilson, Woodrow. Manuscripts Division, Library of Congress, Washington, D.C.

PUBLISHED MATERIAL
Government Documents and Official Histories

Bernachot, Jean. *See* France. Ministère des armées.

Edmonds, J. E., and H. R. Davies. *See* Great Britain. Committee of Imperial Defence.

Edmonds, J. E., and R. Maxwell-Hyslop. *See* Great Britain. Committee of Imperial Defence.

Falls, Cyril. *See* Great Britain. Committee of Imperial Defence.

France. Assemblée nationale. Chambre des deputés. *Journal officiel. . . . Annales de la chambre des deputés,* 1918.

———. Ministère de la guerre. État-major de l'armée. Service historique. *Les armées françaises dans la Grande Guerre.* Tome 7, *Le campagne offensive de 1918 et la marche au Rhin (18 juillet 1918–28 juin 1919).* 2 vols. plus 1 vol. of annexed documents and 2 vols. of maps. Paris: Imprimerie nationale, 1938.

———. Ministère de la guerre. État-major de l'armée. Service historique. *Les armées françaises dans la Grande Guerre.* Tome 8, *Le campagne d'Orient.* 3 vols. plus 3 vols. of documents and 1 vol. of maps. Paris: Imprimerie nationale, 1934.

———. Ministère des armées. État-major de l'armée de terre. Service historique. *Les armées françaises en Orient après l'armistice de 1918.* By General Jean Bernachot. 2 vols. Paris: Imprimerie nationale, 1970.

Germany. Reichskanzlei. *Preliminary History of the Armistice.* Translated by the Carnegie Endowment for International Peace. New York: Oxford University Press, 1924.

———. Waffenstillstandkommission, 1918–1919. *Der Waffenstillstand: 1918–1919.* 3 vols. Berlin: Deutsche Verlagsgesellschaft für Politik und Geschichte, 1928.

Gooch, G. P., and Harold Temperley. *See* Great Britain. Foreign Office.

Great Britain. Committee of Imperial Defence. Historical Section. *Military Operations, France and Belgium, 1918.* By J. E. Edmonds and R. Maxwell-Hyslop. 5 vols. London: H.M. Stationery Office, 1947.

———. Committee of Imperial Defence. Historical Section. *Military Operations, Italy, 1915–1919.* By J. E. Edmonds and H. R. Davies. 4 vols. in 1. London: H.M. Stationery Office, 1949.

———. Committee of Imperial Defence. Historical Section. *Military Operations, Macedonia.* By Cyril Falls. 2 vols. London: H.M. Stationery Office, 1935.

———. Committee of Imperial Defence. Historical Section. *Naval Operations.* Vol. 5, *From April 1917 to the End of the War.* By Henry Newbolt. London: Longmans, Green, 1931.

———. Foreign Office. *British Documents on the Origins of the War, 1898–1914.* Edited by G. P. Gooch and Harold Temperley. 11 vols. in 13 parts. London: H.M. Stationery Office, 1926–38.

———. Foreign Office. Historical Section. *Peace Handbooks.* 155 pts. London: H.M. Stationery Office, 1920. Reprint with 25 vols., Wilmington, Del.: Scholarly Resources, 1973.

———. Parliament. *Parliamentary Debates* (Commons). 5th series. 1918.

Newbolt, Henry. *See* Great Britain. Committee of Imperial Defence.

U.S. Congress. *Congressional Record.* Washington, D.C.: Government Printing Office, 1918.

U.S. Department of the Army. Historical Section. *United States Army in the World War, 1917–1919.* 17 vols. Washington, D.C.: Government Printing Office, 1948.

U.S. Department of State. *Foreign Relations of the United States: The Conferences at Washington, 1941–42, and Casablanca, 1943.* Washington, D.C.: Government Printing Office, 1968.

———. *Papers Relating to the Foreign Relations of the United States, 1898.* Washington, D.C.: Government Printing Office, 1901.

———. *Papers Relating to the Foreign Relations of the United States: The Lansing Papers, 1914–1920.* 2 vols. Washington, D.C.: Government Printing Office, 1939–1940.

———. *Papers Relating to the Foreign Relations of the United States, 1918.* Supplement 1, *The World War.* 2 vols. Washington, D.C.: Government Printing Office, 1933.

———. *Papers Relating to the Foreign Relations of the United States, 1919. The Paris Peace Conference.* 13 vols. Washington, D.C.: Government Printing Office, 1942–1947.

————. *Treaties and Other International Agreements of the United States of America, 1776–1949.* Compiled by Charles I. Bevans. 13 vols. Washington, D.C.: Government Printing Office, 1968–76.

U.S. Office of Naval Records and Library. *The American Naval Planning Section, London.* Washington, D.C.: Government Printing Office, 1923.

U.S. Senate Committee on Foreign Relations. *Hearings. Treaty of Peace with Germany.* 66th Congress, 1st sess., 1919.

OTHER PRIMARY MATERIAL

Baker, Ray Stannard. *Woodrow Wilson, Life and Letters.* 8 vols. New York: Doubleday Page, Doubleday Doran, 1927–28.

Beadon, R. H. *Some Memories of the Peace Conference.* London: Williams, 1933.

Beaverbrook, W. M. Aitken, Lord. *The Decline and Fall of Lloyd George.* New York: Duell, Sloan and Pearce, 1963.

Blake, Robert, ed. *The Private Papers of Douglas Haig: 1914–1919.* London: Eyre and Spottiswoode, 1952.

Bliss, Tasker. "The Armistices." *American Journal of International Law* 16 (1922): 509–22.

Bonsal, Stephen. *Unfinished Business.* Garden City, N.Y.: Doubleday, Doran, 1944.

Callwell, C. E. *Field Marshal Sir Henry Wilson, His Life and Diaries.* 2 vols. London: Cassell, 1927.

Cambon, Paul. *Correspondance: 1870–1940.* Edited by Henri Cambon. 3 vols. Paris: Grasset, 1942–46.

Clarke, Tom. *My Northcliffe Diary.* London: Victor Gollancz, 1931.

Clemenceau, Georges. *Grandeurs et misères d'une victoire.* Paris: Plon, 1930.

Erzberger, Mathias. *Erlebnisse im Weltkrieg.* Stuttgart: Deutsche Verlagsanstalt, 1920.

Foch, Ferdinand. *Mémoires pour servir à l'histoire de la Guerre de 1914–1918.* 2 vols. Paris: Plon, 1931.

Hankey, Maurice Hankey, Lord. *The Supreme Command, 1914–1918.* 2 vols. London: George Allen and Unwin, 1961.

Hardinge, Charles Hardinge, Lord. *Old Diplomacy.* London: Murray, 1947.

Herbillon, Emile E. *Du général en chef au gouvernement: Souvenirs d'un officier de liaison pendant la Grande Guerre.* 2 vols. Paris: Tallandier, [1930].

Houston, David F. *Eight Years with Wilson's Cabinet, 1913–1920.* 2 vols. Garden City, N.Y.: Doubleday, Page, 1926.

International Commission to Inquire into the Causes and Conduct of the Balkan Wars. *Report . . .* Carnegie Endowment for International Peace, Division of Intercourse and Education, Publication number 4. Washington, D.C.: Carnegie Endowment, 1914.

Karolyi, Michael. *Memoirs of Michael Karolyi: Faith Without Illusion.* Translated by Catherine Karolyi. New York: E. P. Dutton, 1957.

Keynes, John Maynard. *The Economic Consequences of the Peace.* New York: Harcourt, Brace and Howe, 1920.

Klotz, L.-L. *De la guerre à la paix: Souvenirs et documents.* Paris: Payot, 1924.

Lane, A. W., and L. H. Wall, eds. *The Letters of Franklin K. Lane, Personal and Political.* Boston: Houghton Mifflin, 1922.

L'Hôpital, Réné M. M. *Foch, l'armistice et la paix.* Paris: Plon, 1938.

Link, Arthur S., ed. *The Papers of Woodrow Wilson.* Vol. 51, *September 14–November 8, 1918.* Princeton, N.J.: Princeton University Press, 1985.

Lloyd George, David. *Memoirs of the Peace Conference.* 2 vols. New Haven, Conn.: Yale University Press, 1939.

———. *War Memoirs.* 6 vols. London: Ivor Nicholson and Watson, 1933–36.

Laroche, Jules. *Au Quai d'Orsay avec Briand et Poincaré, 1913–1926.* Paris: Hachette, 1957.

Launau, Jacques de. *Secrets diplomatiques.* Brussels: Brepols, 1963.

Mermeix [Gabriel Terrail]. *Les négociations secrètes et les quatre armistices.* Paris: Ollendorff, [1922].

Mordacq, Henri. *L'Armistice du 11 novembre 1918: Récit d'un témoin.* Paris: Plon, 1937.

———. *Le ministère Clemenceau: Journal d'un témoin.* 4 vols. Paris: Plon, 1930–31.

———. *Pouvait-on signer l'armistice à Berlin?* Paris: Grasset, [1930].

———. *La vérité sur l'armistice.* Paris: Tallandier, 1929.

Mott, T. Bentley. *Twenty Years as a Military Attaché.* New York: Oxford University Press, 1937.

Napier, Henry Dundas. *Experiences of a Military Attaché in the Balkans.* London: Drane's, 1924.

Nicolson, Harold. *Peacemaking, 1919.* London: Constable, 1934.

Niessel, A. *L'Évacuation des pays baltiques par les allemandes.* Paris: Charles LaVauzelle, 1933.

Pershing, John J. *My Experiences in the World War.* 2 vols. New York: Frederick A. Stokes, 1931.

Poincaré, Raymond. *Au service de la France.* 11 vols. Paris: Plon-Nourrit, 1926–33, 1974.

Recouly, Raymond. *Le mémorial de Foch: Mes entretiens avec le maréchal.* Paris: Éditions du France, 1929.

Repington, Charles à Court. *After the War.* Boston: Houghton Mifflin, 1922.

Riddell, George Allardice Riddell, Lord. *Lord Riddell's Intimate Diary of the Peace Conference and After, 1918–1923.* New York: Reynal and Hitchcock, 1934.

Ruge, Friedrich. *Scapa Flow, 1919: The End of the German Fleet.* Translated by Derek Masters and edited by A. J. Watts. Annapolis, Md.: United States Naval Institute, 1973.

Scott, James Brown. *The Hague Conventions and Declarations of 1899 and 1907.* 3d ed. New York: Oxford University Press, 1918.

Seymour, Charles, ed. *The Intimate Papers of Colonel House.* 4 vols. Boston: Houghton Mifflin, 1926–28.

Snell, John L., ed. "Wilson on Germany and the Fourteen Points." *Journal of Modern History* 26 (1954): 364–69.

Tardieu, André. *The Truth about the Treaty.* Indianapolis: Bobbs-Merrill, 1921.

Tumulty, Joseph. *Woodrow Wilson as I Know Him.* Garden City, N.Y.: Doubleday, Page for the *Literary Digest*, 1921.

Weygand, Maxime. *Foch.* Paris: Flammarion, 1947.

———. *Mémoires.* Vol. 1, *Idéal vécu.* Vol. 2, *Mirages et réalité.* Paris: Flammarion, 1953–57.

———. *Le onze novembre.* Paris: Flammarion, 1958.

Wester Wemyss, Victoria Wemyss, Lady. *The Life and Letters of Lord Wester Wemyss.* London: Eyre and Spottiswoode, 1935.

SECONDARY SOURCES

Ambrosius, Lloyd E. *Woodrow Wilson and the American Diplomatic Tradition: The Treaty Fight in Perspective.* Cambridge: Cambridge University Press, 1987.

Azan, Paul. *Franchet d'Esperey.* Paris: Flammarion, 1929.

Barclay, C. N. *Armistice, 1918.* South Brunswick, N.J.: A. S. Barnes, 1968.

Blake, Robert. *Unrepentant Tory: The Life and Times of Andrew Bonar Law, 1858–1923.* New York: St. Martin's, 1956.

Bourne, J. M. *Britain and the Great War, 1914–1918.* London: Edward Arnold, 1989.

Brook-Shepherd, Gordon. *November 1918: The Last Act of the Great War.* London: Collins, 1981.

Chalmers, W. S. *The Life and Letters of David, Earl Beatty.* London: Hodder and Stoughton, 1951.

Duroselle, Jean-Baptiste. *Clemenceau.* Paris: Fayard, 1988.

Elcock, Howard. *Portrait of a Decision: The Council of Four and the Treaty of Versailles.* London: Eyre Methuen, 1972.

Erlanger, Philippe. *Clemenceau.* Paris: Grasset/Paris-Match, 1968.

Falls, Cyril. *Armageddon, 1918.* Philadelphia: Lippincott, 1964.

Ferrell, Robert H. *Woodrow Wilson and World War I, 1917–1921.* New American Nation Series. New York: Harper and Row, 1985.

Fest, Wilfried. *Peace or Partition: The Habsburg Monarchy and British Policy, 1914–1918.* London: George Prior, 1978.

Flota, Inga. *Colonel House in Paris: A Study of American Policy at the Paris Peace Conference 1919.* Princeton, N.J.: Princeton University Press, 1980.

Fowler, W. B. *British-American Relations, 1917–1918: The Role of Sir William Wiseman.* Princeton, N.J.: Princeton University Press, 1969.

Friedjung, Heinrich. *The Struggle for Supremacy in Germany, 1859–1866.* Translated by A. J. P. Taylor and W. L. McElwee. London: Macmillan, 1935.

Gelfand, L. E. *The Inquiry.* New Haven, Conn.: Yale University Press, 1963.

Grunberger, Richard. *Red Rising in Bavaria.* New York: St. Martin's, 1973.

Halpern, Paul G. *A Naval History of World War I.* Annapolis, Md.: Naval Institute Press, 1994.

Holt, W. Stull. "What Wilson Sent and What House Received: or, Scholars Need to Check Carefully." *American Historical Review* 65 (1960): 569–71.

Howard, Michael. *The Franco-Prussian War.* New York: Macmillan, 1962.

Kent, Bruce. *The Spoils of War: The Politics, Economics, and Diplomacy of Reparations.* Oxford: Oxford University Press, 1989.

Kitchen, Martin. *The Silent Dictatorship: The Politics of the German High Command under Hindenburg and Ludendorff, 1916–1918.* London: Croom Helm, 1976.

Klachko, Mary, with David F. Trask. *Admiral William Shepherd Benson: First Chief of Naval Operations.* Annapolis, Md.: Naval Institute Press, 1987.

Knock, Thomas J. *To End All Wars: Woodrow Wilson and the Quest for a New World Order.* New York: Oxford University Press, 1992.

Krizman, Bogdan. "The Belgrad Armistice of 13 November 1918." *Slavonic and East European Review* 48 (1970): 67–87.

Kruger, Rayne. *Good-bye Dolly Gray.* Philadelphia: Lippincott, 1960.

Lederer, Ivo J. *Yugoslavia at the Paris Peace Conference: A Study in Frontiermaking.* New Haven, Conn.: Yale University Press, 1963.

Link, Arthur S. *Wilson the Diplomatist.* Chicago: Quadrangle, 1963.

Lowry, Bullitt. "Pershing and the Armistice." *Journal of American History* 55 (1968): 281–91.

McDougall, Walter A. *France's Rhineland Diplomacy, 1914–1924: The Last Bid for a Balance of Power in Europe.* Princeton, N.J.: Princeton University Press, 1978.

Maurice, Frederick Barton. *The Armistices of 1918.* New York: Oxford University Press, 1943.

Mayer, Arno J. *Political Origins of the New Diplomacy, 1917–1918.* New Haven, Conn.: Yale University Press, 1959.

———. *Politics and Diplomacy of Peacemaking: Containment and Counterrevolution at Versailles, 1918–1919.* New York: Alfred A. Knopf, 1967.

Miquel, P. *Poincaré*. Paris: Arthème Fayard, 1961.

Mitchell, Allan. *Revolution in Bavaria, 1918–1919*. Princeton, N.J.: Princeton University Press, 1965.

Nelson, Harold I. *Land and Power: British and Allied Policy on Germany's Frontiers, 1916–1919*. Toronto: University of Toronto Press, 1963.

Newhall, David S. *Clemenceau: A Life at War*. Lewiston, N.Y.: Edwin Mellen Press, 1991.

Ormos, Mariá. *From Padua to the Trianon, 1918–1920*. Translated by Miklós Uszkay. Boulder, Colo.: Social Science Monographs, and Highland Lakes; New Jersey: Atlantic Research and Publications, 1990.

Paschall, Rod. *The Defeat of Imperial Germany, 1917–1918*. Chapel Hill, N.C.: Algonquin Books, 1989.

Page, Stanley W. *The Formation of the Baltic States*. Cambridge: Harvard University Press, 1959.

Pedroncini, Guy. *Les mutineries de 1917*. Paris: Presses Universitaires de France, 1967.

Pitt, Barrie. *1918: The Last Act*. New York: Norton, 1962.

Potter, Pitman B. *The Freedom of the Seas in History, Law, and Politics*. New York: Longmans, Green, 1924.

Pound, Reginald, and Geoffrey Harmsworth. *Northcliffe*. London: Cassell, 1959.

Renouvin, Pierre. *L'Armistice de Rethondes, 11 novembre 1918*. Trente journées qui ont fait la France. Paris: Gallimard, 1968.

Ritter, Gerhard. *Staatskunst und Kriegshandwerk: Das Problem des Militarismus in Deutschland*. Vol. 4, *Die Herrschaft des deutschen Militarismus und die Katastrophe von 1918*. Munich: R. Oldenbourg, 1968.

Rothwell, V. E. *British War Aims and Peace Diplomacy, 1914–1918*. Oxford: Clarendon Press, 1971.

Rudin, Harry R. *Armistice 1918*. New Haven, Conn.: Yale University Press, 1944.

Schmitt, Bernadotte E. "The Peace Treaties of 1919–1920." *Proceedings of the American Philosophical Society* 104 (1960): 101–10.

Schwabe, Klaus. *Woodrow Wilson, Revolutionary Germany, and Peacemaking, 1918–1919: Missionary Diplomacy and the Realities of Power*. Translated by Rita Kimber and Robert Kimber. Chapel Hill: University of North Carolina Press, 1985.

Šepić, Dragovan. "The Question of Yugoslav Union in 1918." *Journal of Contemporary History* 3 (1968): 29–43.

Seymour, Charles. *American Diplomacy in the World War*. Baltimore: Johns Hopkins University Press, 1934.

Sherwood, Robert E. *Roosevelt and Hopkins: An Intimate History*. New York: Harper, 1948.

Sibert, Marcel. *L'Armistice dans le droit des hommes*. Paris: Pédone, 1933.

Sigal, Leon V. *Fighting to a Finish: The Politics of War Termination in the United States and Japan, 1945*. Ithaca, N.Y.: Cornell University Press, 1988.

Smythe, Donald. *Pershing: General of the Armies*. Bloomington: Indiana University Press, 1986.

Stevenson, David. *The First World War and International Politics*. Oxford: Oxford University Press, 1988.

————. *French War Aims against Germany, 1914–1919*. Oxford: Clarendon Press, 1982.

Temperley, H. W. V., ed. *A History of the Peace Conference of Paris*. [Royal] Institute of International Affairs. 6 vols. London: Henry Frowde, Hodder and Stoughton, 1920–24. Reprint, London: Oxford University Press, 1969.

Trani, Eugene P. *The Treaty of Portsmouth*. Lexington: University of Kentucky Press, 1969.

Trask, David F. *The AEF and Coalition Warmaking, 1917–1918*. Lawrence: University Press of Kansas, 1993.

————. *Captains & Cabinets: Anglo-American Naval Relations, 1917–1918*. Columbia: University of Missouri Press, 1972.

————. *General Tasker Howard Bliss and the "Sessions of the World," 1919*, Transactions of the American Philosophical Society, n.s., 56, pt. 8. Philadelphia: American Philosophical Society, 1966.

————. *The United States in the Supreme War Council: American War Aims and Inter-Allied Strategy, 1917–1918*. Middletown, Conn.: Wesleyan University Press, 1961.

Unterberger, Betty Miller. *The United States, Revolutionary Russia, and the Rise of Czechoslovakia*. Chapel Hill: University of North Carolina Press, 1989.

Vandiver, Frank E. *Black Jack: The Life and Times of John J. Pershing*. 2 vols. College Station: Texas A&M University Press, 1977.

Volkmann, Hans Erich. *Die deutsch Baltikumpolitik zwischen Brest-Litovsk und Compiègne: Ein Beitrag zur Kriegszeildiskussion*. Köln: Bohlau, 1970.

Weinberg, Gerhard L. *A World at Arms: A Global History of World War II*. New York: Cambridge University Press, 1994.

Weintraub, Stanley. *A Stillness Heard Round the World: The End of the Great War: November 1918*. New York: Truman Talley, E. P. Dutton, 1985.

Williams, Wythe. *The Tiger of France: Conversations with Clemenceau*. New York: Duell, Sloan and Pearce, 1949.

Wilmot, Chester. *The Struggle for Europe*. New York: Harper Colophon, 1963.

Wilson, Trevor. *The Myriad Faces of War: Britain and the Great War, 1914–1918*. Cambridge: Polity Press, 1986.

Woodward, David R. *Trial by Friendship: Anglo-American Relations, 1917–1918*. Lexington: University Press of Kentucky, 1993.

Wormser, Georges. *Le septennat de Poincaré.* Paris: Presses Universitaires de France, 1961.

Zeman, Z. A. B. *The Gentlemen Negotiators: A Diplomatic History of the First World War.* New York: Macmillan, 1971.

NEWSPAPERS AND PERIODICALS

Liberal Magazine 26 (December 1918).

New York Times, 1918.

Times (London), 1918.

Index

ARMISTICE 1918

was composed in 10.5/13 Minion
on a Power Macintosh using PageMaker 6.0
at The Kent State University Press
printed by sheet-fed offset
on 50-pound Glatfelter Supple Opaque Natural stock
(an acid-free recycled paper),
notch case bound over binder's boards
in Kingston natural cloth,
and wrapped with dust jackets printed in two colors
on 100-pound enamel stock finished with film lamination
by Thomson-Shore, Inc.;
designed by Diana Gordy
and published by

THE KENT STATE UNIVERSITY PRESS
Kent, Ohio 44242